The Faces of Janus

The Faces of Janus

*Marxism and Fascism in the
Twentieth Century*

A. James Gregor

Yale University Press   New Haven and London

Designed by James J. Johnson and set in Granjon Roman types by Keystone Typesetting, Inc.

Printed in the United States of America by Sheridan Books, Chelsea, Michigan.

The paper in this book meets the guidelines for permanence and durability of the Committee on Production Guidelines for Book Longevity of the Council on Library Resources.

Library of Congress Cataloging-in-Publication Data

Gregor, A. James (Anthony James), 1929–
The faces of Janus : Marxism and Fascism in the twentieth century / A. James Gregor.
p.   cm.
Includes bibliographical references (p.   ) and index.
ISBN 0-300-07827-7 (alk. paper)

1. Revolutions—History—20th century.   2. Fascism—History—20th century.   3. Communism—History—20th century.   I. Title.   II. Title: Marxism and Fascism in the twentieth century.
JC491.G674   1999
320.53′09′04—dc21   99–28711

A catalogue record for this book is available from the British Library.

10 9 8 7 6 5 4 3 2 1

This book is dedicated to little Gabriel—
as small compensation for his unqualified love

Contents

Preface

The turn of the century is as convenient an occasion as any to take stock of our time. It has been a time of trouble. Two world wars grew out of the "belle epoque"—and by the end of the century, more human beings would be killed by their own governments than would die in those wars. In attempting to understand something of that doleful reality, many have had recourse to the existence, in our century, of "fascism." "Fascism," we are told, was "one of the most glaring examples of political evil in modern history."[1] Fascism, we have been told, was uniquely inhumane. We have been told that "anyone with any concern for human dignity can see the destructive effects of the fascist denigration of human life."[2] The implication of judgments of these kinds is that *fascism*, however that term is understood, is largely responsible for much of the devastation of the twentieth century. More than that, an effort has been made recently to identify "fascism" with "right-wing extremism," and thereby credit the Right with virtually all the infamies of our time.[3] Somehow or other, only the Right figures in the catalog of horrors that make up contemporary history. Yet almost everyone now acknowledges that the regimes of Stalin, Mao, and Pol Pot were stained with the blood of millions of innocent victims—more than those of the extreme right. We are left perplexed.

Even the most generous estimate would make the Left at least partially responsible for the mayhem that distinguishes our century. The political Right and the political Left seem to share something of a common malevolence. All that notwithstanding, some Western scholars continue to treat the political universe as though it were divided between the evil Right and the benign Left.[4]

The thesis of the present work is that much of the literature of the twentieth century devoted to the analysis of violent revolution has failed to appreciate the central issues around which the insurrectionary violence of our time has turned.

The failure of that literature is manifest in its treatment of the revolutions that followed the First World War—and which continue to the present—as being either of the Right or of the Left. Fascism is of the Right and Marxist–Leninist regimes are of the Left.

I will argue that the major systemic revolutions of our time have been of neither the Right nor the Left. Our error has been to attempt to force each revolutionary instance into a procrustean bed of preconceptions. To this day, some in the West remain convinced that while the revolutions of the Right have been unqualifiedly "pathological" and "homicidal," those of the Left have been compassionate and benevolent—and that only extraneous circumstances produced the horrors of the Great Purge, the Great Proletarian Revolution, and the massacre of innocents by the Khmer Rouge.

There are others who, for at least two generations, have argued that the political universe we have known since the Bolshevik and Fascist revolutions has not been divided, primarily, by conflicts between the Right and Left, but between representative democracies and anti-democratic "ideocracies." The contest has been between systems that base legitimacy on electoral results and those whose legitimacy and authority rest on appeal to an ideology considered inerrant, the guidance of a "charismatic leader," and the armed suasion of a hegemonic party. Among the latter movements and regimes there is no Right or Left. There are only anti-democratic systems.

However convenient and informative the distinction between Right and Left may be in local politics, it is largely irrelevant in dealing with the revolutionary movements that have shaped the international environment during the last hundred years. There have been many who have recognized as much.

This work is an effort to restate the case for the latter view. It attempts to supplement the argument advanced a quarter of a century ago that there is more "fascism" in the Left than most Western scholars have been prepared to recognize.[5] Recent developments in post-Soviet Russia and post-Maoist China eloquently make the case.

I attempt to trace the decay of Marxist theory among left-wing intellectuals. Bereft of much of its mummery, Marxist theory reveals itself as a variant of generic fascism. The contest of the twentieth century, which has cost so much in human lives, was not between the Right and the Left. It was between representative democracies and their anti-democratic opponents. It has been an arduous struggle.

The anti-democratic temptation continues to have appeal to those who feel themselves to be oppressed and humiliated. One of the implications of the discussion in what follows is that, at the end of the century, there really is very little convincing evidence that the democracies have won the contest. That does not bode well for the twenty-first century.

Acknowledgments

Preparing an academic manuscript for publication necessarily makes one indebted to many persons and institutions. I owe a deep debt of gratitude to the University of California, Berkeley, for providing me with an intellectual home for most of my professional life. I also owe a great deal to the officers and staff of the Marine Corps University at Quantico, Virginia, for generously allowing me to use their handsome research center for my work. My stay there as Oppenheimer Professor (1996–1997) was stimulating and pleasant.

To my wife, Professor Maria Hsia Chang, I owe access to the Chinese political literature to which I refer in the text. She provided not only access to the Chinese materials, but priceless insights into Chinese political culture. To Mr. Leonid Kil I owe access to the Russian language material, which he knows so well.

Professor Zeev Sternhell of Hebrew University continues to be an inspiration, and Professor Alessandro Campi of Perugia introduced a bit of psychic energy into a life of study that had become more than a little fatigued. Throughout our work together, Mr. John Covell and the staff of the Yale University Press have been more patient and forthcoming than I had any right to expect. I hope this book is worthy, in some small measure, of the contributions of so many good people and fine institutions.

A. James Gregor
Berkeley, California

1

On Theory and Revolution in Our Time

By the end of the twentieth century, it had become clear that academicians in the West, for the most part, had failed to understand the nature of the revolutions that had overwhelmed their time.[1] *Fascism*, for example, frequently invoked as a generic concept, but rarely persuasively characterized, was employed in attempts to comprehend the major social and political dislocations that shaped a substantial part of the century.[2]

Now, in the 1990s, interpretation has become still more problematic as a new generation of scholars have sought to employ the concept *fascism* in an effort to understand something about present and future politics. Unhappily, the term *fascism* has been dilated to the point where its cognitive use has become more than suspect.

In the most recent efforts, the term *fascism* has been pressed into service to identify anything that could in any way be described of as "right-wing extremism"—from any resistance to permissive immigration policies, expressions of religious exclusivity, instances of "hate speech," to the "spewing forth" of "conservative" sentiments.[3] Recently the European Parliament commissioned two major committees of inquiry charged with responsibility for investigating the recruitment and electoral successes of "fascism" on the Continent. The reports that ultimately appeared contained long, doleful recitations of terrorist attacks on foreign workers, assaults on Jewish schoolchildren, incidents of arson at refugee hostels, mindless violence at soccer matches, and advocacy in print of genocidal homicide.[4] Defined as "anti-Jewish violence and racist vandalism," "fascism" was found everywhere.[5]

Communism, in turn, was as frequently invoked as a concept in the discussion of the century's revolutions—and just as frequently addressed in a manner that left one more confused than illuminated.[6] Terms like *communist, Marxist–*

Leninist, or simply *Marxist* were used indiscriminately to identify existing political systems as different as the Soviet Union of Josef Stalin, the China of Mao Zedong, and the Cuba of Fidel Castro.

This kind of confusion was apparent at the very beginning of the "Marxist revolutionary experiment" in 1917. John Reed, the American adventurer and witness to the Bolshevik uprising, was among the first to suggest that Lenin's revolution was the harbinger of what would ultimately be a worldwide "left-wing Marxist future."

That a "Marxist" revolution would occur, in whatever circumstances, in a primitive economic environment, characterized more by peasant life than by proletarian consciousness, did not seem to puzzle very many Western thinkers. Many were clearly disposed, as was John Reed, to see the Bolshevik revolution as a signal of an imminent universal Marxist revolution. V. I. Lenin and his entourage did advertise themselves as Marxists—defenders of the proletariat—and a surprising number of Western scholars continued for seven decades to think of the Soviet experiment as an effort to realize the Marxist dream of equality and peace. There is no other way to explain the admiration with which Western intellectuals like George Bernard Shaw, Sydney and Beatrice Webb, André Gide, Ignazio Silone, Arthur Koestler, or Howard Fast studied the Soviet revolution.

What this contributed to was a systematic difference in the scholarly employment of the two concepts, *fascism* and *communism*. References to fascism were almost always mercurial and fugitive and almost invariably carried moral opprobrium in their train. For the half-century after the end of the Second World War, the term *fascism*, almost without exception, was used to designate "pathological" political phenomena. Fascists and fascism were consistently spoken of as "narcissistic and megalomaniac," as well as "sadistic, necrophiliac" and "psychopathological."[7]

"Marxist," "Marxist–Leninist," or "communist" systems, on the other hand, were rarely treated with such unqualified condemnation. Early in the history of the Soviet Union, E. H. Carr could argue that V. I. Lenin and Josef Stalin really sought to increase "the sum of well-being and human opportunity" through achievements that "impressed the rest of the world."[8]

Even when such systems were convincingly identified with purges, mass murder, and pandemic political violence, they were rarely deemed "psychopathological" or "sadistic." As late as 1984, Norman Mailer could still lament the treatment of the Soviet Union as an "evil force," and others refused to acknowledge that political terror might function in some intrinsic fashion in the communist systems of Josef Stalin, Mao Zedong, or Kim Il Sung. For a very long time, there was an abiding sense, among many Western intellectuals, that the Soviet Union was no more "evil" than the United States.[9]

Fascism was an unmitigated evil, but any such characterization of Soviet or Chinese Marxism–Leninism—for a very long time—was understood to be a product of "paranoia" brought on by the "anti-communist hysteria" of the cold war. For years, between the two world wars, and subsequently throughout the decades of the cold war, many intellectuals in the West seemed to judge Marxist–Leninist regimes, not by facts that had become increasingly available, but in line with wish and utopian fantasy.[10] For an inexplicably long time, the Bolshevik revolution was seen by many Western intellectuals as the fulfillment of socialism's historic destiny—and a promise of the world's salvation.

The collapse of Marxism–Leninism forced everyone, everywhere, to attempt a reassessment of the entire revolutionary experience of the twentieth century. Undertaken in the wrong countries, by the wrong classes, under conditions that Karl Marx and Friedrich Engels insisted could neither foster nor sustain the salvific socialism they anticipated, Marxist–Leninist movements, and the regimes they fabricated, were rarely treated as what they were: historical anomalies, animated by an intellectual pretension for which there was little warrant.[11] The consequence of all this has been to leave modern scholarship without a coherent understanding of what the revolutionary history of the twentieth century was all about. An omnibus "fascism" and a curiously misunderstood "communism" make up much of the political history of our time.

However they understood or misunderstood these terms, most Western intellectuals, throughout the century, decided that some very fundamental differences separated fascist and communist revolutions. Fascist revolutions were inextricably and irremediably of the Right and Marxist–Leninist revolutions of the Left.

Well into the middle of the 1990s, Western academics continued to find humanity and hope in the few remaining left-wing Marxist–Leninist systems that survived the collapse of the Soviet Union in 1991. Left-wing regimes in North Korea and in Castro's Cuba still evoked positive sentiments from some.[12] At the same time, other Western academics were deploring the rise of right-wing "neofascism" in Italy, Germany, France, and the United Kingdom.[13]

Thus, with a certain measure of consistency, scholars in the twentieth century have persisted in distinguishing right-wing revolutions from those on the Left. It has never been altogether clear what the distinction really implied except that, in general, right-wing revolutions necessarily involved unspeakable horrors—while those on the Left, well-meaning if errant, manifested themselves in attempts to lift the burdens of poverty and oppression from the shoulders of the unfortunate.[14]

However emphatic the sentiment that insisted on the distinctions between revolutions of the Right and Left, it is uncertain whether now, at the end of the century, the differences between fascism and communism remain as clear and comprehensible as they were once imagined to be. At the end of the century, it has become almost impossible to determine what the notion *right-wing* means to essayists—except to say that, for many, its reference is "fascism." We are told, with confidence, that "the extreme right's ideology is provided by fascism."[15]

For some, "right wing" and "fascism" both involve "nationalism, hierarchical structures, and the 'leader principle.' "[16] For others, both mean "antiliberalism, anticommunism, and anticonservatism." For still others, both "right wing" and "fascism" are given over to communitarianism, anti-individualism and anti-rationalism, or they entertain a "belief in the authority of the state over the individual; an emphasis on natural community; distrust for individual representation and parliamentary arrangements; limitations on personal and collective freedoms; collective identification in a great national destiny, against class or ethnic or religious divisions; and acceptance of the hierarchical principle for social organizations."[17] Should that be the case, we are left with an abiding puzzlement. We can take little cognitive comfort in the distinctions that such a rehearsal of political traits pretends to deliver.

Once one drops below the high level of abstraction such characterizations offer, one finds denotative right- and left-wing distinctions hard to maintain. We are informed, for example, that "there is overwhelming evidence that the old communist regimes had always harboured sentiments of inherent nationalism and even xenophobic prejudices barely hidden under the cloak of Marxist internationalism."[18] By the mid-1990s, moreover, no one denied the "hierarchical structures" or the predominant role of "leaders" in all communist systems. There is hardly any doubt that Marxist–Leninist systems were, and remain, "communitarian and anti-individualist." Whether they were or are "anti-rationalist" really turns on one's definition of "rationalist."

That Marxist–Leninist systems are or have been anti-liberal and anti-parliamentarian has never really been controversial. That they have argued that their respective nations have a "great national destiny" is hardly a matter of dispute. In fact, for a long time, the distinction between the political Right and Left has been recognized as singularly insubstantial.[19] In 1978, as a case in point, Mikhail Agursky argued that whatever ideology legitimated the regime of Josef Stalin, it was certainly not "left-wing."

Agursky maintained that Soviet domestic and foreign policy was torn between its "radical right nature" and the "radical left legitimacy" of its ideological pretensions.[20] By the end of the 1920s and the beginning of the 1930s, Stalin had created a regime that had abandoned every principle that had presumably typified left-wing aspirations and had given himself over to notions of "socialism in one country"—with all the attendant attributes: nationalism, the leadership principle, anti-liberalism, anti-individualism, communitarianism, hierarchical rule, missionary zeal, the employment of violence to assure national purpose, and anti-Semitism—making the Soviet Union unmistakenly "a cousin to German National Socialism."[21]

We are left with a budget of paradoxes. Given the seeming logic of the proposed classification of right-wing polities—with nationalism, hierarchical political structures, and charismatic leadership as defining properties—both fascism and Marxism–Leninism would seem to be political products of right-wing extremism. Should that be the case, the revolutions undertaken by Benito Mussolini, Adolf Hitler, Josef Stalin, and Mao Zedong were all right-wing endeavors.

Thus, we are told, in fact and for example, that the Romanian Communist regime of Nicolae Ceauşescu, "mixing nationalism and Stalinism," was a regime not of the Left, but of the Right.[22] It was "nationalistic," as all Marxist–Leninist systems appear to have been; it was hierarchical, as all Marxist–Leninist systems have been; and it was informed by the "leader principle," as all Marxist–Leninist systems have been. If Ceauşescu's Communism had been right-wing, all communist systems would have to be right-wing.

Given these evolving notions, it would seem that communism, like fascism—however counterintuitive the idea might be—was a right-wing revolutionary movement. As a consequence, we are now counselled that "perhaps we have tended to misjudge the communist elites of yesterday and failed to notice their latent nationalism all along."[23] And perhaps we never really appreciated the hierarchical character of communist systems, or the role played in the various regimes by the *Vozhd* or the Chairman, the Dear Leader or the *Lider Massimo*.

It is unclear what all that might suggest. It is now generally accepted, for example, that Josef Stalin was an anti-Semite, and that the Soviet Union, whatever its internationalist pretenses, had always been inspired by a form of irredentist and reactive nationalism.[24] The fact is that, throughout the twentieth century, both fascism and communism were committed to the creation of "a new revolutionary order," having nothing to do with "the old, rotten, decadent [antecedent] regime." Fascism, like communism, advocated the achievement of a "new revolutionary order, a new society and, even, a new man." For both fascism and communism, that would necessitate "a general, collective, unitary effort by the whole nation, [requiring that] all the nation's energy . . . be mobilized and channelled to the achievement of its new (and revived) greatness." In both cases, mobilization would be a function of "the leader's charismatic appeal."[25]

Both fascism and Marxist–Leninist systems have demonstrated an abiding distrust of electoral and parliamentary representation. Both entertained the conviction that individuals and groups of individuals must submit to the authority of the hegemonic state—and it would be the hierarchical, nonrepresentative state, in pursuit of "a great national destiny," that would overcome all class, political, ethnic, and racial divisions.[26]

These political properties apply, with varying degrees of faithfulness, as much to Stalin's Soviet Union, Mao Zedong's China, Kim Il Sung's Democratic People's Republic of Korea, and Fidel Castro's Socialist Cuba as they do to Mussolini's Italy. The fact remains that if "right-wing extremism" telescopes into "fascism," then it appears that Josef Stalin's Soviet Union was not only fascist, it was an instantial case of right-wing extremism.

In the years prior to the Second World War, Rudolf Hilferding, the internationally noted Marxist theorist, attempted to bring some clarity into a discussion that had become increasingly opaque. On the issue of left- and right-wing economic strategies, for instance, he pointed out that "the controversy as to whether the economic system of the Soviet Union is 'capitalist' or 'socialist' seems to me rather pointless. It is neither. It represents a totalitarian state economy, i.e., a system to which the [fascist] economies of Germany and Italy are drawing closer and closer."[27]

The fact is that the Soviet Union of Josef Stalin was more like fascism than intellectuals throughout the decades from the 1930s to the 1980s seemed prepared to allow.[28] Only with the collapse of the Soviet Union have an increasing number of specialists shown a readiness to acknowledge the similarities.[29] With its collapse, Marxism–Leninism, at the end of the twentieth century, is being entirely reassessed.

By the 1990s, it was no longer possible to speak, with any intellectual integrity, of the Soviet Union of Stalin as having been informed by a "proletarian" economic system, or possessed of a "working-class" government. No more credence is invested in the Stalinist, Maoist, or Castro "proletarian state" than was invested in the "proletarian" character of the "German National Socialist Workers' Party" or the "Fascist State of Labor."

By the time of its disappearance at the end of the 1980s and the beginning of the 1990s, it was no longer plausible to argue that the Soviet Union offered a clear alternative to the "right-wing extremism" of fascism. In fact, it was no longer clear what "right-wing" or "left-wing" might be taken to mean in terms of the major revolutions of the twentieth century.

If by the end of the twentieth century, some, if not many, intellectuals have been driven to identify both fascism and communism as right-wing revolutionary movements and regimes, how might one explain the fact that for almost the entire century a sharp distinction was drawn between the two on the basis of a right- and left-wing dichotomy? It has become increasingly difficult to explain the persistence of the right- and left-wing distinctions that were so long labored in the academic literature devoted to accounts of revolution in our time.

In fact, during the first years after the termination of the Second World War, there were Western intellectuals, whatever their notions of "left" and "right" political persuasions might have been, who were fully prepared to address that issue. They advised the subsumption of both fascism and communism under the rubric "totalitarianism," arguing that each manifested traits that identified them—however many particular differences may have distinguished them—as members of the same political genus. There were more than a few among Western specialists who resisted the subsumption, insisting that the notion that fascism and communism might share some fundamental properties was an "ideological weapon" in the war against the Soviet Union.[30] For some, the very suggestion that fascism and Marxist–Leninist systems shared any major features was totally unacceptable. Fascism was of the Right; communism was of the Left.

But totalitarianism, as a concept, irrespective of the objections of many academics, remained part of the lexicon of comparative political analysis. The preoccupation was not with the distinctions of Right and Left, but with the shared totalitarian traits. In fact, by the last decade of the twentieth century, we were being told that "all the attributes of totalitarianism had antecedents in Lenin's Russia: an official, all-embracing ideology; a single party of the elect headed by a 'leader' and dominating the state; police terror; the ruling party's control of the means of communication and the armed forces; [as well as] central command of the economy."[31] Totalitarianism, as a political regime, had apparently been as much an invention of the Left as of the Right. A left and a right totalitarianism seemed to share space in the universe of political discourse.

The Stalinism that followed the totalitarian intimations of Lenin's Russia, was not only totalitarian, it was infused by an "almost fascist-like chauvinism," together with a "bureaucratization, absence of democracy, censorship, police repression," and, as has been suggested, by an irrepressible and increasingly intrusive anti-Semitism.[32] By the mid-1990s, it was increasingly acknowledged that left-wing totalitarianism more and more began to resemble right-wing totalitarianism.[33]

The distinction between the totalitarianism of the Left and that of the Right seems to have reduced itself to whatever convictions each entertained concerning private property and the role of the market exchange of goods and services. Even that, however, is no longer considered to be as substantial as once thought.[34] Now that post-Maoist China has permitted the existence, expansion, and protection of qualified property rights under "communist" auspices, the distinctions between right and left political persuasions have become still more diaphanous.

What seems to have become transparent, except to those irremediably doctrinaire, is that the distinction between the Right and the Left, long considered critical to the understanding of revolutionaries and revolutions of the twentieth century, has become increasingly insubstantial.[35] Whatever the putative moral and empirical differences that originally urged the distinction on analysts, an extraordinary measure of confusion continues to stalk any effort to distinguish between the fascist and Marxist–Leninist movements and regimes of our unfortunate time—in terms of discrete right- and left-wing attributes.

By the end of the twentieth century, the distinction between Right and Left has increasingly become a distinction largely without a difference. That seems not to have been apparent throughout much of the last half of the twentieth century. For much of that time, it was the prevailing conviction that fascism, however it was to be understood, was an exacerbated expression of the political Right, while Marxism–Leninism was a product of the "Enlightenment left."

Even at the end of the twentieth century, there were still many intellectuals in the industrial democracies who resisted abandoning the right- and left-wing distinctions with which they had become so familiar. Some remained reluctant to acknowledge that "leftist" regimes were more homicidal than those of the "right." Most commentators, however, had closed a painful chapter in their intellectual history. The long romance with the revolutionary left was largely over.[36] Whatever they would subsequently make of Marxism and Marxism–Leninism, it would never be quite the same.

By the mid-1990s, it had become evident to almost everyone that the application of social science to the study of the "left-wing" Soviet Union, "perhaps the greatest case study of the behavioral age," had been a failure—testimony to a fundamental intellectual problem in the assessment of revolutions in the twentieth century.[37] Western intellectuals seem to have had serious difficulties in taking the measure of revolutionary movements and the regimes they created.

There have been those who have already undertaken to register the moral indifference to the excesses of the Left that seemed to have haunted Western scholars throughout much of the twentieth century. There have been those who have explored the psychological dimensions of the peculiar fascination with communism and communist systems frequently displayed by Western intellectuals.[38] Curiously enough, what has not really been systematically undertaken is a treatment of Marxism–Leninism as itself a "theoretical" system, with social science pretensions, capable of explaining both itself and its opponents.

That is not to say that the study of the intellectual origins of communism has been neglected. A virtual cottage industry has grown up around the production of studies dealing with Marxism and Leninism as intellectual systems. There have even been studies of "Mao Zedong Thought" as intellectual history and scholarly treatment of the stream of consciousness ideology of Fidel Castro.

Marxism–Leninism, we have been told, was predicated on a "coherent" and "systematic doctrine derived from the ideas of Hegel, Marx and Engels, as redefined by Lenin and Stalin." More than that, it "incorporated an economic theory" and a "series of dialectical laws." The clear implication was that Marxism and Marxism–Leninism were theoretical systems capable of providing explanatory and predictive purchase on complex political events.

By the end of the 1980s, concurrent with growing evidence of the failure of "Marxist" regimes, such claims aroused increasing skepticism. It was increasingly recognized that "Marxist categories and arguments [could] be used ideologically to rationalize any situation one pleases."[39] More and more scholars were prepared to recognize that Marxism, as "theory," was singularly empty of any empirical implications. Whatever its intellectual coherence, its economic theories, and its dialectical laws, Marxist theory was incapable of accounting for the major revolutionary changes that have overwhelmed our century.

Worst still, for all its theoretical machinery and "scientific" sophistication, during times of crisis Marxism could apparently do nothing to insulate the regimes it animated from taking on the "common features" of those fascist states it presumably opposed.[40] Marxism, in the hands of its practitioners has been singularly incapable of anticipating systemic crisis in the very systems it operated—or explaining such crises after their passing.

Some Western academics have been fascinated by Marxist theory since its inception in the mid-nineteenth century. A veritable avalanche of volumes devoted to the explication and dissemination of Marxist theory has poured from university presses for over a century. That those same authors who produced that abundance should have sought an explanation, within the body of Marxist speculation, for revolution and the rise of fascism in the twentieth century can be easily understood.

In fact, it will be argued here that it was Marxist and Marxist–Leninist speculation that laid down the first theoretical outlines of an explanatory strategy in the effort to understand revolution in our time. By the end of the first quarter of the twentieth century, doctrinaire Marxists had provided all the recommended conceptual materials, the social science categories, and the compulsory normative assessments, to be invoked in any discussion of "right-wing" and "left-wing" revolutions and regimes.

By the mid-1930s, the judgments of many Western scholars were fixed in just those categories and those assessments. In retrospect, it appears that such dispositions can best be explained by appealing to the principles of the sociology of knowledge, rather than by cataloging whatever evidence was mustered to support such categories and assessments.

It was not the case that throughout the history of Stalinism, Western scholarship knew nothing of Stalin's massacre of innocents, his physical destruction of entire classes of citizens, his political oppression of any opposition, his exploitation of the peasants and workers, and his general denial of civil and political rights to a subject population. Many Western scholars simply chose to interpret the political life of the Soviet Union by an entirely different measure from that applied to Fascist Italy.

Throughout a good part of the history of the twentieth century, fascism, however it was understood, was taken to be an unmitigated evil by Western scholarship. "Marxism," in its various guises, was not. Any suggestion that Mussolini's Fascism and "communism," in whatever form communism manifested itself, might share affinities was repugnant to Western scholarship.

As a consequence, for a very long time, any "Western scholars who had the temerity to link Mussolini . . . with Communism in any way . . . risked harassment."[41] Only with the definitive collapse of Marxist and Marxist–Leninist systems in the 1980s and 1990s were more and more Western academics prepared to tell us, without much equivocation, that "Bolshevism and [Mussolini's] Fascism were heresies of socialism," having both arisen out of the revolutionary aspirations of intransigent socialists.[42] Only then were we told that they shared ideas concerning society, revolution, and the mass mobilization of persons. That, it has been argued, is attested to by the fact that at the founding of the Fascist movement, and throughout its initial revolutionary phase, the largest number of Mussolini's "theoreticians" were former communists and intransigent Marxists.[43] In fact, we are now told that much of the ideological inspiration of Fascism came from revolutionary socialists, and that Mussolini, like V. I. Lenin, was a leader of radical Marxists. More than any other socialist before the First World War, Mussolini resembled Lenin.[44]

By the mid-1990s, "mainstream" opinion among Western scholars had changed. The case for a family resemblance between right- and left-wing revolutionaries was no longer considered exotic. For a variety of reasons, the intellectual environment had been transformed. An account of that transformation cannot be undertaken with any real confidence—but part of such an account would have to include an assessment of Marxism as "theory."[45]

Social science hosts a collection of linguistic artifacts that range from, among others, lexical definitions, through classificatory schemata, to conceptual frameworks and, finally, "theories"—with theories understood to supply explanatory power.[46] Theories are imagined to account for sequences of events that otherwise would remain inscrutable, impenetrable to science.

The term *theory* in social science is generally applied to a body of thought that has at least some predictive pretension. Minimally, "theory" is understood to convey some sense of empirical or normative "understanding" of events.

That social science, in general, is an informal science means, among other things, that the criteria for qualifying as a "theory" are neither particularly rigorous nor systematically applied. In social science it is often the case that any reasonably coherent collection of sentences qualifies as a "theory" as long as it generates in one or another audience an appropriate sense of "understanding."

There are any number of candidate theories in social science, some singularly short-lived, others that have been enduring. All have contributed in some sense and some measure to our comprehension of our time. Among them, Marxist theory has been perhaps the most enduring. How much it has contributed to our understanding of the twentieth century has become one of the major issues of contemporary scholarship.

Karl Marx and Friedrich Engels coined any number of social science predictions in the course of their work during the nineteenth century. Time has failed to fulfill any of them. Nonetheless, some academics have found the ideas of Marx and Engels so attractive—for whatever reason—that they have been loathe to measure them against the requirements of standard science.

The consequence has been that Marxist categories and Marxist normative judgments have survived in the professional literature of social science to an extent that might not otherwise have been expected for a "theory" that enjoys little, if any, empirical confirmation. The very abundance of material left to scholarship by Marx and Engels allowed academics the opportunity, should they be so disposed, to rummage through to find a sufficient number of implicit causes of error, qualifications, and tautologies to insulate the system from final disconfirmation. That many were so disposed was probably a consequence of the fact that classical Marxism was intrinsically seductive. It pretended to deliver not only an elaborate "theory"; it also satisfied the moral sensibilities of academics.

Given Marxism's appeal, by the turn of the twentieth century, there were any number of Western scholars who were prepared to anticipate the increasing "emiseration" of the proletariat at the hands of capitalist oppressors—in just the manner that Marx had predicted. There were any number of Western academics prepared to see in the "proletariat" the "Promethean" class Marx had anticipated. There were "political theorists" who fully expected that the "vast majority" of workers in a capitalist system that had "exhausted its potential" would come to power in the moribund economies of the West, bringing classlessness, peace, humanity, and ultimate fulfillment to humankind. It was a vision so normatively attractive to many that it became a inalienable feature of Western academic life and remains attractive to Western scholars to this day.

The fact is that Marxism has always been more normative enjoinment than social science. Both Marx and Engels were aware that their system was a quasi-deductive "philosophy" rather than an "empiricism." While there was frequent talk of turning Hegelianism, with its "empty idealism," on its head, to provide it with "earthly" content, there was remarkably little empirical observation that might provide substance to conjectures about how the world of economics and class psychology actually functioned.[47] More than anything else, Marxism was a partially formalized deductive system—what has been called a "dialectical dance of categories"—almost entirely devoid of empirical content—consciously or unconsciously designed to support some deeply felt moral convictions.[48]

In general, cosmopolitanism, classlessness, equity, and peace unproblematically recommend themselves to most Westerners. A "theory" that conceives such outcomes to be the "ineluctable" consequence of processes already in act, is one that has irresistible appeal to all right-thinking people. Any political system that purports to be inspired by such thoughts has much to recommend it.

Several considerations, however, urge themselves on anyone with intellectual prudence. Such systems of thought cry out for objective review. So intrinsically attractive are such bodies of rumination that anyone with judgment will suspend commitment until they have been fully inspected.

In retrospect, at the end of the twentieth century, we can look back on the influence of Marxist theory on our efforts to understand what has transpired in what is perhaps the most savage century in the history of humankind. Given the evident reality that has overwhelmed the end of the twentieth century, Western scholars are now prepared to recognize that Marxism could not now serve, and probably never served, as a "metatheory of politics"—as a guide to the interpretation of contemporary revolution.[49] Marxism, in all its theoretical and institutional variations, appears to have contributed very little to the making or understanding of revolutionary movements and revolutionary regimes in the twentieth century.

For all that, it appears that the complexity of its theory and its normatively attractive content shaped Western academic thought about revolution for three-quarters of a century. While many in the academic community were content to limit themselves to the descriptive criterial traits by virtue of which they identified the various revolutionary movements and regimes of our time—"fascist" and "Marxist"—there were others who sought "theoretical" understanding. Dissatisfied with the categories of comparative politics, they searched for a comprehensive account that gave predictive and normative leverage over the complex realities that make up the histories of the fascist and communist revolutions.

As early as the end of the 1920s, the *London Times* recognized the species similarities between Stalinism and Fascism, and in 1934 George Sabine spoke of the Soviet Union, National Socialist Germany, and Fascist Italy as representing a new form of political regime—one governed by "unitary parties" that aspired to "totalitarian" control.[50] The *Times* and Sabine made classificatory and pretheoretical efforts to "understand" a new political phenomenon. For many Western academics, that could hardly be enough. What many sought was theoretical substance, whatever they thought that substance to be. What seems clear is that many conceived Marxist theory as delivering that substance. Observed similarities between fascist and communist systems were dismissed as "superficial." What was sought was theoretical understanding. And that, we were told, was offered by a Marxist theory of revolution.

Only now, at the apparent end of the cycle of "Marxist" revolutions, can one look back and attempt an assessment of the influence of Marxist theory on our understanding of ourselves and our time. Only now do many feel confident enough to raise the question of why the family resemblances between Mussolini's Fascism and Marxism–Leninism had never been fully recognized or acknowledged, or why it took considerable courage to suggest that fascist regimes in any way resembled those of the political Left.[51] What this new independence has suggested to specialists in Soviet history, in fact, is that a more profound understanding of fascism might "shed much light on the regime that emerged from the Russian Revolution."[52]

The present exposition attempts to address some of these issues. The elaborate effort by Marxist intellectuals to understand "fascism" as a political category, and Italian Fascism specifically, reveals a great deal about Marxism–Leninism as a cognitive enterprise. More than that, it reveals a great deal about Fascism.

What this exposition entails is a general review of the Marxist theory of fascism, commencing with the first efforts on the part of Marxist–Leninist theoreticians in the early 1920s. As will be argued, it became obvious early on that the best Marxist–Leninist theorists were never satisfied with their interpretation of Fascism. Initially convinced of Fascism's "reactionary," "counterrevolutionary," and "conservative" character, over the years they progressively discovered its "revolutionary," "anti-conservative" properties. It is the account of that transformation that will occupy us in the first part of the present exposition. It will be devoted to the Marxist interpretation of Mussolini's Fascism as that interpretation transformed itself through seven decades of partisan intellectual activity.

The fact that the Marxist effort at interpretation was partisan renders its assessment of fascism all the more interesting. By the time of the disintegration of the Soviet Union, Marxist theoreticians had begun to evaluate fascism in a totally unanticipated fashion. That, combined with the failure of the Kremlin's theoreticians to foresee the collapse of their own system, offers a special perspective on the nature of Marxist "theory."

More than that, as Marxist theorists were compelled to reinterpret fascism in the light of empirical evidence and political circumstances, the fundamental affinities shared by Marxist and fascist regimes became apparent. Little of this has been discussed by Western specialists at any length; yet it affords precious insight into both the relationship between Marxism and fascism and the quality of Marxist social science.

The fact that Marxist intellectuals were never really satisfied with the time-conditioned interpretation of general and specific fascisms, modifying their accounts to satisfy circumstances and in response to reality, indicates a general failure to really gain durable insights into the phenomena. Marxist "theory" was intrinsically flawed. Conversely, the failure of Western thinkers to appreciate what was transpiring in the course of time, and with the Marxist interpretation of fascism, suggests something about the non-communist intellectual environments in which the "left/right" dichotomy evolved during the interwar years and immediately after the Second World War. The fact that the conviction still persists that one can cognitively distinguish fascist and communist systems on the basis of a left/right distinction is a case study in the persistence of prejudgment.

The argument that follows rests on the conviction that many of the notions that have governed Western political thought have been largely a by-product of Marxist analyses. That Mussolini's Fascism was an "extreme right-wing" response to "proletarian revolution" was really a product of orthodox Marxist–Leninist speculation. While Western scholars, in large part, were not orthodox Marxist–Leninists, they nonetheless succumbed to the "profound theoretical" analysis provided by Marxist–Leninists. From the first quarter of the twentieth century until its close, the influence of Marxist–Leninist "theory" continued to obscure much of the substance of revolutionary thought in our time.

In order to make the case for the influence of Marxist–Leninist theory, a rather detailed exposition of its formulations recommends itself. After that somewhat detailed exposition of the Marxist theories of Fascism, some substantial time will be spent in dealing with the apologetic, theoretical, and interpretative literature generated by Fascist thinkers during the interwar years—with the conviction that such material not only reveals a great deal about their belief system, but documents their awareness of the affinities that united fascist and communist regimes.

Prevalent among "progressive" Western thinkers throughout much of the century has been the conviction that Fascism and communism were fundamentally antithetical—communism rich with intellectual tradition and Fascism entirely empty of serious thought. That, together with the emotional repercussions of a war fought against Fascism, with communism allied to the West, created the conviction that the two were morally and intellectually incomparable. The predictable consequence among intellectuals was that fascism was conceived as both devoid of intelligence and the incarnation of evil, while communism was regarded, in general, as both rich in ideas and involving a flawed attempt to uplift the weary and impoverished.

The result was that "right-wing" Fascism was seen as radically different from "left-wing" Marxism, and that any effort to associate the two was regarded as the product of intellectual indigence or moral perversity. Such efforts were dismissed as both morally repugnant and intellectually benighted.

Only with the catastrophic collapse of the Soviet Union and the critical disillusion that followed in its train has Western scholarship shown any disposition to reevaluate the entire communist tradition—and its relationship to fascism in general and Fascism in particular. It was the total disintegration of institutionalized socialist ideology, revealing its fundamental lack not only of coherence, but of relevance for a revolutionary political community undergoing the stresses of accelerated economic growth and industrialization, that has led to a reevaluation of Marxism–Leninism as a belief system.

The fact that a form of fascism has made its appearance in the former Soviet Union has reopened the entire issue of the affinities between the Marxism and fascism of the twentieth century.[53] That the fascism that has arrested the attention of international scholarship was, and is, in substantial part, a product of "critical Marxists" is of particular significance in attempting to understand revolution in our time.[54]

Over time, critical Marxists in the Soviet Union became increasingly uncomfortable with the disjuncture between Marxist rhetoric and the reality of established communist systems. They identified the transparent hypocrisy of what purported to be a "classless society" in which a self-selected "new class" of state functionaries, using monopoly party control, governed in a fashion that resulted in the exaction of more tribute from subjects than any class-based autocracy in history. It was they who compared the promise of "humanity" and "liberation" found in the writings of Marx and Engels to the reality of the totalitarianism that Marxism–Leninism had constructed. It was they who recognized the dysfunctional nature of the economic system and the prevalence of nationalist sentiment in a polity that promised "unlimited abundance" and celebrated the resolution of "all national questions." It was they who revealed not only the intellectual poverty of Marxism–Leninism, but its incompetence as a guide to conduct as well.

By the end of 1989, in a conference held in Moscow, sponsored by the Central Committee of the Communist Party itself, several speakers expressed profound misgivings about the relevance of Marxism's "historical and dialectical materialism" to the making of social policy.[55] There was a clear recognition that classical Marxism, with all its talk of "proletarian" and world revolution, actually had very little to say to the first Bolsheviks, or their heirs, who found themselves facing the armed hostility of advanced industrial nations with only a relatively retrograde agrarian economy, peopled largely by peasants, at their disposal.[56]

The response of Soviet intellectuals took essentially one of two alternative courses: (a) rejection of the Soviet system as a non-Marxist caricature of "true Marxism"; or (b) search for an ideology that better represents the character and intent of the system that made Russia one of the great world powers of the twentieth century. The first course provided the world with the "democratic reformers" who have rejected the old system in its entirety; the second course is represented in the "nationalist opposition" that, at the turn of the century, threatens an emerging Russia with the recreation of a non-democratic, authoritarian, elitist, and developmental future.

In the dying Soviet Union, as will be argued, critical Marxists began to put together an alternative ideology for "national salvation." They began to appeal to latent nationalist and patriotic sentiments. They spoke of authoritarian and elitist modalities to salvage the nation from the wreckage of catastrophic failure. They invoked determination and heroism, leadership and discipline.

Once the implications of all this are understood, the entire question of whether socialism in the twentieth century was of the Left or of the Right can be profitably examined. If scholars are now prepared to acknowledge that Stalinism was "utterly irrational"—the system created by Marxism–Leninism fundamentally "pathological"—then what used to provide the moral grounds for distinguishing between the political Left and the political Right can no longer serve.[57] If "mass murders," numbering in the millions, are now "freely attributed to Stalin, who [is] acknowledged as one of the greatest criminals in history," it becomes increasingly difficult to draw the traditional separation between "humane" communism on the Left and "homicidal" fascism on the Right.[58] Marxism–Leninism can no longer be conceived as uniquely "rational and constructive," and Fascism as uniquely "irrational and destructive."[59] The major markers employed to distinguish the political Left from the political Right in the past are forfeit.

The search for an adequate, general account of socialist revolutions in the twentieth century arises out of the intellectual crisis that attends the contemporary reemergence of "fascism" in Eastern Europe and the former Soviet Union. One aspect of this crisis is reflected in the inability of scholars to settle on any one account of what the Russian Revolution of 1917 was all about.

There will be those, of course, who will continue to attempt a more-or-less "orthodox" interpretation of the revolutionary history of the twentieth century— with "Marxism" on the Left and fascism on the Right—but it is unlikely that such attempts will be anything more than hapless and helpless. More promising, perhaps, is pursuit of what the now acknowledged affinities between Fascism and Bolshevism might mean. This involves moving outside the customary grooves of standard twentieth-century historical interpretation, using Mussolini's Fascism as a paradigmatic instance of what revolution in our time might be taken to mean and drawing out whatever that might imply.

In the litter of what were once socialist states, contemporary historians and political scientists have identified the delusions that confused half a century of analysis. Marxism, the idea with an army at its back, became flesh in the wrong country, leading the wrong people, pursuing goals that were unattainable. In the course of their revolution, the Bolsheviks betrayed, or were soon to betray, almost every political principle they had proclaimed in their struggle for power. As an inescapable consequence, it will be argued, Marxist socialism transformed itself into something that only fascists, and some few Russian and Western intellectuals, could recognize. It became an identifiable variant of fascism.

Fascists had early anticipated the advent of the total state and its function in a world of unequal competition, in which each nation found itself compelled to pursue economic growth, industrialization, self-sufficiency, resource acquisition, and the search for space. The advent of the total state was predicated on neither "reaction" nor the preservation of privilege; it was understood to be neither a "tool of capitalism" nor a device for the slaughter of innocents. Whatever else it was conceived to be, it was seen as a functional response to the demands of less-developed countries in their unequal contest with the established "plutocracies."

In that sense, Fascist concepts were neither of the Left nor the Right.[60] They represented a complex conception of the nature of revolution in the twentieth century that remains instructive to this day. Western intellectuals, caught up in the synthetic dichotomy of Left and Right, have generally failed to appreciate the revolutionary authenticity of Fascist thought, and have thereby lost whatever leverage they had in terms of seeking to understand not only what was transpiring during the years between the First and Second World Wars, but during the entire period of the cold war as well.[61]

Given the truth of such an account, fascism in general and Mussolini's Fascism in particular have been almost universally misperceived, and, as a consequence, their relationship to Marxist–Leninist systems has been almost entirely misunderstood. The attempt to make a plausible case for these contentions will take the present discussion into the literature and history of "Marxism" and "fascism" as contested concepts. The course of exposition will commence with Marxism's first theoretical efforts to understand fascism, undertaken in the language of orthodox Marxism–Leninism as that language was understood by Western scholarship.

It was "theoretical" Marxism that mesmerized Western intellectuals and imposed on them the conviction that what scholarship was dealing with was a meaningful distinction between Right and Left. In fact, it will be argued that the proposed distinction was an artifact of Marxist–Leninist "theory" itself. The distinctions made were quasi-deductive derivations of entirely abstract, empirically untested notions. In fact, so little did Marxist–Leninists understand fascism that they failed to anticipate its reappearance at the end of the cold war. For all its intellectual pretensions, Marxism–Leninism offered very few cognitive insights into some of the most important events of the twentieth century. In fact, it failed to appreciate some of the most important political and intellectual developments within Marxism–Leninism itself.

At the conclusion of the brief history of Marxist ideas concerning Fascism, an attempt will be made to present the Fascist interpretation of what was transpiring in the twentieth century.[62] For Fascism, the revolutions of the twentieth century were those of poor, less-developed nations mobilizing their populations against the "demoplutocracies," the privileged nations that had acceded to industrialization, with all its attendant benefits, in the nineteenth century or early in the twentieth. The revolutions of "poor nations" anticipated by the Fascists were, and would be, revolutions that found their inspiration in neither the political Left nor the political Right. They were mass-mobilizing movements of reactive nationalism that sought a place in the sun for economically backward and industrially retrograde communities. They were, and would be, aggressive revolutions prepared to fight for what they considered, and today consider, equity and justice in the international arena. If the Fascists were right, we will yet see more members of the species.

2

The First Marxist Theories of Fascism

For whatever reason, by the end of the First World War many intellectuals in the West found Marxist "theory" fatally attractive. It was complex and seemingly profound. It augured a world without war, in which the meek and the disadvantaged would share, without distinction, the anticipated material and spiritual abundance generated by advanced industrial capitalism.

The horrors attendant on the first world conflict apparently left intellectuals in the West hungry for assurances that humankind might effectively gain control of its destiny—and that the future would bring a surcease from pain, want, and oppression. The Marxism of Karl Marx and Friedrich Engels seemed to promise just such an eventuality.

Orthodox Marxism was so seductive in those circumstances that many of the major intellects of the first years of the twentieth century became transfixed by the ideas found in the tomes left as an intellectual legacy by Marx and Engels. The First World War was conceived of as the product of reactionaries and chauvinists, all in the service of monied interests. They were the forces of the Right. The forces of the Left, the socialists, humanists, internationalists, and feminists, all opposed war, nationalism, imperialism, and invidious class distinctions.

By the end of the First World War, those notions were deeply embedded in the consciousness of many Western intellectuals—and they supplied the matrix into which Marxists were to insinuate their first "theories" of Mussolini's Fascism, to subsequently extend their coverage to generic fascism as well. That Marxists chose to characterize Mussolini's Fascism as "right-wing," "reactionary," and "counterrevolutionary" at the time of the confrontation between Marxism and Fascism on the Italian peninsula was only to be expected. Political circumstances on the Italian peninsula, at the conclusion of the First World War, had made Fascism the bitter enemy of Italian Socialism and Communism.

Those socialists who had followed Mussolini into Fascism had been "interventionists," advocates of Italy's entry into the First World War. They had taken on all the coloration of nationalism and had sought the resolution of national problems through international conflict. For Marxists, they must surely be of the "right." As early as 1915, when Mussolini and the syndicalist "subversives" of the Italian "radical left" joined in the clamor for war, the leaders of Italian Socialism had indicted Mussolini and those around him as "Marxist renegades"—Marxists who had rejected the official party position with respect to Italy's participation in the First World War. As though that were not enough, Fascism's first recruits, at the conclusion of the first world conflict, were violently opposed to the anti-nationalism of official Socialism and the newly organized Italian Communist Party. As survivors of the war, the socialist interventionists were committed to nationalism, a defense of Italy's victory, and "restoration" of Italy's "lost territories." For Marxists, all that was irremediably "bourgeois"—hence, "rightist."

Furthermore, the first Fascists were opposed to organized socialist and communist political institutions. That could only be "counterrevolutionary" and "reactionary." All of that was particularly galling to Marxists. The first Fascists were almost all Marxists—serious theorists who had long been identified with Italy's intelligentsia of the Left. Mussolini, himself, had been a leader of the Italian Socialist Party and was an acknowledged leader among Marxist intellectuals.[1]

It was the issue of Italy's intervention in the First World War, not right-wing versus left-wing dispositions, that, at first, deeply divided Italian Marxists.[2] In 1914 and 1915, the majority of organized Italian Socialists championed neutrality in the war that had broken out in Europe, while a small but aggressive minority of socialists, for a variety of reasons, advocated Italy's entry into the conflict on the side of the Allied powers.

Ultimately, the Italian government did enter the war, on the Allied side. The subsequent heavy losses suffered by the Italian military and the continued denunciation of the war by the official socialist organizations generated intense feelings among those who had lost comrades in the carnage. The issue of the war created venomous dissension in the ranks of Marxist theoreticians, with some of the most intellectually accomplished joining the first Fascist squads. The final insult for Marxists was the defeat by Fascism of both domestic Socialism and Leninist Communism, in a test of strength that concluded, on the Italian peninsula, with the Fascist march on Rome in October 1922.

The enmities bred by the dispute ultimately reached such intensity that Marxists of whatever variety and nationality refused to acknowledge the heretical Marxist origins of the first Fascism. Italian Marxists simply attributed the "defection" of some of their foremost intellectuals to venality and opportunism.

For their part, most foreign Marxists never even knew of the Marxist origins of the first Fascism.

For Italian Marxists, the next step in the logic of denial was to conceive of Fascism itself, together with its Marxist "apostates," as venal and opportunistic. The final step was to see Fascism, in its entirety, as the suborned "tool of reaction"—since only monied "reaction" could offer sufficient benefits to those who sought to profit from their apostasy.

Almost immediately after the Fascist seizure of power in Italy, Italian Marxists and Marxist–Leninists began to produce theoretical literature that pretended to explain the necessarily "reactionary" and "right-wing" character of revolutionary Fascism. The very first extended treatments of Fascism that shaped the conceptions of Western intellectuals were those produced by domestic Italian Marxists. Almost immediately, intellectuals in Austria, Germany, France, and England began to contribute to the formulation of an elaborate account of why Fascism was reactionary, right-wing, and, of necessity, inhumane.

Those formulations fit so well into the entire roster of preconceptions entertained by many Western intellectuals that, for most of our century, they were part of the folk wisdom of political science. Those notions succeeded in defining the greater part of the political universe for many Western scholars for three-quarters of a century. Fascism was to be forever a "right-wing, reactionary, and inhumane" excrescence, while Marxism–Leninism was to be "left-wing, progressive, and humane."

Confronted by one of the most arresting political phenomena of the early twentieth century, Western Marxists of all kinds rummaged through the relatively informal body of literature left to them by the nineteenth-century founders of their movement in the effort to attain some measure of understanding of what was transpiring. They sought explanations in the abstract speculations of Karl Marx's neo-Hegelianism.

Karl Marx and Friedrich Engels left their intellectual heirs a loosely formulated, quasi-deductive set of convictions about economic matters, society, and revolution. Composed of essentially nonempirical conjectures about the nature of material production, the sources of the intrinsic value of commodities, the lawlike relationship between increments in the production of wealth and decrements in the general standard of living in capitalist society, together with a faith in the "inevitable" positive outcome of all those processes, classical Marxism was more morality play than science. Because critical terms were ill-defined, and the relationship between independent and dependent variables was frequently cast in terms of metaphor and analogy, very few, if any, of the propositions of classical Marxism were or are testable.[3]

The central notions of classical Marxism left Marxism's intellectual heirs, a set of beliefs about society and the nature of material production that reinforced every preconception entertained by leftist Western scholarship. Marxists believed that the Marxism they had inherited provided a "theoretical" understanding of the generic fascist phenomenon when Mussolini's Fascism first manifested itself on the Italian peninsula after the conclusion of the Great War of 1914–18.

However much they were welcomed by some Western scholars, whatever their convictions, Marxist theories of fascism, from their very first appearance, were largely derivative products, attempts to account for complex empirical events by drawing out the entailments of premises inherited from a nineteenth-century intellectual tradition. All this notwithstanding, many Western scholars were not concerned with empirical truth or falsity. They wanted affirmation of their visions of the future.

Before the middle of the nineteenth century, Marx had convinced himself that modern society had irreversibly divided itself into two, and no more than two, diametrically opposed, historically relevant classes—the bourgeoisie and the proletariat. The former were "reactionary" agents of the prevailing "relations of production," while the latter represented the rapidly burgeoning "forces of production."[4]

For Marx and Engels, human history was, in essence, the interplay between material productive forces and the relations of production. Productive forces were employed in providing goods, and relations of production governed their distribution. As long as the one was "compatible" with the other, society was in a relatively stable state. When the forces of production outgrew those relations, social change was inevitable.

At some stage in the evolutionary process that governs economic systems, according to Marx, the relations of production that govern the allocation of goods produced would increasingly act as a "fetter" on the forces of production. In capitalist society, as a case in point, the benefits produced by the system are allocated in accordance with the laws of property and private profit. Given the existence of private property, the argument continued, production in modern society is geared exclusively to the generation of profit—to the satisfaction of the needs and wants of the ruling class, the owners of the means of production. As long as the economic system was responsive only to the requirements of class rule, the forces of production could not develop fully nor freely. Ultimately, Marx contended, the forces of production would no longer be capable of developing at all.

In his mature account, Marx argued that only *living labor* was capable of creating value. "Constant capital"—the instruments of production, the investment in plant, the cost of rent, and fixed assets in general—was *dead labor*, incapable, in and of itself, of creating value. Of the value generated by living labor, part is employed as "variable capital," distributed as wages necessary to maintain a suitable work force. Variable capital provides the "minimum subsistence wage" necessary to sustain the work force and provide for its replacement in the normal course of events. The amount of value remaining after the payment of wages and the expenses involved in the cost of acquiring, maintaining, renewing, and expanding the material means of production and their ancillaries, Marx identified as "surplus value"—which, to all intents and purposes, constitutes capitalist profit.

In *Das Kapital*, Marx argued that as the "organic composition" of capital changed (the measure of dead versus living labor), not only would the ratio of constant to variable capital change, but that the rate of profit (the ratio of surplus value to the sum of constant and variable capital), over time, would tend to fall.[5] Given enterprise competition and the technological change that competition generates, modern production becomes increasingly capital-intensive, the organic composition of capital changes, and the rate of profit must necessarily decline. When the rate of profit approximated zero, as Marx argued it eventually must, the entire system would shudder to a halt.[6]

At that point the vast majority of humankind in capitalist society—the "proletariat"—would seize the means of production and turn its products to human use rather than profit for an exiguous class of capitalists. The accession of the proletariat to power and the abolition of private property and private profit would create circumstances that would signal the end of war, privation, and oppression. Human beings would no longer compete for space and sustenance. Humankind would make its "leap from necessity to freedom." A classless society would be ushered in by the "ineluctable" processes of history. In effect, in Marx's judgment, there were forces intrinsic to the capitalist mode of production that would ultimately and "inevitably" lead to the collapse of the system. The capitalist mode of production would ultimately prove dysfunctional and, given the anticipated course of history, reactionary.

For Marxists, in general, history has a goal. Its ultimate goal is the lifting of the burden of inequality and exploitation from the shoulders of the vast majority of humankind through "proletarian revolution"—the uprising of the "ninetenths" of the population of moribund capitalism. "History" had established that when the profit rate of the capitalist mode of production fell to zero, industrial capitalism could only become irremediably "reactionary," and that only the success of the proletarian revolution could salvage the future. Only the proletarian revolution was indisputably "progressive." The eschatology of final ends that so appealed to the normative desires of many Western scholars was given its "theoretical" vindication. Many would never abandon the dream.

These were the central convictions that animated Marx's heirs in the Second International and engaged the commitment of many, many Western intellectuals. After the death of Engels in 1896, the Second International became the major exponent of Marxist views in Europe and throughout the world. By that time, Marx's conjectures concerning the capitalist mode of production and its supersession by proletarian socialism had become articles of faith for many leftist Western intellectuals and were central to the propaganda of the Second International.[7]

For all its complexity, Marx's "theory" was empty of empirical content. It trafficked on definitions and their entailments. The entire system was little more than a quasi-deductive set of claims derived from suspect premises. Although all Marx's conjectures were advanced with the calm assurance of prophecy, they were neither self-evident nor amenable to confirmation. With or without confirmation, however, the Marxism of Karl Marx provided his intellectual successors in the early twentieth century with an entire vocabulary of emotive and evocative terms that could be used to good effect against real or fancied opponents.

The availability of that entire system of linguistic devices left many scholars in the West without critical judgment. As a consequence, entire periods of history and the most complex series of events were dismissed with loosely framed "explanations." Distinctions were made where no differences existed, and realities were overlooked in the service of fancy.

The empirical vacuity of Marxist theory became fully apparent only in subsequent history. Only the catastrophic collapse of Marxist–Leninist systems, the total inability of Marxist theoreticians to anticipate events, and the utter failure of Marxism–Leninism's "predictions" finally convinced most Western intellectuals that Marxist speculations were largely without empirical merit.

Until that realization, however, Marxists and leftists, in general, continued to interpret both Fascism and fascism as though Marxist thought had concrete application. Only gradually did it become obvious to the orthodox Marxist–Leninists in the Soviet Union that the "Marxist–Leninist theory of fascism" was fundamentally flawed.

Throughout the period from its inception until its abandonment, however, the Marxist–Leninist theory of fascism influenced not only Soviet, but also Western, intellectuals. The intellectual Left needed an account that accorded with its notions of a political world divided into "reactionaries" and "progressives."

A few days after the Fascist march on Rome in October 1922, Julius Braunthal, an Austrian Marxist intellectual, published a piece entitled, "Der Putsch der Faschisten" in the Social Democratic Party journal *Der Kampf*. Braunthal employed all the evocative language of "theoretical" Marxism, instinctively identifying the Fascism of Mussolini as "reactionary" and a "brutal expression of the property-owning classes' desire for domination." Without citing any empirical evidence whatsoever, he described Fascism as "counter-revolution in its modern form of militaristic violence."[8]

That Bolshevism had employed "militaristic violence" in its revolution was a matter of little concern. That there were more victims in Russia at the hands of the Bolsheviks than elsewhere at the hands of Fascists was irrelevant. Since Fascism arose in Italy as a declared opponent of "proletarian" revolution, it could hardly have been anything other than "reactionary." For Marxists, to be "reactionary" meant to oppose oneself to the "progressive" unfolding of history. Since Marxists accepted the notion that only a revolution undertaken by a class-conscious proletariat could be truly progressive, Fascism was, by definition, reactionary. Although by the time of the march on Rome there were more industrial workers in the ranks of Fascism than there had been in the Bolshevik ranks at the time of Lenin's revolution, Fascism was still deemed "reactionary," and the workers in its ranks as impaired by "false consciousness."

Early in 1923, another Marxist intellectual, Julius Deutsch, offered his own interpretation of Italian Fascism. As might be anticipated, he found that Fascism was a force enlisted in the service of "profit-mad capitalist reaction."[9] Without the suggestion of empirical evidence that could tie Fascists to "profit-mad capitalists," he was prepared to make his claim with absolute assurance. He further embellished his account with the suggestion that Fascism had succeeded in imposing itself on Italy not only by serving "profit-mad capitalists," but also by "fanaticizing" petty bourgeois and "adolescent" elements of the population with the kind of "dark mysticism" so appealing to "Latin psychology." Fascism was not only the "tool of reaction," it was irrational in its appeals.

The petty bourgeois and "adolescent" elements in the population were moved by irrational appeals to serve the fully rational, if occult, interests of "reaction." All this was true for Deutsch because it was evident to him that any *rational* appeal to any and all classes, or fragments of classes, other than "monopoly capitalists," would necessarily recommend the proletarian revolution anticipated in Marx's apocalyptic vision of the "ineluctable" course of history.

It is difficult to imagine how any of this could possibly pass as credible, but all of it continued to provide the substance of the initial Marxist notions about Fascism for the European intellectual community. The Fourth World Congress of Lenin's Third International, held immediately after Mussolini's accession to power, correspondingly declared Fascism to be an "instrument" of counter-revolutionary reaction consciously employed against the "working masses" by the "agrarian capitalists" of the Po valley.

Not long after, however, it was decided that Fascism was not simply the reactionary instrument of the landed bourgeoisie. By that time "rural Fascism" had engulfed the major urban centers. Empirical fact, not theory, convinced

Marxists that Fascism was not a weapon in the service of the agrarian bourgeoisie, but part of the "political offensive of the [entire] bourgeoisie against the working class."[10]

At about the time that European Marxists had apparently settled on the judgment that Fascism was a tool of the entire bourgeoisie, the Hungarian intellectual Gjula Sas published (under the pseudonym Giulio Aquila) his *Der Faschismus in Italien*, in which he affirmed that Fascism represented, in "essence" and "historically," neither an instrument of agrarian capitalists nor a weapon of the entire ownership class; rather, Fascism was a tool of Italy's "industrial bourgeoisie."[11]

For the first few years following its advent, each Marxist identified his own element of the reactionary bourgeoisie as the "real master" of Fascism. It remains uncertain what evidence was used in making those determinations. Neither documentary nor empirical evidence linked Fascism with any element of the "ruling class," but European intellectuals were, nonetheless, certain that Fascism must necessarily be reactionary. Marxist theory left no alternative to identifying Fascism as reactionary and the tool of the forces of oppression.

That Mussolini's Fascism was understood to be reactionary was the simple consequence of holding true some of the central conjectures of classical Marxism. That Fascism was "counterrevolutionary" was simply a recognition of the fact that, among many other things, Fascism had declared itself unalterably opposed to any of the then prevalent forms of socialism. Beyond that, the first Marxist theoreticians who attempted to provide insight into Fascism had very little to say that was either empirically confirmed, particularly novel, instructive, or persuasive. For Marxists, any form of government other than the "dictatorship of the proletariat" was necessarily reactionary, counterrevolutionary, and fundamentally irrational.

Thus, it was perfectly predictable that the first Marxist interpretations of Fascism would unanimously identify Mussolini and his movement as reactionary and counterrevolutionary. For Marxists, *any* government other than that of the "revolutionary proletariat" could be nothing other than "a committee for managing the common affairs of the whole bourgeoisie."[12] It followed that Mussolini's Fascism could be nothing less. To have said that is not to have said a great deal. Notwithstanding, the interpretation became the substance of the Western understanding of Fascism.

In order to make the entire account more persuasive, a more elaborate presentation would be required. If Mussolini was to serve as the conscious tool of reactionary purpose, the logic of their position required that Marxists identify, somewnere among all the disparate elements of the bourgeoisie, the real "masters" of Fascism. However clear the intellectual imperative, the first Marxist interpreters of Italian Fascism could not seem to decide, with any conviction, in whose specific service Mussolini's reactionary labors were undertaken.

In Marx's lexicon, the bourgeoisie, as a class, was fairly inclusive.[13] It included all those who owned the "means of production." Besides the familiar owners of assets and equity, this included subclasses like the landed gentry, the rentier class, and established professionals. The "grand bourgeoisie," in turn, was composed of industrial and finance capitalists. For its part, the petty bourgeoisie was composed of a variety of subgroups, including peasants, academics, artists, artisans, craftsmen, small shopkeepers, petty merchants, and salaried bureaucrats.

Given the abundance of candidates, it remained uncertain in whose service Italian Fascism, as the "paid agent" of the bourgeoisie, was employed. Since the petty bourgeoisie were being "fanaticized," they could hardly qualify as the "masters" of Fascism. That still left an abundance of possibilities, but there was hardly enough evidence available during the first years of Mussolini's regime to allow Marxists to make a responsible choice.

Irrespective of the lack of convincing evidence, however, Aquila decided not only that Mussolini was a "conscious agent of the bourgeoisie," but, more specifically, that he was the agent of the "magnates of heavy industry" who could provide the movement and its leader the support essential to victory.[14] Aquila, consequently, understood Fascism to be an agent primarily, if not exclusively, of Italy's industrial capitalists. In the more than half-a-century since the passing of Fascism, scant evidence has been produced to support such a contention; but lack of evidence has never proved a handicap as far as Marxist pronouncements are concerned.

The lack of evidence clearly did not inhibit Aquila. At best, his claims were inferential and as compelling as his premises were true. In fact, his premises were the speculative premises of classical Marxism.

Fascism did conduct a long, violent struggle against socialist revolutionaries, and under the established regime capitalists did make profits, and property rights were secured. None of that, however, established the fact that Mussolini was the conscious and venal instrument of the bourgeoisie in general or of industrial capitalism in particular. Least of all did any of that make Fascism a "right-wing" movement or a "right-wing" regime unless "right-wing" is taken to mean, by definition, any movement or regime that does not serve the "revolutionary proletariat."

However well or poorly supported, Aquila's arguments were so well received by Western intellectuals, many of whom were foreign members of Lenin's Third International, that they passed, almost without any change, into the report delivered by Clara Zetkin to the executive meeting of the Communist International held in Moscow in June 1923. In fact, Zetkin's *Der Kampf gegen den*

Faschismus was little more than a synopsis of the account provided by the Hungarian intellectual Aquila.[15]

Not only are the general theses of Zetkin's communication identical with those of Aquila, but whole phrases from Aquila's essay reappear in Zetkin's prose. For Aquila, Mussolini's Fascism was not a "simple victory of arms, but an ideological and political victory" over the working class movement. For Zetkin, Italian Fascism was not a "military phenomenon," but an "ideological and political victory over the working class movement."[16] Moreover, in providing the data she advanced as evidence of Italian Fascism's "bourgeois" essence, Zetkin simply repeated, with only the slightest modification, the events and the catalog of legislation bearing on political, social, fiscal, and military affairs forthcoming under the Fascist regime to be found in Aquila's account.[17] It was clear that by 1923 European intellectuals had already put together a set of convictions that characterized Fascism as a product of right-wing reaction.

Zetkin's case, like that of Aquila, depends on there being only *one* interpretation of the data offered in support. If the intent of the legislation and the political decisions of the Mussolini regime could be given no more than a single interpretation, then the case advanced by Zetkin and Aquila might have been persuasive. In retrospect and in fact, Mussolini's behavior and the legislation of his regime have been variously interpreted, and no single interpretation of their intent has been generally accepted.

Whatever the case, it soon became evident that not even the theoreticians of Lenin's Third International were content with the account provided by Aquila and Zetkin in 1923. By 1926, the Italian Communist Party prepared a more generous official version. That version agreed with the one of Aquila and Zetkin insofar as the "inherent weaknesses of capitalism" remained the critical necessary conditions for the appearance and success of Fascism. According to their rendering, capitalism, no longer sustainable and facing imminent proletarian revolution, created and unleashed Fascism.

The version of 1926, like that of Aquila and Zetkin, argued that the immediate contingent condition for the victory of Fascism was the "betrayal" of the proletariat by the reformist Social Democratic leadership of pre-Mussolinian Italy. While the workers were being abandoned by their reformist socialist leaders, Fascism was recruiting and "fanaticizing" the petty bourgeoisie of the urban areas and the "new petty bourgeoisie" of the rural regions. What was different in the version provided by Italian intellectuals in 1926 was the identification of Fascism as the "instrument" not of the "industrial bourgeoisie," but of "an *industrial and agrarian oligarchy*."[18]

In the account of 1926, Italian Fascism was conceived of as an "industrial-agrarian reaction" to "revolutionary communism" that resulted in an "industrial-agrarian dictatorship."[19] The change was significant. For Aquila, Mussolini's Fascism served a "progressive function" in dismantling the old political system that reflected "financial and agrarian interests." Aquila saw those interests conflicting with the growth requirements of "heavy industry." In pursuit of their interests, the barons of industry assigned Mussolini the task of dealing with those representatives of the financial and agrarian bourgeoisie who obstructed the passage of the industrial development on the peninsula.

Because of her dependence on Aquila's account, Zetkin seemed to entertain a similar perspective. Zetkin's interpretation had Italian Fascists responding to the objective needs of the "North Italian industrial bourgeoisie" and against those of the "agrarian and finance capitalists."

All this apparently made Fascism appear far too rational and progressive for the intellectuals of the Italian Communist Party in 1926. According to their Marxist prejudgments, Mussolini's Fascism could not possibly serve any progressive function. Fascism was deemed totally reactionary, functioning as an unqualified dictatorship for *both* industrial and agrarian capitalists.

By 1928, the Communist International had settled on a suitably negative interpretation of Fascism. Mussolini's Fascism was simply "the terroristic dictatorship of big capital." Fascism was conceived to be the institutional expression of the "undivided, open and consistent dictatorship [of] *bankers*, the *big industrialists* and the *agrarians*."[20] Fascism was no longer considered exclusively or essentially the reactionary, right-wing "tool" of agrarian capital or the industrial bourgeoisie. Nor was fascism the joint dictatorship of both the industrial and agrarian bourgeoisie. By 1928, fascism had become a "joint dictatorship" of a collegium of "big capital."

Thus, in 1928, Palmiro Togliatti repeated most of the central theses of Aquila and Zetkin, insisting, however, that Fascism was not the lackey of "industrial capitalism," but served the interests of the entire "big bourgeoisie" (*la grossa borghesia*).[21] In Togliatti's judgment, the Fascist movement did not initially intend to serve as a dictatorship of "industrial and finance capital." But since its "social base," the petty bourgeoisie, possessed neither a "political consciousness" nor a will of its own, Fascism, in order to survive, was driven into the service of the "great bourgeoisie and the agrarians." Ultimately, Mussolini's Fascism lost whatever autonomy it had and was compelled to effect, with "brutality and without reserve," the political purposes of "finance capital" and "big industry." Mussolini had become the tool of "finance capital and heavy industry (*la grande industria*)."

Because Togliatti was a member of the Third International, his formula, whatever its cognitive merit, had to be politically acceptable to the Executive Committee. Togliatti went on to indicate that Italian Fascism was not simply the "dictatorship of heavy industry" or the "dictatorship of heavy industry and agrarian capitalists"—it was the "dictatorship of financial, industrial and agrarian capital."[22] The Marxists of the Third International, together with many European intellectuals, were putting together a standard version.

Needless to say, such a generous reformulation of the theses of Aquila and Zetkin indicates the porosity of the original "theory." More than that, such a reformulation generated some real empirical and theoretical tensions for the Marxist interpretation of Fascism. Not only was it impossible for Marxist theoreticians to produce documentary evidence to confirm Mussolini's "conscious decision" to serve as a "paid tool" for the bourgeoisie, but it was evident that any dictatorship that attempted to satisfy all the demands of all the financial, industrial, and agrarian interest groups in the national community would find itself severely tested.

It is an economic commonplace that agrarian interests, in general, are best served by free trade policies, while the representatives of nascent or destabilized national industries favor import substitution strategies. Some agrarian interests (like Italy's beet sugar and sugar refineries), of course, tend to favor protection. Similarly, it is generally argued that industrial capitalists, with well-established industries enjoying a heavy volume of export trade (like Italy's textile factories of the period), tend to favor free trade to reduce the threat of retaliation on the part of trading partners. Noncompetitive industries (like Italy's maritime industry), in turn, tend to favor protection, while those industries which, even if only marginally established, depend on the importation of essential raw materials (like the steel industry of Italy), tend to favor free trade. Some financial groups tend to favor inflationary fiscal policies, while some others oppose them. Any dictatorship that attempted to serve as a tool for all such disparate interests would not enjoy a long half-life. It could not possibly serve all its putative patrons.[23]

It could be argued, of course, that such problems might be resolved through negotiation among the constituent elements of the "dictatorship"—and the bourgeoisie might prefer some such arrangement to one in which the representatives of organized labor or the public at large might intrude themselves. If class warfare threatened the survivability of the system, the bourgeoisie might prefer a Fascist dictatorship, whatever its inconveniences, to any "liberal bourgeois" arrangement. All that would be required to confirm such conjectures would be some relevant documentary or trace evidence. In the case of Fascist Italy, very little has been forthcoming.

Quite independent of the fact that Marxists have never produced anything like the required evidence, the Marxist accounts of 1928 were far from convincing for other reasons as well. The fragmentary evidence in support of their thesis was laced together by a tissue of suppositions and prejudgments that involved chiliastic speculations about history, as well as an unsupported faith in the reality of complex conspiracies.

All of this became increasingly obvious to intellectuals in the West. By the mid-1930s, the intellectuals closest to the Third International began to put together more comprehensive accounts of a "reactionary," "right-wing" generic fascism. Not only had such a task increasingly urged itself upon the European intellectuals of the period, but it was during this period that Hitler's National Socialism began to assume center stage. "Fascism" was no longer a Latin eccentricity; it loomed large in one of Europe's most important nations.

In 1935, the Stalinist Communist International was prepared to formulate a public statement concerning its interpretation of generic fascism. In that year, Georgi Dimitroff delivered his report on fascism to the Seventh World Congress of the Communist International. He informed his audience that fascism was a product of the "most profound economic crisis," the "sharp accentuation of the general crisis of capitalism." Within the secular decline of industrial capitalism, characterized by the progressive reduction in its overall rate of profit, a "sharp accentuation" had provoked the "ruling bourgeoisie" to undertake "exceptional predatory measures against . . . toilers" everywhere. "Imperialist circles," in order to solve their problems of diminishing returns, conjured up the forces of fascism. "Fascism, in power" was understood to be "the open terrorist dictatorship of the most reactionary, most chauvinistic and most imperialist elements of finance capitalism."[24]

However articulate the reports of the Communist International, what was required was a comprehensive treatment of a subject that had become critical for the world communist movement. It was evident that a coherent major effort would be required.

In Europe, what resulted were two major interpretive works: one by the French Trotskyist Daniel Guerin, *Fascism and Big Business*, and the other, *Fascism and Social Revolution*, by the Anglo-Indian Rajani Palme Dutt.[25] Those books, and others like them produced by leftist intellectuals during the period, attempted to develop a more cognitively satisfying "Marxist theory of fascism" than any that had been forthcoming. In those accounts, it was recognized that it was not enough simply to identify fascism as a "capitalist reaction" to the threat of "proletarian revolution" in circumstances of a "general crisis of capitalism." There had been "capitalist reactions" to the threat of "proletarian revolution" ever since the mid-nineteenth-century Paris Commune. What was needed was a coherent, persuasive explanation of why "capitalist reaction" had taken on a specifically fascist form at that specific time.

As early as the late 1920s, Nikolai Bukharin, Leon Trotsky, and Palmiro

Togliatti had all identified the first two decades of the twentieth century as a "new epoch" in the historical evolution toward the anticipated socialist society.[26] Capitalism had begun its "general crisis"—its ultimate, irreversible contraction.

Fascism was the frenzied resistance of industrial capitalism in its final agony. Marxist–Leninist thinkers, both Trotskyist and Stalinist, sought to explain the origins, the advent, and the success of fascism by conceiving of it as the real-world product of Karl Marx's speculations about the inevitable conclusion of contemporary industrial history.

As has been suggested, for Marx, the "inevitable" victory of the proletariat was predicated on a number of "theoretical" considerations. Marx argued that industrial capitalism was destined to destroy itself because, ultimately, its frenetic activity would not be able to sustain an appropriate rate of profit. At some stage or another, capitalism was destined to sink into a fatal torpor because it would no longer be able to profitably empty its inventories. There were "iron laws" to which capitalism was compelled to conform. Among these was the irreversible secular decline in the rate of profit that would condemn industrial capitalism to systemic collapse—an inability to complete its required cycles of expanded reproduction. Incapable of sustaining a requisite rate of profit, the system could not survive. Ultimately, modern industrial capitalism would lapse into irremediable crisis.[27]

Given this set of convictions, Daniel Guerin began his classic interpretation of fascism with the affirmation that fascism was the "spawn" of capitalism in irreversible and fatal decline—it arose at a point when the "economic crisis" that had descended on the industrialized democracies after the First World War had become "acute," and the "rate of profit sinks toward zero."[28] Guerin was making a specific claim that was to serve as a central conviction for almost all subsequent Marxist interpretations during the 1930s.[29] According to Guerin and those of his persuasion, fascism appeared in Europe because industrial capitalism had entered the final, inevitable phase of its senescence. In those circumstances, the "captains of heavy industry," wedded to the "magnates of high finance" with a "stake in heavy industry," sought salvation in fascism.[30] Caught in the "iron laws" of capitalist senescence, facing a rate of profit that approximated zero, those who controlled finance and industry attempted to sustain the system by having recourse to fascism. Fascism was assigned responsibility for salvaging the profits of heavy industry and finance capitalism at the cost of barbarizing society and exploiting the working classes.[31]

Because Marx had argued that only living labor produced the surplus value that made up the substance of profit, he could plausibly maintain that the secular rate of profit for industrial capitalism would be expected to decline as more and more of the system's resources were committed to fixed capital investments in "dead labor"—in plant, technology, and machines. Around this predictable, irreversible, and secular decline were the periodic business cycles that testified to capitalism's inability to generate enough demand to profitably empty its inventories.

According to the original Marxists, the ebb and flow of unemployment, the precariousness of the lives of workers, the inability of small businesses to survive in competition with increasingly large manufactories, all attested to the "contradiction" between the enormous productive power of modern industry and the inability of modern society to distribute its benefits. But, beyond that, there would be the final descent into systemic stagnation and decay as the rate of profit declined to zero. As the rate of profit approximates zero, the resistance of capitalism's "wage slaves" increasingly threatens the survival of the system. Capitalism's ruling "magnates of finance and industry" become desperate. They gamble on fascism.

It was R. Palme Dutt who provided the full account of the Marxist–Leninist interpretation of fascism that was to become standard in the literature and constitute the substance of the leftist interpretation of fascism's reactionary right-wing character. Like Guerin, Palme Dutt sought to draw out of Marx's account of the inevitable decline of industrial capitalism and the equally inevitable rise of the revolutionary proletariat an interpretation of fascism.[32]

Like Guerin, he identified the first decades of the twentieth century as the end time of industrial capitalism. By the end of the First World War, capitalism was presumably in its final throes of internal disintegration. The "inner laws of capitalist development" had "inevitably" led to a catastrophic economic crisis such that capitalism could no longer profitably operate the productive forces at its disposal. As early as the first years of the 1920s, Marxist–Leninists insisted that modern industrial capitalism could no longer develop the forces of production. Capitalism's historic functions had been fulfilled. The "forces of production" had been throttled by incompatible "relations of production." Industrial capitalism had reached a stage of irreconcilable conflict with the material needs of humankind.[33] As needs increased, the capitalist industrial system contracted. In its effort to resist the inevitable, capitalism conjured up fascism. However confusing fascism may have appeared to others, Marxist–Leninists understood that fascism's "objective," "reactionary" responsibility was to serve as "guardian of a capitalism which [had] collapsed."[34]

Since fascism's tasks ran counter to the course of history, fascism was not only reactionary, it was irrational. The forces it was compelled to conjure up to discharge its reactionary responsibilities could only be barbaric and inhumane. By the mid-1930s, all this had been given something like academic expression in the works of Guerin and Palme Dutt. For Guerin, fascism was "the monstrous product of the capitalist system in decline."[35] For Palme Dutt, fascism was "the most complete expression of the whole tendency of modern capitalism in decay."[36] As the profit rate of industrial capitalism approached zero, the system had become increasingly pathological. Fascism was the product of an attempt to sustain an entirely irrational economic, social, and political arrangement.

According to this thesis, the old techniques of governance, the old methods of intensifying the rate of exploitation of labor, the old strategies of increasing market share, and the old devices for maintaining monopoly prices no longer worked. Capitalism could no longer be sustained without extraordinary measures. Only fascism offered "big business" and the "magnates of high finance" what seemed to be a solution.

This entire interpretation of fascism hung on the truth of the conviction that the final "general crisis of capitalism" had overwhelmed the industrialized West—and that the "rate of profit" of Western capitalism approximated zero. These were the notions that provided the theoretical foundation for the work of both Guerin and Palme Dutt and constituted the intellectual core of the interpretation of fascism as a "right-wing," "reactionary," "pathological" phenomenon.

Palme Dutt argued that since capitalism had entered the final, fatal crisis predicted by Marx, only desperate measures afforded the "big bourgeoisie" any prospect of salvation. No longer capable of realizing profit through the production of commodities for competitive exchange, Palme Dutt continued, the entrepreneurial bourgeoisie was compelled to employ extraordinary measures. One of those measures was to systematically restrict output, curtail technological innovation, and stabilize production at the level of simple reproduction. Expanded production would be precluded, and consumption would be confined to artificially low levels. Cartelized or monopolized production would be distributed only in quantities and at prices fixed at levels that maximized profit.[37] Fascism was assigned just such reactionary tasks. Fascism was charged with the task of reducing society's productive capabilities to an artificially low level in order to optimize the profits of monopoly capitalism. Fascism was charged with returning modern society to preindustrial barbarism.

Such an interpretation was plausible only if one accepted as unqualifiedly true all the major theses of classical Marxism. It was plausible only if the private ownership of the means of production revealed itself as inherently "incompatible with the further development of production and utilization of technique," and if industrial capitalism had entered its final crisis.[38] It was credible only if the profit rate of capitalism was, in fact, approximating zero.

By the mid-1930s, Palme Dutt could confidently maintain that all this was true. As a consequence, the only alternatives open to Western society were clear: either the modern world chose "progressive" communism, or humanity was to be abandoned to "reactionary" fascism. Fascism would not only restrict production and abandon science and technology, it would also undertake "the systematic destruction of all science and culture . . . [and lead] the revolt against education." Without the salvation that would come in the train of the proletarian revolution, the industrialized West would have to accustom itself to a "return to handwork"—a "return to the Stone Age." That would constitute "the final logical working out of the most advanced capitalism and fascism."[39]

In retrospect, it is clear that there was very little substance to any of this. Economists have never found evidence of a secular decline in the rate of profit in advanced industrial systems. Industrial capitalism has survived repeated business cycles, and while theoreticians regularly lament capitalism's failures, few argue that a final collapse of the system is to be anticipated. Throughout the 1930s, irrespective of the protracted dislocations of the Great Depression, industrial capitalism continued to operate without ratcheting down production to some artificially low profit-maximizing level, or destroying science, culture, or education—and nowhere in the capitalist world, National Socialist Germany and Fascist Italy included, did material production fall anywhere near the levels predicted by Palme Dutt.[40]

Without the support of Marx's economic prognostications, the Marxist–Leninist interpretation of fascism, standard in the 1930s, really had very little to say about fascism other than that it was to be seen as an attempt by the generic bourgeoisie to maintain its privileges in the face of what Marxist enthusiasts imagined was imminent proletarian revolution. Even that would have to assume that contemporary society was objectively "rotten-ripe for the social revolution," and that the bourgeoisie had no hope of salvation other than to throw in their lot with fascists.[41]

That society was "rotten-ripe for the socialist revolution" was predicated on the conviction that profit rates in the system approximated zero—that sustainable rates could not be restored—and that the class-conscious proletariat understood all this and was prepared to assume the responsibilities of rule. Only in those circumstances would the characterization of fascism as the reactionary armed guard of capitalism take on any plausibility.

Only if all the speculations that made up Marxist–Leninist "theories" of the world are accepted as true, might one conceive of fascism as discharging the responsibility of protecting the survival of the system by supervising an overall reduction in industrial output, restricting the growth in fixed capital assets, cartelizing the entire economy, and imposing monopoly prices throughout. This would entail the unpleasant business of reducing the gross national product, mandating and maintaining extremely low wage rates, curtailing social services, and imposing draconian discipline. The entire system would wind down to a "lower technical and economic level" to satisfy the requirements of senescent capitalism.[42]

All this flew in the face of fascism's evident preoccupation with the possibility of war. Whatever else it was, fascism was committed to making Italy a "great power." In pursuing that goal, Fascists expected resistance on the part of the "plutocracies"—resistance that might involve military conflict. Given that recognition, Fascists sought the rapid growth and industrialization of their economies in order to provide the weapons systems and weapons platforms necessary to sustain conflict in the twentieth century.

The entire standard Marxist–Leninist account of fascism during the interwar years was, at best, a caricature of the actual political and historical sequence. To suggest that Italian Fascism was "financed, controlled and directed" by the "big capitalists," the "big landlords," the "big industrialists," or "finance capital" is so simplistic that it hardly merits analysis.

We know that Mussolini received subventions from agrarian and industrial interests in their respective efforts to contain and neutralize the revolutionary socialist movement. But we also know that Mussolini assiduously maintained his political independence. While he cultivated support from a variety of entrenched interests, he maintained an independent political posture.

That Mussolini, in the course of the Fascist revolution, received the passive or active support of the constabulary, the magistracy, and the military was a consequence not of a "capitalist conspiracy" to preserve suitable levels of return in the face of the declining rate of profit; it resulted from the fact that the Socialists in Italy had succeeded in alienating almost everyone by 1920.[43] They had defamed the military and attacked and abused war veterans. They had stigmatized the constabulary as the "venal agents of the bourgeoisie." They had made a display of their contempt for the "petty bourgeoisie"—the professionals, intellectuals, small landholders, shopkeepers, artisans, and salaried state employees—all the "parasitic and nonproductive interstitial" strata of capitalist society. Moreover, by 1921, large sections of the working class itself had become disillusioned with socialist strategies. Most independent intellectuals recognized as much.

Thus, it was not necessary to invoke obscure notions regarding a conspiracy of finance capitalists and Italian Fascists to explain the passive or active support that Fascist squads received in Italy after the high wave of "proletarian" revolutionary activity had crested in 1920.[44] Nor is it necessary to suggest that Italian Fascism could not have come to power without the active intercession of "the big bourgeoisie." However one chooses to construe the standard Marxist–Leninist version of generic fascism, the candidate explanation remains unconvincing. We know that Italian industrialists and "big capitalists" interacted with Italian Fascists from a position of strength; we also know that their interests and the interests of the Fascists coincided at critical and broad junctures. But all the evidence we now have at our disposal indicates that the industrialists were never able to "control," much less "direct," Mussolini's Fascism.

Fascism frequently, if not regularly, compensated the organized industrialists and financiers of Italy for their submission to control, but the evidence clearly indicates that business and banking interests almost always remained subordinate to Fascist political priorities. Fascism's political priorities often prevailed over capitalist interests when a choice had to be made.[45] Not only did Mussolini sometimes sacrifice business and financial interests when it served Fascism's purpose; he did not hesitate to dismiss, and in significant instances exile, influential business leaders in whom he had no confidence. Mussolini's alliance with business, agrarian, and financial interests was always based on political considerations.[46] This was particularly true with respect to foreign policy, where he operated with almost absolute independence.[47]

Beyond that, it is clear that Fascism neither intended nor succeeded in winding down Italy's industrial or agrarian production.[48] By the mid-1930s, Fascist Italy had achieved an irregular rate of real economic growth in which some sectors had made quite spectacular gains. So evident was this fact that, after the Second World War, one Marxist commentator simply reported that "fascism really represented a development of *capitalist forces of production*. . . . [Fascism promoted] the *expanded reproduction* of the conditions of capitalist production."[49]

The total volume of agricultural production, for example, rose in Fascist Italy from the base index of 100 in 1922 to 147.8 in 1937, while population growth, similarly indexed, had risen only to 111. By 1937, Fascist Italy was producing 15.5 quintals of wheat per hectare, whereas it had produced only 9.5 quintals per hectare in 1922. For the first time in its modern history, Italy was producing enough wheat for its domestic population.[50]

The aggregate indices of industrial production in Fascist Italy suggest measurable advances. There was a general improvement, with the index rising to 182.2 in 1934. The metallurgical, building, automotive, aircraft, textile, and hydroelectrical generating industries all showed advances. As early as the mid-1930s, American economists reported that Fascist Italy had "made considerable progress in the expansion of some of her industries."[51]

The standardized figures that became available after the end of the Second World War indicate that Fascist Italy sustained a credible rate of real economic growth when compared to the resource-favored capitalist countries. By 1938, the enormous costs of the intervention in Spain and the war in Ethiopia notwithstanding, the index of aggregate volume of output (using 1913 as a benchmark) was 158.8. This compared favorably with that of France, which, similarly indexed, stood at 109.4, and with Germany, whose index stood at 149.9. By 1938, the aggregate index for output per capita stood at 145.2 for Fascist Italy, 136.5 for France, 122.4 for Germany, 143.6 for the United Kingdom, and 136.0 for the United States. The aggregate index for output per man-hour stood at 191.1 for Fascist Italy in 1938, as compared with 178.5 for France, 137.1 for Germany, and 167.9 for the United Kingdom.[52]

Whatever else might be said, it was clear that Fascist Italy did not "suppress" or "restrict" the forces of production; nor did it "stabilize" at the level of the "simple reproduction of capital."[53] By 1938, in Fascist Italy, 15.9 percent of the gross national product was employed in fixed asset formation, as compared to 11.5 percent in the United Kingdom and 14 percent in the United States.[54]

Monumental errors were made in the Fascist governance of the peninsula's economy, but, given Italy's total lack of essential resources, the absence of fossil fuels, iron ore, and critical minerals, and the impact of the worldwide depression after 1929, the performance could hardly be characterized as a "winding down" of the national economy to a "lower technical and productive level." If the calculating capitalist conspirators who "controlled and directed" Italian Fascism were compelled by the inherent laws of capitalism to "wind down" the economic system, they seem to have failed. If "decaying" capitalism requires a "suppression" of the productive forces, and the magnates of "high finance" are required to engineer a system to effect that "suppression," then they and Fascism seem to have been singularly unsuccessful.

All this was only part of the problem with the standard Marxist–Leninist interpretation of fascism. Many Marxist thinkers not caught up in the requirements imposed by the Third International took exception to much of the Marxist–Leninist standard version.

Throughout the 1930s, a number of reasonably independent Marxist scholars attempted to formulate interpretations of generic fascism that bore more correspondence to political reality. August Thalheimer, for example, an "opposition" member of the Communist Party of Germany, insisted as early as 1930 that fascism could be most coherently understood as an *autonomous* mass mobilizing political movement of the petty bourgeoisie that arose in social, economic, and political circumstances that found the "big bourgeosie" incapable of ruling effectively. As a consequence, the ruling bourgeoisie was compelled to surrender political power to the fascists in the frantic hope that fascism would protect their economic and social position.[55]

Arthur Rosenberg, in turn, accepted the principal outlines of the Marxist–Leninist standard version, but insisted that the "progressive task" of Mussolini's Fascism (naturally at the behest of industrial and finance capital) was to "further develop the productive forces of Italy." He insisted that there was clear evidence that Italian Fascism had "systematically spurred" development in heavy industry, in chemicals, automotive and aircraft industries, and the maritime trade.[56] Rather than "winding down" productive output, Fascism had created conditions for its acceleration.

Otto Bauer, in 1936, insisted that generic fascism constituted too strong a force to be contained by the established capitalist elites. It could not possibily be employed as "a simple tool of the bourgeoisie." "Fascism," he maintained, "grew over the heads of the capitalist classes." The bourgeoisie may have imagined that they could dominate fascism, but fascism extended its power over all classes. Bauer insisted that, ultimately, fascism came to terms with the capitalist elites, but he also indicated that the confluence of interest between fascism and its non-fascist allies was at best temporary and contingent.

In Bauer's judgment, the foreign policy of fascism, with its disposition to military adventure, predictably worked against the vested interests of broad segments of the capitalist class. It is clear that for Bauer, the relationship between fascism and the possessing classes was far more complex than anything suggested in the standard Marxist–Leninist version of Palme Dutt.[57]

Perhaps the most significant variation in this general tradition was expressed in an essay by Franz Borkenau in 1933.[58] Borkenau denied that conditions in Italy in 1920 were "ripe" for socialist revolution. He insisted that in an "objective sense," it was not that Fascism was "reactionary," but that the demands raised by the maximalists and the Leninists in the post–First World War Italian situation threatened "progress." What Italy required after the termination of the First World War was not proletarian revolution, but a rapid increase in overall productivity. The wage demands and the ill-conceived political innovations demanded by the self-selected "leaders of the working classes" at that time augured ill for the weakened and only partially developed economy of post–First World War Italy. What Italy required at that time was a control on nonproductive consumption, in order to assure that available assets could be devoted to basic industrial growth and agricultural modernization. Italy required an increased "tempo of accumulation," a period of intensive "primitive capital accumulation," that would be requisite for a drive to industrial and agricultural maturity.

Fascism, Borkenau insisted, was alive with a modernizing fervor typified by the presence in its ranks of the Futurists, who were machine fetishists, and the technical bourgeoisie, who advocated a rapid growth in the industrial potential of the peninsula. Fascism, in Borkenau's judgment, was not the tool of industrial or finance capital. Italian Fascism arose in a partially developed economy and embodied all the "contradictions" common to such circumstances. However "contradictory" Fascism's political character, one of its purposes was the intensive and extensive growth of the Italian economy. Fascism was committed to the creation of the preconditions for, and fostering of, the development of industry. It was not the product of "rotten-ripe" capitalism; it was a perfectly comprehensible response to delayed development and thwarted industrialization.

In those circumstances, the industrial and finance capitalists were hardly Mussolini's masters; they were his allies at best and his dependents at worst. For Borkenau, political Fascism was made up of a collection of strategies and economic modalities designed in large part to perform a time- and circumstance-conditioned "historic function." Just as any knowledgeable Marxist might expect, Italian Fascism sought the steady expansion of industrial capabilities in an economic environment in which the material forces of production remained laggard.

Under Mussolini's regime, electrification was undertaken and rapidly expanded. The automotive and textile industries flourished. The communications system was expanded and rationalized. The banking system was centralized and rendered more efficient. The independence of traditionalist agrarian financial interests of the south were compromised in the service of northern industrialists. Agriculture was modernized, and extensive road building and land reclamation were undertaken. To accomplish all this, Borkenau maintained, the defense capabilities of organized labor had to be broken, wages kept to a minimum to underwrite the rapid accumulation of investment capital, and collective enthusiasm kept at a high pitch to sustain the levels of energy required for modernization.[59] Fascism, in Borkenau's judgment, was a mass-mobilizing developmental dictatorship under single party auspices. It was a "transitional" form of rule developed in an environment suffering marginal industrial development and agricultural stagnation.

By the end of the 1930s, it was no longer certain what "right-wing" might be taken to mean. Even fascism's identification with "reaction" was no longer certain. Independent Marxist intellectuals had begun to suggest an interpretation of fascism that differed markedly from that urged by the Leninist Third International.

Fascism was understood to be a kind of "Bonapartist" dictatorship that enjoyed considerable autonomy in an environment characterized by the "equilibrium of class forces" that existed, in general, in modern or modernizing industrial society.[60] Otto Bauer, the Austrian Social Democrat, argued that some contemporary communities found themselves lodged between the class rule of the bourgeoisie and the rising proletariat. In such circumstances, a "balance" had been struck between the two classes that Marx had identified as the only real historical protagonists, and the state, which had previously been the "executive arm of the bourgeoisie," suddenly obtained a measure of autonomy.

In substance, Bauer rejected the notion that capitalism had entered its final phase. Rather, the steady emergence over time of the proletariat had created an equilibrium of social forces in which a relatively thin stratum of bureaucrats, together with a specific political leadership, achieved a measure of independence from the bourgeoisie. Thus, for Bauer, "Italian Fascism . . . [was] the modern counterpart of French Bonapartism in 1851. In each case, an adventurer, supported by bands of adventurers, sent the bourgeois parliament packing, ousted the bourgeoisie from its position of political supremacy and established . . . dictatorship over all the classes."[61]

Bauer's interpretation was a far cry from that of doctrinaire leftist thinkers. What Bauer was addressing was the possibility, evident at the time and fully confirmed by subsequent evidence, that neither Adolf Hitler nor Benito Mussolini were the "supine servants" of their bourgeois "masters."[62] Independent Marxists recognized that fascists acted with considerable autonomy in dealing with the critical issues of the period. It was hard to conceive of fascism as nothing but the simple "tool" of capitalism. It was harder still to conceive of it as "identical with capitalism, representing only a special method to maintain its power and hold down the workers."[63]

Whatever else fascism was, it certainly was not the simple tool of the "reactionary magnates of capital." It evidently was not simply another form of capitalist rule. And it clearly was not the "open and terroristic dictatorship of the most reactionary, most chauvinistic and most imperialistic elements of finance capital."[64]

There are very few non-Marxist economists who accept the claim that modern industrial society is dominated by "finance capital," or that banks control the daily operations of contemporary capitalism. Without some such agency in control, it is hard to imagine how the bourgeoisie could simply "put fascism in power" or control it when it was there. There were many independent Marxist theoreticians who found it difficult to invest confidence in such notions.

Borkenau never acceded to the notion that "finance capitalism" somehow controlled contemporary society. He suggested that fascism, free to pursue its interests in an environment in which simple class rule, in whatever form, was no longer possible, sought industrial development and technological maturity, if for no other reason than to maintain political initiative and provide for an assertive foreign policy of expansion. It was clear that Italian Fascism, for whatever reason and with whatever efficiency, sought the industrial development and economic modernization of the Italian peninsula.[65]

All these notions began to come together in the outlines of an alternative interpretation of fascism that was quite original. As early as 1924, Otto Bauer recognized that in the Soviet Union Lenin's Bolshevism had become a "dictatorship of a governing caste set above all classes in society, just like [Italian] Fascism."[66] By the mid-1930s, even Trotsky was prepared to recognize the "fateful similarities" between Italian Fascism and Stalinism.[67]

What was emerging was an interpretation that conceived fascism as one form, among many, of developmental dictatorship under unitary party auspices. It was uncertain what that class of regimes might be called. Trotsky, for example, was prepared to recognize the features shared by Italian Fascism and the system created by Stalin in the Soviet Union. He was prepared to admit that the Soviet Union had been transformed under the ministrations of Josef Stalin. What he was not prepared to admit was that what had been intended as a "proletarian democracy" had become a dictatorship of a bureaucratic stratum of technocrats, political hacks, and place-holders in a system committed to the rapid development and rationalization of a developmentally retarded national economy. If that were the case, how could one distinguish "right-wing reaction" from "left-wing progressivism"?

A perfectly plausible case can be made that Stalinism was the ideology of a developmental *national socialism*—the "socialism" of an economically backward nation. As such, it shared more than superficial similarities with the Fascism of Mussolini. Years later, Bruno Rizzi was to suggest that "that which [Italian] Fascism consciously sought, [the Soviet Union] involuntarily constructed."[68] The real question was, What, in fact, had been constructed in both the Soviet Union and Fascist Italy?

Early in the history of the Fascist regime in Italy, both Giuseppe Prezzolini and Rudolfo Mondolfo had remarked on the attributes that characterized both Fascism and rapidly evolving Bolshevism.[69] The similarities included an intense nationalism, the instauration of an authoritarian and anti-liberal state under a "charismatic leader" who activated "masses" that included all "sound" and "productive" elements of the population, a domestication of labor, and state control of the means of production through the employment of an enterprise and managerial bureaucracy enjoying differential income and privileged access to the levers of power.

All this took place within the confines of a political system dominated by a unitary party monopolizing the articulation and aggregation of interests. Control over the means of communication and the prevalence of special means of social surveillance completed the picture of functionally analogous political systems. All that was now required was a specification of what purpose all this was to serve.

Borkenau had suggested that at least one purpose of these political and institutional arrangements was the rapid economic development and industrial modernization of less developed economies. In circumstances in which industrialization had proceeded to the level of the most advanced systems, something like fascism might emerge where a society sought to escape the real or fancied restrictions imposed by history—lost wars, unequal treaties, foreign impostures, and the loss of national territories—burdens that followed as a consequence of an eccentric past and unequal competition with more powerful neighbors.

Borkenau argued that the peculiar social, economic, and political history of Germany, for example, left it bereft of "typical" bourgeois institutions and "typical" bourgeois behaviors.[70] Further, the defeat that followed the Great War of 1914–18 left Germany without the flexibility typical of mature economies and mature political systems. Without independent sources of raw materials, without secure export markets, burdened by onerous repatriation responsibilities, Weimar Germany, with its fragile representative democracy, lapsed into a political dictatorship subsequently identified as "fascist."[71]

For Borkenau, German fascism was manifestly different from that found in Italy—but whatever the differences, by the beginning of the Second World War, the first outlines of an inclusive class of nationalistic, mass-mobilizing, antiliberal and multi-class developmental movements and regimes had made their appearance. What was unclear was whether such systems were "right-wing" or "left-wing" in character.

These were the notions with which Marxists progessively faced the political and revolutionary problems of the interwar years. Initially, Marxist theoreticians pieced together the most simple-minded conjectures in order to dismiss Fascism as capitalist reaction.

Over the years, this thesis became increasingly difficult to defend. Acknowledging this, the more independent Marxists sought to provide a more plausible rendering of then contemporary events. But these intellectual developments were overtaken by the Second World War. Little survived the war. Fascism, on the "right," had been defeated, while socialism on the "left," had allied itself with the victors. Fascism was "reactionary"; Marxism was "progressive."

Leftist intellectuals in the West acknowledged none of the developments that typified the early history of the Marxist theory of fascism. Had they done so, it might have become clear that the Marxist–Leninist interpretation of fascism was fundamentally flawed, and that the entire notion of a left-wing Marxist revolution in the Soviet Union and a right-wing revolution in Fascist Italy could hardly be defended.

Decades were to pass before the insights of Bauer and Borkenau were taken up again to offer the outline of something like a competent interpretation of what had transpired in Russia and Italy between the two world wars. In the interim, the notion that fascism was nothing more than right-wing reaction, to be forever distinguished from the political left wing, dominated most of the learning institutions of the West. Curiously enough, it was among orthodox Marxist thinkers in the Soviet Union that the first major reassessment of fascism took place.

3

The Marxist Theory of Fascism
after the Second World War

The victory of communist arms on the battlefields of Europe and Asia during the 1940s did little to improve the quality of the Marxist–Leninist interpretation of fascism. Soviet academics had little immediate incentive to try to produce a more cognitively satisfying account.

For their part, academics in the West were generally prepared to treat fascism as a simple study in political pathology, better left to criminal justice than intellectual reflection. In the passion and horror of the Second World War, Mussolini's Fascism had been swallowed up in the enormities of Hitler's National Socialism. All distinctions were lost, and academics, East and West, were perfectly comfortable dealing with a selective notion of "fascism" that included within its compass only those movements and regimes somehow identified with the "radical right"—to the exclusion of anything on the "left."

For some time after the end of the Second World War, Western scholars were no more disposed to undertake a serious review and reconsideration of fascism than were their Marxist–Leninist counterparts. Often as not, fascism was simply consigned to history as an unhappy parenthesis in the history of civilization.

In the years immediately following the conclusion of the Second World War, Soviet scholars, with some rare exceptions, seemed content to repeat all the stolid implausibilities that made up the standard Soviet interwar interpretation of fascism. In the Soviet Union, the postwar *Brief Philosophical Dictionary* persisted in defining fascism as the "open terroristic dictatorship of finance capital" as though nothing had transpired in the world or in Soviet intellectual circles since 1930.[1]

Little changed until the 1960s. In 1965, Soviet commentators began to complain of the lack of intellectual independence they had suffered under the Stalinist "cult of personality." Stalin, according to Soviet Marxists, had forced the discussion of fascism to assume an artificial and abstract character. Scholars revealed that they had been compelled to neglect the obvious realities of their time and "replace concrete study" with the "repetition of this or that general resolution of the Communist International."[2] The 1960s revealed to Soviet thinkers that they had been denied intellectual independence. In fact, the story was much more complicated than that.

In 1970, Alexander Galkin published an interpretation of fascism that could only count as a substantial revision of the original interwar standard version.[3] In the revised version, fascism was no longer identified with the *final* or *general* crisis of capitalism. That thesis was abandoned, together with the conviction that the world faced only one of two options—the dictatorship of the revolutionary proletariat or the terrorism of fascism.

By 1970, Soviet theoreticians were prepared to acknowledge that real and potential alternatives existed between the dictatorship of the proletariat and fascism. Those alternatives might take on a variety of forms. Industrial capitalism, Galkin argued, had not lapsed into its final crisis at the conclusion of the First World War. Whatever Marxist theorists had written, there was no empirical evidence to support the contention that, by the time of the Great War, capitalism had exhausted its potential for extensive and intensive growth. The impressive expansion of capitalist production after that war, renewed growth after the Great Depression, and accelerated increases in yield during the years following the end of the Second World War had made all that abundantly clear. "Bourgeois capitalism" had not only survived the First World War, it had prospered. One of the major premises of the original standard interpretation of fascism could no longer be defended.

For the purposes of discussion, it is interesting that the revised account was prepared to acknowledge that market-governed industrial systems still retained the potential for significant growth, and that fascism was not simply a final desperate strategy to salvage moribund capitalism. Whatever else it was, fascism was not the final defense of reaction; nor could it be identified with a government that had been compelled by the "intrinsic laws of capitalism" to confine its domestic economic system to negative growth and technological primitivism.

It had taken Soviet intellectuals two decades after the end of the Second World War to undertake a revision of the standard interpretation of fascism. The revision took on some interesting features. What Soviet theoreticians affirmed was that in the changed circumstances of the twentieth century, capitalism required the extensive support of the state to sustain itself. The state began to play a major, nonsubstitutable role in the maintenance and expansion of capitalist productive systems. Fascism was only a special variant of the state monopoly capitalism required by advanced industrialization.

In order to suitably discipline its subject population, and to accumulate the resources necessary to make the transition to a higher productive level, capitalist economies required the institutionalization of a new state system. According to this thesis, *all* capitalist states shared at least some of those features, but only fascism exemplified them all.

Galkin argued that because the "ruling bourgeoisie" of many nations found fascism to be a very risky alternative, they had found ways of making the transition to a new level of economic growth and modernization without abandoning "one or another form of bourgeois democracy." Fascism was not a question of "fatal inevitability, but a variant of the way of development."

What had become manifestly clear was that Soviet thinkers, by the mid-1960s, had put together a new interpretation of fascism. In the new account, fascism was a variant of state monopoly capitalism with certain properties. Like all forms of state monopoly capitalism, fascism represented a new state form that gave expression to special economic strategies designed to attain "new levels" of growth and development.

Fascism distinguished itself by its ready recourse to anti-democratic coercion, systematic violence, and a willingness to embark upon military adventure. Fascism was state monopoly capitalism without the restraint common to bourgeois polities.

For Galkin, fascism was a relatively rare by-product of "bourgeois" rule. It had arisen during one of the recurrent crises of industrial capitalism, and it succeeded in shepherding some capitalist states through those crises, but only at the expense of violating some of the cardinal rules of bourgeois society. Fascism satisfied special bourgeois requirements in the "late imperialist period"—but only at a terrible price.

Fascism was a form of state monopoly capitalism that had proved itself capable of putting together the instrumentalities that would protect capitalist society during periods of serious dislocation. More than that, fascism, as a special variant of state monopoly capitalism, fostered and/or sustained a transition from one level of economic development and modernization to another.

According to the new interpretation, fascism, within the confines of the "capitalist mode of production," was a form of modernizing movement that embodied itself in one type of modernizing regime. What distinguished fascism from other variants was its specifically anti-democratic character and its ready recourse to genocidal violence.

When Galkin addressed himself specifically to the Italian case, he noted that Mussolini's Fascism had arisen as an autonomous movement in circumstances of special crisis, and that only subsequently had the "ruling circles" of the peninsula recognized that it might serve their particular interests. The fact that Mussolini's Fascism had an independent origin and pursued an independent course clearly posed problems, in Galkin's judgment, for the "capitalist ruling class." While Italian Fascism did satisfy some of the basic "interests of the ruling class and its upper crust as a whole," it nonetheless "inevitably entailed infringement of the concrete interests of its separate representatives and entire factions."

Soviet Marxists were prepared to argue that fascism was a singularly strange "bourgeois" regime. Fascists operated with independence, often at the expense of the bourgeoisie. Galkin acknowledged that Italian Fascism, during its tenure, extended its bureaucratic control over a very substantial part of the economic system, and that "the settlement of questions which for centuries were the prerogative of the big capitalists, in some measure [became] the function of the state bureaucratic agencies." In the fascist state, power was concentrated in the hands of the fascist leadership, and, as a result, "the handing over of power [by the ruling classes] to the fascists implied at the same time subordination to the regime."

Furthermore, since "the transfer of leadership implied a change in the form of power, it inevitably led to a reconstruction and, in a number of cases, to a breakup of the old party political mechanism. This ran counter to the intrinsic conservatism of the bourgeoisie and dictated renunciation of its former political sympathies and ties." All this meant not only that the "ruling bourgeoisie," composed as it was of heterogeneous interests, would regularly find itself suffering "inconveniences and at times tangible losses," but that fascism would violate its intrinsic "conservatism." Under the circumstances, the bourgeoisie, as the "ruling class," afforded Italian Fascism, more frequently than not, little more than "friendly neutrality."[4]

What the new interpretation succeeded in accomplishing was a *discrete separation of political power and control from the ownership of property.* In principle, Mussolini could act as an arbiter of Italy's fate quite independently of the "ruling propertied class." However much Fascists might accommodate themselves to the "ruling class," Fascism, in principle, remained its own master. In effect, Fascism's political power afforded it control over the propertied classes of the peninsula.

By the mid-1960s, Soviet Marxists were prepared to accept the thesis that the control of property did not ensure political control of the system. Marxist–Leninist theoreticians had put together an interpretation of fascism that conceived of it as a modernizing movement that arose spontaneously in times of socioeconomic crisis. The movement that had been considered the simple lackey of finance capital by the theoreticians of the Third International was conceived of, by the end of the 1960s, as capable of violating the interests and outraging the sensibilities of those who owned the means of production. The "finance capitalists," who, in the standard version of the Third International, had created and controlled fascism, disappeared into a vague, omnibus "ruling class," a class that not only did not dominate Mussolini or Hitler, but suffered at their hands. The fascism that had been "supinely subservient" to the "big bourgeoisie" in the account of Marxist–Leninists during the interwar years, had become an autonomous political power to which the capitalist class accorded, at best, only "friendly neutrality."

Outside the Soviet Union, there had already been a suggestion of substantial revisions in the standard version by Soviet-friendly Marxist–Leninists. In the early years of the 1960s, Paolo Alatri, an Italian Marxist–Leninist, warned that the "mechanical" and "rigid" interpretation of Italian Fascism must be abandoned. Moreover, he argued that it was absurd to suggest that the modern world faced only two alternatives in its future: either the "proletarian revolution" or fascism. Fascism, Alatri contended, was only one of the forms available to "antiproletarian reaction." Further, "no one could dream of thinking that Mussolini was purely and simply the executor of the directives of Italian industrialists." During his tenure Mussolini was, in Alatri's judgment, "the absolute master of Italy."[5]

In Alatri's presentation of the revised standard version, the "finance capitalists" of Italy made only a fleeting appearance. It was the omnibus ruling classes, not the finance capitalists, who conspired with Mussolini—and even they were "deluded" into believing that Fascism could be domesticated to their purposes. In Alatri's assessment, Fascism in Italy could not be domesticated, because it operated from a position of strength. It had its own multi-class demographic base, because, as Alatri acknowledged, specific class consciousness could be absent only where "the objective conditions for the [proletarian] revolution had not yet been realized."[6]

Implicit and explicit in Alatri's account was a recognition of the separation of ownership of the means of production in any given socioeconomic system and the exercise of political power. In Italian Fascism, political control had been separated from ownership. The revised interpretation of fascism suggested that attention be paid less to the economics of a system, than to its politics.

This change in focus was reflected in the work of Reinhard Kuehnl. In 1971, his work *Formen buergerlicher Herrschaft: Liberalismus-Faschismus* provided a German rendering of the Soviet revised standard version. Kuehnl was not disposed to go as far as Galkin or Alatri on some issues, but he did grant that fascism created a "qualitatively new" form of political structure, one of whose functions was to maintain a high profit rate for industrial and agricultural enterprise[7]—a guarded, elliptical way of saying that the Fascist state in Italy provided an opportunity for rapid capital accumulation and the attractive investment environment necessary for industrial expansion, technological improvement, and agricultural modernization.

Kuehnl's account was largely an affirmation and confirmation of those of Alexander Galkin and Paolo Alatri. Whatever the variations, the revised version of the Marxist–Leninist interpretation of fascism unmistakably conceived of fascism as largely autonomous in origin, multi-class in character, revolutionary in principle, developmental in function, modernizing in effect, and administered at considerable expense to the "bourgeois ruling classes." The full implications of the new Marxist–Leninist interpretation became abundantly clear in the early 1970s, when *Telos* published a chapter of a forthcoming book by Mihaly Vajda, a researcher for the Hungarian Academy of Sciences in Budapest.[8]

For Vajda, as for Galkin, fascism was a mass-mobilizing movement that, for a variety of reasons, assumed responsibility for resolving some of the nation-specific *developmental problems* of industrial capitalism under particular crisis conditions. Critical to understanding the dynamics of fascism, according to Vajda, was recognition that the movement and its leaders were involved in initiating, fostering, and sustaining "the development of the forces of production" during capitalism's transition to a higher developmental level.[9] It was clear to Vajda that all this occurred in the context of an industrial capitalism that had not yet reached the limits of its "historical development."[10]

Vajda argued that in order to accomplish the further development of productive forces, fascism advocated an ideology of national reconciliation calculated to unite all elements of the community in a demanding enterprise.[11] Fascism sought to mobilize the human and material resources of a given political community in the service of rapid technological development, industrial rationalization, and agricultural modernization. In pursuit of that purpose, fascists rejected all the traditional "bourgeois conceptions" of individuality, liberty, and equality. Fascism was manifestly "anti-bourgeois" in conception and anti-democratic in practice.

Vadja argued that fascism, while serving some abstract conception of the "general interests" of the "bourgeoisie," was a singular form of political arrangement. It provided the institutional agencies that facilitated the transition from one level of market-based economic development to another often, if not always, at the cost of the propertied classes. A number of alternative arrangements might have succeeded as well, but under the peculiar conditions of the period, fascists chose to employ modalities that left, within the system, qualified protection of person or property.

In Italy, Fascism arose not because capitalism had exhausted its potential and was senescent, but because agricultural and industrial capitalism was weak and only partially developed. By the turn of the twentieth century Italy had, in fact, only just begun its economic development and modernization. In those circumstances the "petty bourgeoisie" found itself marginalized in a system that no longer provided place, much less upward mobility, for peasant farmers, artisans, and small shopkeepers.[12]

Italian Fascism arose in an economically retrograde environment in which the domestic labor movement had been anachronistically infused with revolutionary enthusiasm. The petty bourgeoisie had been marginalized and alienated, and the possessing classes were threatened from all sides. The working masses, had they been successful, were fully capable of paralyzing production.[13] Such a paralysis would have ensured the continued deterioration of the life circumstances of both the petty bourgeoisie and the agricultural and industrial capitalists. Under these conditions, it was the dissatisfaction and restiveness of the petty bourgeoisie that provided mobilizable masses prepared for systemic change, and the surrounding anarchy that prompted the threatened "big bourgeoisie" to provide the financial, material, and moral support for a revolutionary political movement led by "declassed" veterans who had survived the Great War. Given the primitive state of economic development on the Italian peninsula, "proletarian revolution," rather than fascist victory, would have been theoretically, as well as practically, "untimely."

What this suggested to Vajda was that the demands of Italy's "proletarian" masses immediately following the First World War were, in "objective fact," "reactionary." Had their demands been met, the burdens imposed on the community would have "hinder[ed] the development of the economy." Conversely, Mussolini's Fascism, with its modernizing fervor and clearly industrial biases, offered the weak industrial bourgeoisie a potentially powerful ally in the effort to industrialize the Italian peninsula. Fascism was not the creature of the "ruling bourgeoisie," it was a singular political response to objective historical and economic conditions.

In Vajda's judgment, at the conclusion of the First World War, Mussolini's Fascism "remained the only progressive solution" to the crisis of Italy's economic underdevelopment. Fascists, acting with independence, chose a "progressive" political course in response to prevailing crisis conditions that "consisted in the capitalization of the economy." This course was pursued not because it was dictated by the propertied bourgeoisie, but because any other alternative would have been "reactionary."

Vajda maintained that, in Italy, "the defense of democracy against Fascism from the position of proletarian democracy [would have been] reactionary, since the alternative between bourgeois democracy and Fascism was one between economic stagnation and economic development."[14] Neither bourgeois control nor bourgeois democracy typified Mussolini's Fascism, because, in Vajda's judgment, both would have been "reactionary" in the prevailing circumstances.

As a Marxist, Vajda recognized that only the full maturation of the productive forces and the material abundance they assured could provide the objective economic foundation upon which socialist productive relations and a socialist superstructure could be erected. Fascism, instrumental in the development of the productive forces, was "progressive" insofar as it contributed to the creation of the preconditions for socialism. What becomes evident in all this is that, in some sense or another, fascism and socialism were united in the "logic of history."

More important than anything else, the revised Marxist–Leninist interpretation separated the notion of "fascism" from any direct connection with the ownership of the means of production. "As soon as they came to power," Vajda reminded his readers, "both Italian and German fascism removed the traditional ruling classes from political power."[15] The fascists exercised political control, although they themselves did not own the "means of production."[16]

By the 1970s, fascism for many Marxist–Leninists was no longer the "inevitable" economic and political product of the "rotton-ripe" last stage of monopoly capitalism; it was an ideological and political novelty designed to sustain the growth and sophistication of an economy poised to achieve a new station of growth. In the course of its instauration, fascism seized power from the traditional bourgeoisie and operated with significant independence. Its leaders were the autocratic masters of the new state form.

Of course, much of the revised version of the Marxist theory of fascism that emerged by the 1970s owed a great deal of its substance to the "nonorthodox" Marxist interpretations of the interwar years. Vajda, for example, regularly referred to the interpretation offered by Franz Borkenau to support his own position.[17] For Vajda, as for Borkenau, Italian Fascism was conceived of as "progressive" in the sense that "the task of Italian Fascism was precisely that of assuring the accumulation of capital necessary for the extensive growth of the prevailing economy—something that the Italian bourgeois democracy had shown itself entirely incapable of accomplishing."[18] Fascists were enlisted in the service of the productive forces, not the ruling classes, and, as a consequence, qualified as "progressive."

By the 1970s, the orthodox Soviet interpretation of fascism had been transformed. While fascism was still understood to somehow serve the "historic interests of capitalism"—some of its major features were identified as "progressive" and, in a significant sense, "revolutionary." Within the "capitalist mode of production," fascism fashioned a "new state system" sufficiently different from the classic "bourgeois state" to qualify fascism as "revolutionary."

What is difficult to understand is why the new interpretation came into being when it did, and why it had the character it had. Clearly, a great many of the insights that passed into the revised version had been recognized for some time by both Marxist and non-Marxist theoreticians. As has been suggested, there were notable non-Soviet Marxists in the 1930s who had made arguments that appeared in the new version with remarkably little change. What had been rejected as a fundamentally flawed interpretation of fascism by Soviet scholars in the 1930s was found acceptable to Marxist–Leninists in the 1960s and 1970s.

That the revised version was formulated and accepted by the intellectual leadership in the Soviet Union was not without cost. Certainly, the new account generated a sense of paradox among Marxist–Leninists. Galkin, Kuehnl, and Vajda admitted that, whatever else it was, generic fascism was very threatening to traditional capitalist elites, wresting from them the prerogative of resolving political issues and radically diminishing their control over their own properties. They all granted, explicitly or implicitly, that the bourgeoisie, in permitting fascists to seize political power, had lost control of their political environment. Irrespective of that recognition, representatives of the postwar interpretation of fascism maintained that the regime remained, nonetheless, a "form of bourgeois rule." Although fascism "ran counter to the intrinsic conservatism of the bourgeoisie," it remained, for all that, "bourgeois."[19]

All the evidence of fascism's use of political coercion and ultimately its use of terror against individuals and whole segments of the "big" and "petty" bourgeoisie notwithstanding, there remained an insistence that fascism was somehow tethered to the interests of the "possessing class." Even though Italian Fascism had so much autonomy that Mussolini, during his time, exercised something like totalitarian control over many aspects of economic, political, and social life, there remained the insistence that fascism somehow was forever enlisted in the service of the "big bourgeoisie."

What is manifestly clear is that the revised Soviet standard interpretation of fascism separated political power from ownership of the means of production. Political power was understood, under certain conditions, to operate independently of the ownership of property. *Fascism* had become a concept defined in terms not of property relations, but of overt political behavior.

Only the notion that *fascism* was to be defined in terms of overt political behavior could diffuse the sense of paradox that accompanied the new interpretation. Italian Fascism had arisen in industrially retrograde Italy; yet it was somehow seen as the product of "late capitalism." It was an industrializing movement in an essentially agrarian environment that was both modernizing and reactionary. It had violated all the norms of traditional bourgeois society and in the end had threatened the "socialization" of private property in its nationalist drive to create a collectivistic "Greater Italy." Yet, somehow or other, Fascism was a defense of capitalism and the enemy of the socialist revolution.

The revised interpretation of fascism, produced by Soviet and Soviet-friendly scholars in the 1960s and 1970s, created significant theoretical tensions for many Marxist intellectuals. Nonetheless, it was sanctioned by the leadership in the Kremlin. In retrospect, it seems clear that the new interpretation of fascism served other than strictly intellectual and explanatory functions. The concept *fascism* was to be pressed into service for other than cognitive purposes. That purpose can perhaps best be appreciated by considering yet another version of the revised interpretation of fascism that came out in the 1970s.

At that time a book appeared in the West that was identified as a special contribution to the "controversies on the left" concerning the interpretation of fascism. Upon its publication, Nicos Poulantzas's work *Fascism and Dictatorship* was identified as "the first major Marxist study of German and Italian fascism to appear since the Second World War." As will be argued, it was certainly not the first Marxist study of fascism to appear after the Second World War. What it was, in fact, was a study of fascism from an *anti-Soviet Marxist* point of view. It was to provide a new and "rigorous theory" of fascism as "an emergency regime for the defense of capital" *from a Maoist perspective.*[20]

In terms of the revised Soviet Marxist "general theory" of fascism, Poulantzas offered very little that was new. Fascism was understood to be but "one form of regime among others of the exceptional capitalist state."[21] No less had been said by Galkin and Alatri—and by Borkenau and Otto Bauer several decades before. Like those who preceded him, Poulantzas maintained that fascism was the product of a peculiar "conjuncture of the class struggle," a political crisis taking place during the "imperialist stage of capitalism."[22] That stage involved the full articulation of monopoly capitalism as state power. The bourgeois state, under the demands of "imperialist monopoly capital," assumes new interventionist responsibilities within the economy. Nothing less had been said by those Soviet Marxists who had already revised the interwar standard version.

Poulantzas lamented the "theoretical failures" of the interwar Third International. He argued that the international of the 1930s had succumbed to a vulgar form of "economism," in which fascism was the consequence of the "mechanical decomposition of capitalism, the miraculous contradiction between the productive forces and relations of production." Galkin had said little less.

According to the privative notions of the Third International, Poulantzas complained, fascism had been "reduced to [an] inevitable need" of "moribund capitalism." Poulantzas explicitly rejected, for example, the notion that fascism was intrinsically related to the "tendency towards a *falling rate of profit*" that heralded the imminent disintegration of advanced capitalist systems in the "era of imperialism." Nothing less had been argued by that time by the Marxist–Leninists in the Kremlin.

Poulantzas was fully familiar with the work of the major theoreticians of the Third International. He distanced himself from "the Third International's econ-

omist catastrophism, predicting [as it did] the imminent disintegration of capitalism . . . based . . . on its conception of [the] tendency towards a falling rate of
profit as an 'inevitable law' " of modern industrial society.[23]

For Poulantzas, fascism was not to be explained as an epiphenomenon of
economic factors. He argued that fascism was a very complex reality. Fascism,
rather than being a "paid tool" of capitalism in decline, "really represented a
development of *capitalist forces of production.* . . . It represented industrial development, technological innovation, and an increase in the productivity of labor." One of the fundamental mistakes entertained by the orthodox Marxist–
Leninists of the interwar years, according to Poulantzas, was to "define" fascism
as "a 'retarding' and 'retrograde' phenomen[on]," as a simple tool of "finance
capitalism" facing economic extinction.[24]

By the early 1970s, the Kremlin's revised standard version of the Marxist–
Leninist theory of fascism had already said as much. What distinguished Poulantzas's account was his emphasis on the role played by "the politics of class
struggle" in the emergence, victory, and endurance of fascism. Poulantzas was
emphatic about the primary role played by the politics of class struggle, rather
than economics, in the history of fascism.[25]

As though to support his thesis, Poulantzas pretended to be able to identify,
without equivocation, not only the fundamental class interests that fascism
served, but also how political class struggle found expression in particular institutions in the fascist state. Thus, in the intense political class struggles that
shaped the history of Italian Fascism, Poulantzas insisted that the educational
apparatus created by the ministerial reforms of Giovanni Gentile served as the
"refuge of medium capital." "Medium capital" somehow seized control of education in Fascist Italy and somehow or other used it in defense of its interests.

The Roman Catholic Church, in turn, was a "stronghold of the *landowners.*"
Poulantzas was convinced that the landed bourgeoisie of Italy had used the
Roman Catholic Church as a weapon in their own defense. The Italian mon-
archy, in Poulantzas's certain judgment, "was allied with medium capital," while
Mussolini was the spokesman for the "urban petty bourgeoisie."[26] Thus, while
the fascist state, in Poulantzas's assessment, was essentially under the control of
the "hegemonic class"—"big capital"—"nonhegemonic classes," in the course of
"class struggles," politically controlled certain branches and institutions of the
state.[27] Poulantzas knew all this with the assurance of a sleepwalker. One could
only understand Italian Fascism in particular and fascism in general by understanding *the politics of class struggle.* This conviction was absolutely central to
Poulantzas's new interpretation.

Once again, it is not the affirmation that is of interest, but the evident lack of
empirical confirmation. References to other Marxist authors constituted the bulk

of the "evidence" that Poulantzas provided in support of his claims. Throughout his text, Charles Bettelheim, Paul Baran, Paul Sweezy, Antonio Gramsci, Clara Zetkin, Leon Trotsky, Karl Radek, Palmiro Togliatti, Karl Kautsky, Paolo Alatri, Angelo Tasca, Arthur Rosenberg, and Daniel Guerin are referred to with metronomic regularity. Non-Marxist historians are cited with some frequency as collateral support, but there is none of the direct empirical evidence required for the confirmation of his claims. Given the lack of empirical support, one can only wonder why Poulantzas was so insistent on affirming and defending his particular thesis.

What distinguished Poulantzas's version of the Marxist–Leninist interpretation of fascism from others was his discovery of the primary role played by specifically *political* struggle, expressed through institutions, rather than simple economic factors. What is important is that Poulantzas identified this discovery with the influence upon him of the "thought of Mao Zedong."[28]

For Poulantzas, it was Mao Zedong who "introduced *new and crucially important* elements into Marxist–Leninist theory and practice."[29] It was the thought of Mao that moved contemporary Marxist theory beyond the economic determinism implicit in the orthodox emphasis on the "material productive forces." It was Mao, according to Poulantzas, who revealed the importance of both the "relations of production" and "superstructural elements" in the revolutionary history of our times. It was he who rejected the "metaphysical primacy given to the 'productive forces'" and emphasized the significance of the "contradictions" between the "economic base" and the "superstructure" of any given society.[30]

In its simplest form, what all this meant was that Poulantzas, like Mao, chose to make class struggle a central notion in revolution and the analysis of revolution. Poulantzas sought a place for individual and collective strength of will, conviction, ideas, and ideology as they found expression in class struggle.

Volition, conviction, ideas, and ideology have always been identified as "superstructural" elements among Marxist theoreticians. It was Mao who contended that they were a central issue. It was he who identified the failure of his enemies with moral and ideological failure.

In the history of Marxism, there has been a protracted dispute between those who held that economic factors exert preeminent influence on the outcome of events and those who insisted that "class consciousness" and political leadership served as determinants.[31] Marx argued that the "relations of production" into which human beings enter "correspond to a definite stage of development of their material productive forces." The development of the material productive forces, together with their corresponding productive relations constitute the "economic base" upon which the "superstructure" of legal, political, and intellec-tual life is erected.[32]

For more than a century and a half, many competent Marxists interpreted all this to mean that the development of machinery and its attendant technology constituted the foundation of social change. The relations of production—the arrangements through which the material yield of the forces of production are distributed—simply "correspond" to the available levels of output. The intellec-tual life of a community, in turn, "reflects" the economic base.

Should all this be accepted, it would seem that, as Marx suggested, in the final analysis, "the productive forces . . . are the basis of all . . . history."[33] Productive relations would "correspond" to those forces; and "superstructural elements" would be epiphenomenal. Thus, Marx maintained that "in acquiring new pro-ductive forces, men change their mode of production; and in changing their mode of production, in changing the way of earning their living, they change all their social relations. The hand mill gives you society with the feudal lord; the steam mill, society with the industrial capitalist. The same men who establish their social relations in conformity with their material productivity, produce also principles, ideas and categories, in conformity with their social relations."[34]

However much Mao Zedong and Nicos Poulantzas may have objected, the fact is that these "theoretical" notions provided the grounds for what Poulantzas called the "economism" of the Third International's interpretation of fascism. If fascism marked a new stage in the evolution of capitalist society, Marxism rec-ommended a study of changes in the productive base. Marxism suggested that fascism could best be understood as a "reflection" of major alterations in the productive foundation of capitalist society.

As has been indicated, the argument during the interwar years was that the productive forces of capitalism had outgrown the existing property relations of capitalist society. The evidence for that was the putative secular decline in the rate of profit. The declining rate of profit served as an indicator of the economic decay of the system. Fascism was interpreted as an effort to postpone the evident and inexorable disintegration of the productive base of the system. Because of its intention to forestall an inevitability, it found expression in irrationality. Its irrationality was the product of the fruitless effort to arrest what the Soviet Marxists of the period interpreted as the irreversible decomposition of industrial capitalism.

Once that account was abandoned, an alternative explanation was necessary. If fascism could not be understood as a function of economic factors, recourse would have to be made to alternative explanatory strategies. Poulantzas was prepared to conceive of fascism as a product of political class struggle. It was class conflict, not economic factors, that ultimately governed the advent, success, and survival of fascism in the modern world. What Poulantzas was arguing was that an understanding of fascism required not scrutiny of the productive forces, but reflection on the relations of production and the superstructural components of modern capitalist society. This necessitated assessment of class relations and the *ideological* conflicts that typify contemporary society. In Poulantzas's new, fascism could be understood only by applying the insights of the thought of Mao Zedong to modern history.

Whereas Mao had found his "class" enemies in a society in which private property had been abolished, so Mussolini's Fascism was to be understood not as a by-product of economic factors, but in terms of political consciousness. Mao had provided Poulantzas the key to understanding fascism. All this, needless to say, was exceedingly curious. Mao knew very little, if anything, about European history. He knew even less about fascism. Worse still, it is not at all evident that he knew much more about classical Marxism.[35] At best, his Marxism was exceedingly thin.[36] Nonetheless, Poulantzas found what to him was the secret to the interpretation of fascism in the insights provided by Mao Zedong.

In fact, Poulantzas's interpretation of fascism had very little to do with serious theory construction. It had more to do with what was transpiring among the leaders of the Marxist–Leninist systems that had survived and prospered after the Second World War. By the time Poulantzas wrote his book, Maoism had supplanted the Marxism–Leninism of Josef Stalin as the ideological compass for many non-Soviet Marxists. By then, there had been the denunciation of the "excesses" of Stalinism at the Twentieth Party Congress of the Communist Party of the Soviet Union. More than that, Nikita Khrushchev, with his proposed "de-Stalinization," had traumatized Marxist intellectuals everywhere. Traditional Marxism–Leninism seemed to have entered into eclipse. Revolutionary "Marxism–Leninism Mao Zedong Thought" began to appear increasingly attractive to alienated Marxist intellectuals in the West.

For a variety of reasons that need not detain us, Mao had early begun to have difficulties with the leadership of the Soviet Union. After 1960, the tensions between the two Marxist–Leninist regimes had become common knowledge.[37] More significant for the present discussion, by the turn of the decade the radicals of the "Great Proletarian Cultural Revolution" in China were identifying the Soviet Union, itself, as a "fascist dictatorship."[38] By the late 1960s and the early 1970s, Marxist theoreticians in both the Soviet Union and the People's Republic of China began to employ the concept *fascism* in their criticisms of each other's system. Whatever motivated the employment, it became clear that the concept *fascism* would have to be tailored to its new uses.

What appeared to be a simple matter of political interpretation to many Western academics became a major practical political issue in the rapidly escalating Sino–Soviet dispute. More and more frequently, Soviet academics and their Chinese counterparts invoked "fascism" to explain the controversy that threatened armed conflict between Soviet and Chinese Marxism–Leninism. What appeared to be intellectual grotesquerie to outside observers was, in fact, an issue thick with implications for Marxist–Leninist practitioners. The Sino–Soviet dispute had compromised "proletarian internationalism." The universal socialist revolution had foundered on a dispute between two Marxist–Leninist systems. Marxist–Leninist theoreticians were compelled to attempt an explanation of the unanticipated sequence of events that threatened the very integrity of Marxism.

What emerged from the Sino–Soviet conflict was a revised standard version of the Marxist–Leninist interpretation of fascism that, in principle, allowed the application of the concept *fascism* to what were deemed failed socialist systems. The new interpretation allowed an autonomous "revolutionary" and "modernizing" political leadership, whose power was independent of property ownership, to be identified as "fascist" even if that leadership ruled in a system that had abolished private property and the market exchange of goods. No longer tied to ownership of the means of production, "fascists" were conceived of as controlling political institutions in the service of some remote "bourgeois" purpose—even in systems legally devoid of private property.

The new interpretation allowed a system to be "fascist" if it could be characterized, in some manner or other, as a variant of "state monopoly capitalism." Such a system, dominated by an autonomous political party, mobilizing a subject population to controlled, accelerated economic growth and industrial development, might well be "fascist"—however it chose to identify itself—as long as it resisted the "true socialism" of the Soviet Union or Maoist China.

Within the new interpretation, one might expect to find "fascism" in otherwise "progressive" (Soviet or Maoist) political arrangements, as long as those arrangements threatened war against "proletarian internationalism," compromised Marxism, and/or deflected world society from its ultimate communist goal. In principle, in the new interpretation of fascism, it was possible to find fascism in the most unexpected places, including those socioeconomic systems of the Left that otherwise identified themselves as Marxist–Leninist. That Marxist–Leninist intellectuals in the late 1960s and early 1970s undertook a revision of the earlier Marxist–Leninist interpretation of fascism was in part the result of the growing Sino–Soviet ideological and policy conflict. Marxist intellectuals were obliged to explain how "proletarian revolutionary systems," presumably united by the one true social science, could find themselves poised on the brink of armed conflict. Those were the circumstances in which intellectuals like Galkin, Alatri, Vajda, and Poulantzas sought an interpretation of fascism that had contemporary relevance, one that might account for a sequence of events that had shattered the intellectual pretensions of Marxism as a social science theory.

As early as the first years of the 1960s, the Chinese Communist Party had denounced the Soviet Communist Party for its failure to adhere to Marxism–Leninism.[39] In a world presumably moving ineluctably toward communism, a Marxist–Leninist regime had abandoned Marxism. At the same time, Soviet thinkers charged Maoism with having given itself over to "a variety of anti-communism, petty-bourgeois counter-revolutionism and reactionary national-ism."[40] Maoism was seen as "a fusion of nationalism with great power chauvin-ism and the theory of violence."[41] Initially, Soviet thinkers were to discover in the economic backwardness and massive poverty of the People's Republic of China the reason behind Mao Zedong having turned "the Communist Party of China from the Marxist–Leninist stand to a petty-bourgeois, nationalist ideological and political platform."[42] Soviet intellectuals argued that if the superstructure of a society must conform to its economic base, then China's superstructure, its system of laws, beliefs, and convictions about Marxist theory, must be impoverished and primitive indeed.

Chinese Marxists, for their part, argued that the corruption of Marxism–Leninism in the Soviet Union was the result of "bourgeois" influence. As early as 1957, Chinese Marxists argued that some sort of political "right-wing opportun-ism" and "revisionism" had surfaced in the Soviet Union and had caused "sectar-ianism" and "dogmatism" to undermine the Marxist integrity of the system. The deviance was ascribed to "bourgeois influences" that had somehow survived the socialist revolution.[43] It was a bourgeois influence independent of the existence of bourgeois property. It was the political expression of a subterranean "class strug-gle" that somehow persisted even after the abolition of private property and the suppression of the market exchange of commodities. Maoists were soon to dis-cover that defenders of capitalism had survived not only in the Soviet Union but in the People's Republic of China as well.

The theme of "bourgeois" influences in socialist society was to play a central role in the violence of Maoist China's "Great Proletarian Cultural Revolution." Mao Zedong mobilized the masses to defend his revolution against a "reaction-ary bourgeoisie" that had inexplicably survived in the very ranks of the Commu-nist Party itself, in spite of the socialist revolution, the abolition of private prop-erty, and more than a decade of violent suppression.

In the course of the violent "class struggle" that tormented China for almost a decade, a substantial number of Communist Party leaders were discovered to be themselves "bourgeois capitalist roaders" attempting to "restore capitalism" in

China. The "state monopoly capitalism" they sought to impose on "revolutionary China" was nothing other than a form of fascism. That so many in the leadership ranks of the Communist Party of China had given themselves over to the service of fascism threatened not only the integrity of the revolution, but its rationale as well.

The argument put together by Mao and his entourage to explain the defections was that, irrespective of the fact that "bourgeois property relations" had been abolished in Communist China by the revolution, bourgeois elements had somehow survived, and "new bourgeois elements appeared daily."[44] The Marxists of China had found that "a considerable number of . . . anti-Party and anti-socialist representatives of the bourgeoisie" had not only survived in Communist China, but had infiltrated the Central Committee of the Party itself. They had compromised the government at every level.[45]

Almost twenty years after the succession of Mao Zedong to power in China, the Marxist–Leninists there found themselves involved in what was subsequently to be characterized as "a life-and-death struggle, under the dictatorship of the proletariat, between the two major antagonistic classes, the proletariat and the bourgeoisie."[46] Maoist China found itself locked in class conflict in a socialist environment devoid of private property and the private ownership of the means of production. The bourgeoisie, as a class, was apparently more durable than the "capitalist mode of production" itself.

What had taken place, of course, was a Maoist redefinition of class. Class was no longer defined in terms of an ownership relationship to the means of production. It was defined instead in political terms of "consciousness"—determined by whether or not one possessed "proletarian" or "bourgeois" consciousness. Consciousness itself was no longer related to "material life circumstances," but to one's commitment to the "thought of Mao Zedong."[47] Anyone who "mastered Mao Zedong thought" was "proletarian." Anyone who understood that "Every sentence by Chairman Mao" was "the truth, and [carried] more weight than ten thousand ordinary sentences" was "proletarian."[48] Only armed with such a "moral atomic bomb" might humans become truly "proletarian."[49] Only then could the proletariat defeat "fascism," "social imperialism," and the "bourgeoisie" that was their ultimate source.

For the Maoists of the period, "proletarians" and "anti-fascists" were those who defended and followed Chairman Mao's teachings. Alternatively, the "bourgeoisie" were those who "malign[ed] Mao Zedong thought, extol[led] . . . bourgeois culture and strove for the restoration of capitalism."[50] Class consciousness was at the center of the conflict between socialism and fascism.

However uncertain orthodox Marxism had been in discussing "class" and class membership, the "thought of Mao Zedong" did absolutely nothing to enhance the clarity of the subject or the credibility of the enterprise. By the time of the Great Proletarian Cultural Revolution, "class" and "class struggle" had little objective meaning to Chinese Marxist–Leninists. In effect, the relationship of classes to the material productive forces was no longer a matter of any consequence. What mattered was what one *thought* about the world and society. What was essential was one's *ideological* commitments. Anything other than Maoism was irrevocably and irremediably "bourgeois." Politics was in command.

All this was apparently what Poulantzas, and those like him in the West, found so illuminating.[51] These were what Poulantzas considered the "new and crucially important theoretical elements" that Mao Zedong supplied to contemporary Marxism–Leninism. They were the insights that allowed Poulantzas to produce the interpretation of fascism that conceived of it as the *political* product of an *ideological* "class struggle."

Fascism was not the final defense of moribund capitalism; in socialist environments it was the resistance of the "bourgeois" to the "thought of Mao Zedong." Given that notion, Maoists could argue that because the leadership in Moscow had raised objections to Maoism, socialism in the Soviet Union had been transformed into a "fascist dictatorship."[52] What Maoists had discovered was that while it was relatively easy to "drive out the landlords and capitalists," it was extremely difficult to offset the counterrevolutionary influence of the bourgeoisie in general and those "petty bourgeois" elements generated by "small production" in particular.[53]

By the time Poulantzas's book appeared in English translation, China's Maoists had put together a notion of fascism that saw it as the product of ideological class struggle in any environment, capitalist or socialist, in which "bourgeois elements" were capable of politically defeating the "proletariat." In the Soviet Union, such bourgeois elements had succeeded in accomplishing what Hitler had attempted, but failed, to do. The bourgeoisie in the Soviet Union had defeated the Marxist "dictatorship of the proletariat" and had there undertaken the "all-round restoration of capitalism" and the imposition of a "fascist dictatorship."[54] These were the "new and crucially important theoretical" insights into fascism provided by the "thought of Mao Zedong."

By the time he wrote his major study of fascism, Poulantzas had accepted the substance of Maoism. He confidently spoke of the "class struggle" being conducted in the Soviet Union half a century after the revolution had destroyed private property. Poulantzas was convinced that "desperate class struggles" had savaged the Soviet Union throughout its history. In a society that no longer suffered private ownership of the means of production, the class struggle was between the ideological "bourgeoisie" and the ideological "proletariat."[55]

By the mid-1970s, it was clear to anyone who was not an uncritical enthusiast that theoretical Marxism was in a state of advanced putrefaction. Within that general decay, the Marxist–Leninist interpretation of fascism that had begun so confidently half a century before had been reduced to a collection of poorly defined, loosely articulated convictions about class, class consciousness, class interests, imperialism, and capitalism. It had become victim to political struggles between two Marxist–Leninist systems.

The entire notion of "class" was no longer associated with ownership of the means of production—or of having only one's labor power to sell. "Class" had become a function of consciousness, and fascism was identified as any "bourgeois" ideological and political effort to defend, sustain, or restore the kind of "capitalism" to be found in the Soviet Union of Nikita Khrushchev and Leonid Brezhnev. If, for Poulantzas, understanding fascism required an appreciation of "the conjuncture of the class struggle" during a specific historical period, it is very difficult to see how the "thought of Mao Zedong" could have been of any serious assistance in any such undertaking.[56]

However intellectually unconvincing the Marxist–Leninist interpretation of fascism was in the interwar years, by the 1970s it was almost completely devoid of interpretive substance. That Marxist–Leninists of whatever persuasion found merit in the accounts delivered after the mid-1960s speaks well for ideological enthusiasm, but says little about theoretical competence. That some Marxists found something theoretically important in Maoism is a testament to political loyalty. It tells us very little about fascism.

In the turmoil of the Sino–Soviet dispute, there were other Marxists, Marx enthusiasts, and fellow travelers who were to take up the new interpretation of fascism and attempt its development. At the very commencement of his account of fascism, Poulantzas alludes to the work of the "New Left" that had made its appearance by the early 1970s.[57]

The fact was that there were some "neo-Marxists" in the West who attempted new "theoretical" developments. Those attempts were predicated on features of Maoism that became increasingly popular among "anti-imperialists" around the time of the Vietnam War. The "neo-Marxist" thought of the North and South American, European, and African "New Left" represented a major attempt to restore the relevance of Marxism–Leninism to the contemporary world by infusing it with Maoist and "neo-Maoist" substance.

By the mid-1970s, China's Maoists had succeeded in reducing the Marxist–Leninist interpretation of fascism to a list of simplisms. "Fascism" signified any attempt to defend capitalism in the industrialized democracies or any effort made to restore capitalism in socialist systems. Such "anti-Marxist" undertakings were still more emphatically fascist if they were enlisted in the service of "imperialism." For Maoists, fascism, in its most fundamental form, was an ultimate defense of the capitalist mode of production in a world irresistibly moving toward socialism.

Given such notions, Maoists were prepared to affirm that the Soviet Union had transformed itself into a fascist regime. The "bourgeois elements" that had seized control of the Communist Party of the Soviet Union had pursued a fascist policy of capitalist restoration, serving the "social imperialism" that was central to the ultimate interests of their class. In so doing, whatever their protestations, they were the "objective allies" of international imperialism. For Maoists, "imperialism" was the taproot of fascism.

The "neo-Marxists" and "neo-Maoists" who surfaced in the West during the first years of the 1970s were to contribute to the articulation of that particular aspect of the new interpretation. Like Maoists, what theoreticians like James Cockcroft, André Gunder Frank, and Dale Johnson discovered was that fascism was, indeed, the product of the "reactionary bourgeoisie." It was the offspring of the "class struggle" wherever that struggle was to be found, and it was the desperate defense of the capitalist system wherever that system survived or could be restored.

What was distinctive about the New Left interpretation was that the bourgeois base of fascism was to be found almost exclusively in the industrialized "metropole," while the revolutionary proletariat—identified with the peasant masses of the Third World—hunkered down on the periphery of the world capitalist system. The class struggle that shaped the world was an *international* class struggle against imperialism, in which the revolutionaries on the periphery made war on the exploiting metropole.[58]

There was something of an echo of Lenin's rationale for the "Eastern policy" of the Third International in all this. But it had substance of its own as well. The revolutions on the periphery were no longer seen as "bourgeois national"; they were genuine "anti-imperialist" revolutionary movements. They were not harbingers of the forthcoming proletarian revolution; they were the liberating revolution itself.

In the global conflict envisioned by the theoreticians of the New Left—the "dependency theorists" of the 1970s—the reactionaries of the metropole dispatched paid mercenaries to the peripheral countries to defend international capitalism against attacks by indigenous "anti-imperialists." The United States troops in Vietnam, in the Philippines, in Central or South America were mercenaries who, we were informed, were "fascists," performing the same "class functions" as the original *squadristi* of Mussolini.[59]

Some perverse semblance of coherence had been restored to the original Marxist–Leninist interpretation of fascism—but only at the cost of jettisoning almost all the theoretical integrity of classical Marxism. Under the influence of

Maoism, the neo-Marxists saw fascism as an immediate by-product of international imperialism. It was not a domestic result of economic developments, but a consequence of *international* class struggle.

For neo-Marxism, the class struggle was no longer a domestic phenomenon, but was conducted on a world stage. The oppressed class was not the proletariat of the advanced industrial countries, in which Karl Marx had invested so much confidence. The oppressed class was the revolutionary peasantry of economically underdeveloped countries. If rural denizens were irremediably counterrevolutionary for classical Marxism, they were the real revolutionaries for neo-Marxists of the 1970s.

Anyone who resisted the revolutionary efforts of the peasantry in economically retrograde and industrially backward environments was a "fascist." Thus, for the more enthusiastic neo-Marxists, the United States, as the hegemonic imperialist power, was the progenitor of fascism everywhere in the world.[60]

The Maoist-inspired neo-Marxist interpretation of fascism constituted more than an abandonment of some secondary claims to be found in the classical Marxist literature. Neo-Marxism rejected some of the central tenets of Marx's interpretation of world developments. For Marx and Engels "the bourgeois mode of production" was the first productive system in history driven by its own impetus to extend itself over all humankind. In doing this capitalism would provide the material conditions for its own transcendence. The worldwide maturation of industrial capitalism would produce the economic abundance upon which socialism would be erected.[61]

In 1848, the first Marxists maintained that modern industry would be compelled by its intrinsic needs not only to establish a "world market," but to supervise an "immense development [in] commerce . . . navigation, [and] communication," which would accompany the global "extension of industry." Driven by the necessities of the system itself, capitalist production would "nestle everywhere, settle everywhere, establish connections everywhere," drawing "even the most barbarian nations into civilization." Industrial capitalism would "compel all nations, on pain of extinction, to adopt the bourgeois modes of production. . . . In one word, it [would] create a world after its own image."[62]

The expansion of industrial capitalism was for Marx and Engels the necessary condition for the ultimate victory of socialism. It was the "infinite" productive potential of machine industry that capitalism brought with it that held the promise of socialism. Without universal industrialization, the entire tragic conflict of classes, the curse of poverty, and the exploitation of man by man, could not be overcome.

The first Marxists understood "colonialism" and the attendant spread of the capitalist mode of production as the necessary antecedent to world revolution.

"Colonialism" and/or "imperialism" would destroy the "mummified" economies of the less developed portions of the world and create in their stead an industrial foundation that would constitute the "material basis of the new world"
anticipated by the founders of modern "scientific socialism."[63]

Moved by Maoist insights, neo-Marxists were to deny all that. For neo-
Marxists, the advanced industrial countries, rather than transferring industrial
potential to less developed peripheral economies, were seen as creating inequities
in multilateral trade that assured their lack of development. International capitalism sought not the industrialization of the less developed world, but its
perpetual underdevelopment, in order to ensure that the nonindustrial regions
remained forever market supplements and resource repositories for the developed metropole.

According to neo-Marxists of the 1970s, the oppressive and exploitative bourgeoisie of the advanced industrial nations employed "client fascist" instrumentalities to preclude the possibility that industrialization might take root on its
periphery. Rather than bringing development to the less developed portions of
the globe, the industrialized nations of the world at the end of the twentieth
century used deceit, corruption, oppression, and violence to make that industrialization impossible.[64]

According to the analysis, only those less developed communities that break
out of any trade or capital investment relationship with the advanced industrial
nations could avoid becoming "client fascist" states. Only revolutionary communities like economically backward "proletarian Cuba" and industrially retrograde "socialist China" could resist fascism.

At the time of its articulation, neo-Marxism sought to give some kind of
theoretical expression to the foreign policy postures of Mao Zedong and his
"theory" of "Three Worlds," in which only the peasant Third World was truly
revolutionary.[65] It was an attempt to provide some theoretical coherence to Lin
Biao's quixotic conviction that only the marginally developed "colonial countries," engaged in a "people's war," could defeat "world imperialism."[66]

What had been attempted by neo-Marxist and dependency theorists of the
1970s was an effort to give substance to the vagaries of "the thought of Mao" as
that thought found expression in the Great Proletarian Cultural Revolution.
What they produced, as we shall see, was the theoretical analog of the Fascist
conviction that revolution in the modern world was rooted in the struggle of
"proletarian nations" against the "plutocracies."

The Marxist–Leninist interpretation of fascism that emerged in the 1960s
and 1970s was the captive product of the Sino–Soviet dispute. It arose with that
dispute and left little behind at its conclusion. It proved to be neither cognitively
satisfying nor particularly helpful in understanding modern revolutions. As will

be argued, what it did, in its own fashion, was to reconfirm the relevance of fascism for our time.

A review of the treatment of the concept *fascism* employed by the protagonists in the course of the adversarial exchanges that embittered the relationship between Communist China and the Soviet Union in the years following de-Stalinization is instructive. Intellectuals, however much their efforts were compromised by service to one or other regime, generally sought to make their accounts as coherent as possible, in possession of as much substance as their primary obligations would allow. Because of the peripheral need on the part of intellectuals to satisfy at least some of the independent measures of competence that governed their enterprise, it will be argued that, in a curious and unintended way, the variants of the Marxist–Leninist theories of fascism that emerged in the course of the Sino–Soviet conflict succeeded in providing a distorted insight into the rationale of historic fascism.

Fascism and Marxism–Leninism in Power

By the end of the 1960s, interaction between the People's Republic of China and the Soviet Union had become increasingly hostile. Why the two major Marxist–Leninist powers entered into the long period of contention that at one point saw Chinese and Soviet troops in armed conflict along their borders is a question too complex to attempt to adequately address here. What is of relevance here is that as a consequence of the expanding conflict, theoreticians in Beijing and Moscow each sought to justify respective national policy by appealing to *fascism* as an explanatory concept.

Marxist–Leninist thinkers believed that they had legitimate occasion to employ the concept *fascism* in coming to understand regime deviance in one or other "proletarian" regime. Soviet Marxists discerned elements of fascism in the political system that took shape under the ministrations of Mao Zedong, and Chinese Marxists saw fascism in the developments of the post-Stalinist Soviet Union.

For more than a decade after the end of the Second World War, academics everywhere seemed to have been content to deal with fascism as a problem of descriptive discrimination. Fascism was understood to be an essentially "right-wing," nationalistic, anti-democratic, anti-Marxist, and potentially genocidal political system, characterized by the "leadership principle," insistent elitism, an appeal to violence as a legitimate tool of change, totalitarian aspirations, substantial state control of the economy, the imposition of an exclusivist formal ideology, a pervasive anti-intellectualism and anti-individualism, emphatic voluntarism, and the exploitation of a mystique of military heroism and personal self-sacrifice in the service of a "revolutionary community."[1]

For some considerable length of time, Western academics at least pretended to be able to identify instances of a generic fascism by appealing to such a constellation of descriptive traits.[2] While Western academics rarely accepted much of the substance of Marxist theory *per se*, there was considerable overlap in the conceptual vocabulary employed.

For both Marxists and non-Marxists, fascism was characterized as an "open terroristic dictatorship" that was "reactionary" and "opportunistic" in essence. Everyone seemed content, except for the troubling fact that Marxists began to identify a fascism on the Left. Most Western thinkers simply chose to overlook such anomalies. Whether of the Left or the Right, fascism continued to mean dictatorship, reaction, irrationality, terror, and mass murder.

What all this suggests is that theoreticians of whatever persuasion had very little purchase on a credible *theory* of fascism. That was true in general, and it was particularly true with respect to Marxist theory. By the mid-1960s, it had become evident that the entire issue of how fascism was to be understood cried out for elucidation. By then, the issue had become more than just a matter of intellectual interest. In the years since Nikita Khrushchev's denunciation of Stalin at the Twentieth Party Congress of the Communist Party of the Soviet Union, relations between the Soviet Union and Communist China had become increasingly strained. Khrushchev's revelations concerning Stalin served as a catalyst for what was to become a dramatically changed relationship between the two Marxist–Leninist powers.

Between the end of the 1960s and the early 1980s, theoreticians in the Soviet Union supported their nation's policies with a revised interpretation of fascism. Throughout the decade, as we have seen, more and more of the interwar Soviet interpretation of fascism was jettisoned. The entire elaborate theoretical infrastructure—with its "labor theory of value," the increasing "organic composition" of capital, the declining rate of profit, the "inevitable" growing misery of the proletariat, together with notions regarding a "final crisis" of industrial capitalism—was unceremoniously abandoned.

According to the revised version, nonsocialist industrial systems could, in fact, grow—but only under the auspices of "state monopoly capitalism." Under such a regime, political power was discretely separated from ownership of the means of production, and under fascism, a singular form of "state monopoly capitalism," political power determined the distribution of system benefits.

Such an exploitive system could foster increments in production, to serve essentially military needs. Such a system was chauvinistic, bellicose, militaristic, and irredentist, animated by a disposition to solve domestic and foreign problems through the deployment of organized violence. Political repression typified the system, and the "leader" was accorded the status of sage, prophet, and inerrant guide to behavior.

These kinds of assessments shaped Soviet responses to Chinese Communist criticisms of Soviet domestic and international policies. A chain of events prompted the Chinese to consider Khrushchev's de-Stalinization initiatives at the Twentieth Communist Party conference in the Soviet Union to have been more than ill considered. Unrest in Poland and rebellion in Hungary followed shortly after Khrushchev's denunciation of Stalin. A suspicion was afoot that Khrushchev's policies had reawakened and fostered a substantial anti-communist reaction within the bloc of Marxist–Leninist and Marxist–Leninist–friendly states.

Differences of interpretation concerning the Leninist notion of the "inevitability" of war between the socialist and capitalist states further inflamed exchanges between Moscow and Beijing. Dramatic damage was done to relations between the USSR and the People's Republic by Moscow's withdrawal of support for Mao's drive to industrialize. The violation of contractual agreements undertaken in good faith and projects abandoned for lack of technical assistance all contributed to the increasing bilateral hostility. The subsequent rancor and bitterness drove the two communist countries further and further apart.[3] The rift between the two Marxist–Leninist states became so deep that analysts spoke of the possibility of war.[4]

The Soviet Union and the People's Republic of China were operating in an international environment in which perceptions had become as important as reality. Both Moscow and Beijing were compelled by prudence and considerations of prestige and power to attempt to fully explain their respective positions to an anxious international audience. Their explanations were expected to be delivered in terms of their presumably common ideological commitments. The leadership of both countries believed that command of the "forces of international revolution" hung in the balance.

Such considerations had become urgent by the mid-1960s. It became increasingly necessary for theoreticians in each country to explain the divergences between the two "proletarian" powers. The Marxist–Leninist leadership in both countries pretended to base their individual policy decisions on a single infallible "theory of social development."

Attempting to explain, in Marxist terms, what had transpired proved a daunting task. Each party in the dispute sought to explain what had happened without threatening the integrity of Marxist theory as an impeccable guide to "world revolution."[5] It was during those years, as we have seen, that Soviet theoreticians undertook a review and reassessment of their standard theory of fascism. Soviet intellectuals were charged with the responsibility of explaining why one Marxist–Leninist power found itself so profoundly opposed by another. More than that, it was expected that the forthcoming explanation would employ the traditional Marxist–Leninist "class analysis." That was no mean task.

In general, what the Soviet theoreticians concluded was that politics in the People's Republic of China had succumbed to "petty bourgeois revolutionary adventurism," and that its source was Mao Zedong, whose very origins were "petty bourgeois."[6] More than that, in a nation in which "true proletarians" numbered no more than 0.05 percent of the work force at the time of the revolution, one could hardly expect anything other than petty bourgeois influences to dominate.[7]

For the Marxist–Leninist thinkers of the Soviet Union, all this intimated that one might expect, sooner rather than later, distinctive reactionary traits to emerge. Capitalists, merchants, and "bourgeois" elements of all sorts would be cultivated, and workers oppressed, by a petty bourgeois political party that pretended to leftist revolution.[8]

Intimations of a "Chinese fascism" began to surface in Soviet literature. By the end of the 1960s, Soviet theoreticians were prepared to argue that the "Chinese leadership" had transformed itself into an "anti-Marxist, anti-socialist, chauvinistic and anti-Soviet . . . bourgeois-nationalistic" movement of reaction. Maoism was a movement of "obscurantism and barbarism," committed to a "personality cult" that exploited "the basest instincts" of humankind.[9]

In their account, Soviet thinkers had recourse to the same list of descriptive traits that Western academics had employed for some considerable time to identify fascist political and social systems.[10] The descriptive properties that had become commonplace in the literature were sufficiently vague and general to allow any number of political systems to be identified as "fascist" in some sense. The "class analysis" that was supposed to distinguish the Marxist–Leninist account from the account of non-Marxists proved to be of very little cognitive use.

Whatever Soviet Marxist–Leninists objected to in Maoist policies was immediately identified as "petty bourgeois." Thus, if Maoists were "Great-Han hegemonists" and "racists," it was because the Chinese population consisted of "petty artisans, traders and non-proletarian elements." The hegemonism, nationalism, chauvinism, and racism of Maoism were "ultimately due to the fact that most of the members of the Communist Party of China were of peasant origin."[11] How the "class origins" of political leaders or "popular masses" might determine their policies was never explicated. That Lenin and Stalin were both of "petty bourgeois origin" did not determine their politics, it seems. That Mao Zedong was petty bourgeois apparently did.[12] That the Bolshevik revolution was undertaken by nonproletarian masses did not determine its outcome, apparently. That Mao's revolution was similarly nonproletarian did, it seems.

None of this seemed to deter Soviet thinkers. However the term "fascism" was defined, and whatever the analysis employed, the term was always associated with opprobrium. That seemed to be a more important consideration than generating a coherent, intellectually satisfying analysis of the political struggle between the communist powers.

During and after the Second World War, the term *fascism* always served as an invective. This fact could only recommend its use to Soviet intellectuals in their struggle with Maoism. Among academics and those responsible for formulating public argument, however, there had to be at least the pretense of a serious assessment in accounting for the political behaviors of an entire economic, political, and social system.

The fact that generic fascism had been characterized as a class of political movements or regimes in which members were held to be committed to a formal set of exclusive ideological beliefs, nationalist in inspiration, etatist, elitist, anti-democratic, hegemonic in inclination, voluntaristic, anti-intellectual, and disposed to the employment of violence and terror, afforded Soviet theoreticians an easy opportunity to identify Maoist China as an exemplar of the class. The traits that constituted the admission criteria for the category had been so formulated that it was not difficult for Soviet theoreticians to find evidence of a "rightist" fascist presence in Mao's "leftist" China.

Marxist theorists argued that Maoists had used the entire notion of "class struggle" to suppress their political opponents—opponents who were often of proletarian provenance. "Class struggle" was a "trick" to "intimidate and terrify the Chinese people . . . used to justify the Maoists' political reprisals and to discredit their opponents."[13] The entire Maoist system was predicated on anti-working-class violence—an expression of a philosophy of force, an exaltation of mayhem.[14] "Superimposed on this was Mao's cruelty. . . . It was, we would say, a specifically imperial cruelty, the cruelty of *fuehrerism*, prepared to sacrifice the lives of millions."[15] Maoism was a form of generic fascism.

As such, Maoism was an exacerbated form of nationalism, dedicated to the recreation of the millenial "grandeur" of China—the undoing of a century of humiliation at the hands of the imperialists. As such, Maoism was neither Marxist nor internationalist. It was "anti-Marxist" in theory and "anti-Soviet" in practice.[16]

But there was more to the theoreticians' responsibilities than identifying Maoist chauvinism, reactive nationalism, and anti-Marxism. Soviet scholars had inherited the interwar account of fascism that conceived of it as anti-developmental and charged by the most reactionary of the bourgeoisie to limit economic growth and technological development to the level of precapitalist "barbarism." Given that Soviet theoreticians had confidently identified Chinese communism with industrial development through the 1950s, if Maoism was to be identified with fascism, the association of fascism with anti-developmentalism would have to be abandoned or substantially qualified.[17] As we have seen, the revision of what had been the standard Soviet interpretation of fascism throughout the interwar years began about the time of the Sino–Soviet dispute. At that juncture, Marxist theoreticians were prepared to recognize the modernizing and developmental character of fascism in general and Italian Fascism in particular.

By the 1960s, there was enough independent evidence to warrant the revision, but it seems evident that Soviet theoreticians needed the appropriate, time-conditioned incentives to undertake the task. By the time Soviet intellectuals were prepared to associate Maoism with fascism, the standard Soviet interpretation of the interwar years had been sufficiently revised to accommodate the notion that fascist systems might be, in part and in some intelligible sense, progressive and developmental.

By the mid-1960s, Soviet theoreticians were prepared to argue that fascists had supervised the economic growth and industrial development of their systems and that the interwar interpretation had been flawed. Like Mao, Mussolini had been in one sense or another, while always in the service of the "bourgeoisie," a modernizer, shepherding his system from one economic level to a "higher" one. Like Mao, Mussolini had introduced "productivism," developmentalism, and "state monopoly capitalism" into what had been a retrograde economic system.

For Soviet Marxists, both Italian Fascism and Maoism had undertaken to accelerate industrial and technological growth of their respective laggard economies. In both instances, the enterprise was undertaken in order to ensure the availability of weapons in a program of irredentism—the restoration of "lost" national territories—and the militarization of the nation in the pursuit of "hegemonism."[18] In that specific sense, Soviet Marxists were prepared to argue that Mao's approach to foreign policy "smacked of the hare-brained aspirations of Mussolini."[19]

Like fascism, Maoism conceived of the international community as divided along "class lines," with the impoverished "Third World"—less developed communities—forever pitted against the advanced industrial democracies—an approach that, according to Soviet Marxists, "in no way differs from fascism."[20]

By the end of the 1960s and the first years of the 1970s, the revisions in the standard Soviet interpretation of fascism allowed the Marxist–Leninists of the Soviet Union to suggest that Maoism was a variant of fascism without intellectual discomfort. What was more difficult for Soviet Marxist theoreticians was to formulate an argument to the effect that the domestic and international policies of Mao Zedong, like those of Mussolini and Hitler, somehow served the ultimate interests of finance capitalism and imperialism.

If Mao were to be considered a fascist, it would not be enough simply to rehearse his "petty bourgeois" origins, allude to the primitive state of the Chinese economy, or catalog the traits that his system shared with the fascism of the interwar years. The nationalism, the elitism, the statism, the disposition to employ violence, and the anti-intellectualism of the regime were not sufficient to render the characterization persuasive.[21] Mao would have to be shown to be the "tool" of the international financial bourgeoisie. That, after all, had always been an essential aspect of the Marxist–Leninist characterization of fascism.

During the long years between the two world wars, Marxist theoreticians, justifying the Eastern policies of the Comintern, were prepared to see China's "national bourgeois" and Kuomintang revolutionaries as "objectively anti-imperialist" members of the rising tide of anti-capitalist world revolution. As long as the early followers of Sun Yat-sen and Chiang Kai-shek, during the 1920s through much of the 1940s, were real or fancied allies of the Soviet Union, Stalin and his immediate entourage resisted any temptation to identify them as "fascists." However petty bourgeois they may have been, they were apparently not fascists, because they were seen as "anti-imperialist."

By the beginning of the 1960s, China was no longer led by the "national bourgeoisie." By that time, Marxist–Leninists ruled a "proletarian" China. For all that, China had begun to loom large as a potential threat to the Soviet Union. In those circumstances, the interests of the leadership in the Kremlin recommended a very different assessment of revolutionary China. Soviet theoreticians were called upon to explain how China, hitherto an "objective ally" of the international proletarian revolution, could be reasonably characterized as "fascist."

The first response among Soviet commentators to what they perceived as China's hostility toward the Soviet Union was to argue that Mao's policies were simply mistaken, the result of Mao's ignorance or his petty bourgeois conceit. The Great Proletarian Cultural Revolution, during which the Soviet Union was excoriated as a "revisionist" power, was understood to be the result of politically induced mass hysteria—a great wave of stupidity and destructiveness conjured up by the leaders of China in the course of a protracted, violent, intraparty struggle for power.[22] By the end of the 1960s, however, this seemed hardly sufficient to explain what was transpiring. Soviet theoreticians began to speak of Maoism as an anti-Marxist, militaristic, chauvinistic "petty bourgeois nationalism," animated by voluntarism and an appeal to violence.[23]

To Soviet analysts, Maoism was a personalist and hierarchical dictatorship, supported by a form of "anti-socialist" ideological "infantilism" and an action-oriented "primitivism" born of the anti-intellectualism of Mao's petty bourgeois background.[24] In the effort to delude the masses, Mao had created a "cult of personality" with few parallels in the history of modern political systems. He was given to autocratic rule, animated by the conviction that will and "heroic" violence could resolve problems of whatever magnitude. He infused the primitive masses of China not only with the conviction that his "thought" was the "acme of Marxism–Leninism," containing "truths that conform to the laws of development of ... society ... [and] nature," but further, that his thought was a kind of moral talisman that assured China's prevalence against any enemy, as well.[25] In order to prevail against any opponent, China need only impose iron discipline and insist on ideological conformity from its population.[26]

All this could easily be identified with fascism. Even the Maoist insistence on "class warfare," which was supposed to distinguish Marxist from "bourgeois" alternatives, was understood by Soviet Marxists as a pretext for repression and imposed political conformity that worked most hardship on the working classes.[27]

When Mao spoke of China, he entertained few class-based distinctions. People were revolutionary, not because of their class identification, but because of their adherence to the "thought of Mao Zedong." It was obedience to the "thought of Mao" that made people "proletarian." In principle, Mao considered the Chinese people a "blank slate" upon which he was to work his artistry.[28]

Soviet Marxism considered Maoism to be an expression of "aggressive great Han chauvinism," intent upon provoking a third world war from which China would emerge as world hegemon.[29] Most damning of all, however, was the conviction that the "Chinese leadership ... [was] making advances to imperialist circles of the West" in order to oppose the Soviet Union.[30] Maoist Chinese foreign policy was not only weakening the "united front" against imperialism, the Marxists in Moscow argued; Maoists hoped to exploit the occasion of any international conflict to fulfill their "dream of world domination."[31] Soviet-friendly Marxists in India could thus condemn Maoists for "playing the shameful role of accomplice of the rabid warmongering circles of imperialism."[32]

By the early 1970s, even the anti-Soviet Trotskyists identified China's relationship with the United States as "China's Alliance with U.S. Imperialism."[33] According to Soviet and Soviet-friendly Marxists, Mao's China had become a tool of international finance capitalism. The clinching element had been added to the picture of Maoist China as nothing other than a variant of European fascism.[34]

By the mid-1970s, Soviet theoreticians pretended to have discovered in Maoism all the overt species traits of fascism as fascism was understood by both many Western academics and leftist theoreticians. The catalog of descriptive traits that Western thinkers had employed to identify fascism as "right-wing extremism" was mapped over the final years of Maoism in China. In the confusion that resulted, it has never been made quite clear whether Maoism was a form of "right-wing extremism" or a "left-wing adventure," which suggests that the distinction was never very clear nor convincing.

At the same time as this kind of analysis was being generated by Marxists in

Moscow, Maoist theoreticians were using the Marxist theory of fascism for their own purposes. If nothing else, Marxist theory has shown itself to be remarkably fungible. If Soviet propagandists had little difficulty tailoring theory to the needs of their time, theoreticians in Communist China were no less adept. By the early 1970s, theoreticians in the People's Republic of China were unequivocally characterizing the Soviet Union as a "fascist type dictatorship" that had grown out of the objective necessities of the "state monopoly capitalism" created by the anti-Marxist "revisionism" of Nikita Khrushchev. Chinese Marxists argued that the ideological corruption of the Soviet Union had commenced with Khrushchev's attempts at "de-Stalinization."

For theoreticians in Beijing, the dictatorship that grew out of Soviet revisionism found itself inevitably and inextricably in the service of "world imperialism."[35] Chinese Marxists understood all this to have been the perfectly predictable result of the "objective laws of social development."[36] If anything, the Chinese account of emergent Soviet fascism was somewhat more complex and sophisticated than the Soviet theoreticians' explanation of the rise of Maoist fascism.

Loath to abandon the elaborate arguments put together in the 1930s out of the speculations of classical Marxism, Chinese theoreticians attempted to salvage what was salvageable. Chinese Marxists argued that after the death of Stalin, a "renegade clique" in the Soviet Union had undertaken the restoration of capitalism.[37] Why they did so was unclear, except that, in Chinese eyes, "bourgeois elements" seemed to enjoy the capacity to reproduce themselves any and everywhere under any and all conditions.[38] But whatever the case, the putative restoration of capitalism in the Soviet Union allowed Chinese theoreticians to reinvoke some of the familiar arguments employed by Marxists in the interwar years, in their new effort to explain the rise of fascism in a socialist environment.

Whatever their origin, the "renegades" in the USSR had undertaken to reintroduce profit incentives into the socialist command economy and were attempting to insinuate market determinants into the socialist system of resource management and commodity distribution.[39] Differential wages were introduced to act as a stimulus to increased productivity, and state enterprises, to a substantial extent, would be operated on what Maoists called a "commercial, i.e. profit-oriented, basis." The net result, according to Maoist theoreticians, could only be compromise of the command economy of socialism and the corruption of the infinitely malleable consciousness of the masses. For Maoists and Maoist-friendly Marxists, this constituted a "restoration of capitalism" in the USSR—the consequence of a "coup" by Nikita Khrushchev.[40]

Maoists maintained that those who dominated the system in the Soviet Union, in the course of time, had been transformed or had transformed themselves into a "new bourgeoisie." To assure themselves of the real and anticipated profits associated with the restoration of capitalism, these "capitalist roaders" in authority were compelled to impose dictatorial rule on the exploited masses. Although private property no longer existed as an institution in the Soviet Union, an exiguous minority of Communist Party officials controlled the means of production. There were "persons in authority" who were leading the Soviet Union down the "capitalist path."

The "new bourgeoisie" did not own the means of production, but they could profit from their control over them. Even though the ownership of the means of production had been socialized, control remained in the hands of a bureaucracy that, after the passing of Stalin, chose to exploit the circumstances to its own advantage. When the national leadership of the Soviet Union opted for a "capitalist restoration," with its commodity production and market exchange, its profit motive and differential income, the bureaucracy emerged as the functional equivalent of a new bourgeoisie, pursuing personal profit and class advantage. A "functional stratum" had become a "class."

The "new bourgeois" elements in charge of the system served as the equivalent of the domestic "big bourgeoisie" and "finance capitalists." This, in turn, created the economic base for the emergence of a "fascist dictatorship."[41]

As an inevitable consequence, the people of the USSR were to be exploited as never before. As evidence, Maoists cited Soviet legislation strengthening the domestic security forces, enforcing draconian penal codes, and imposing sweeping administrative regulations that, among other things, incarcerated dissidents for political "reeducation."[42] The dictatorship that was thus institutionalized provided a defense for a form of "state monopoly capitalism" that shared all the central political and economic features of traditional monopoly capitalism in exaggerated form.[43] For Chinese Marxists, the extreme form of state monopoly capitalism was a "fascist dictatorship."

Revisionism in the Soviet Union had produced a "bourgeoisified privileged stratum" that was compelled by the "objective laws of social development" to exploit its own domestic working class in order to pursue policies of military adventure.[44] For Maoist theoreticians, revisionism had thus produced the perfect analog of Italian Fascism in the Soviet Union.

Since capitalism had been restored to the Soviet Union, according to Maoist theorists, its system was subject to the same "objective laws" that Marx had discovered to be operative in the advanced industrial democracies of the nineteenth century. As capitalism ages, the argument proceeded, its profit rate must inevitably decline. Marx had taught no less. According to Maoist theoreticians, the Soviet state monopoly capitalists faced the same "objective" inevitabilities. The traditional Marxist argument of an inevitable declining rate of profit for mature capitalist industry made its appearance in the anti-Soviet literature of Maoist theoreticians, who were more conservative than their Soviet counterparts. However discredited the notion of the declining rate of profit for modern industrial systems might be, Chinese Marxists found it serviceable. They maintained that as the domestic wealth of the Soviet "revisionist clique" diminished because of the declining rate of profit, the clique would be "ineluctably" driven to scramble for international sources of raw materials, market outlets, and investment opportunities. The leaders of the Soviet Union, under the banner of socialism, would produce a "fascist dictatorship" that would threaten the place, security, and resources of its neighbors.

Pursuing this thesis, Maoists made recourse to the Leninist notion that monopoly capitalists, attempting to maintain a suitable rate of return on their investments, seek not only to control territories rich in resources, but also to maintain favorable conditions of international trade. Following Lenin's lead, Maoists argued that, on the pretext of extending aid, for example, Moscow, like all imperialists before it, imposed exorbitant rates of interest on its foreign loans. Like any other imperialism, an imperialist Soviet Union dictated self-serving terms of trade to its trading partners.[45]

Like any other imperialist, the Soviet imperialists attempted to suppress competition from other industrialized or industrializing communities. They sought to exploit the resources of the nations on their periphery and in the Third World, and, in order to fully secure their dominance, they must ultimately embark upon "wars of redivision." This was the Maoist explanation of the Soviet Union's policies toward China.

The argument was that there was not "much difference between the state monopoly capitalism in the Soviet Union and that in capital-imperialist countries. The only difference [was] that the former, transformed from socialist state ownership, is the more intensified in the degree of concentration and monopolization. State monopoly capitalism is the base of the dictatorship of the Soviet bureaucrat monopoly capitalist class and the economic root cause of the external aggression and expansion by Soviet revisionist social-imperialism and hegemonism that it pushes."[46]

According to the Maoists of the period, the Soviet Union, driven by the economic imperatives of monopoly capitalism in its final stages, had taken the path of exploiting its domestic working class in order the fuel its aggressive military expansion. Moscow's investment in its massive military machine was a corollary of its economic regression to monopoly capitalism. By restoring capitalism in the Soviet Union, the bureaucratic leadership had recreated the economic base for a fascist "predatory imperialism."[47]

The very logic of such a system, according to Maoist theorists, required the conquest of contiguous territories. Neighbors of the Soviet Union had experienced Moscow's fascist aggression and the violation of their sovereignty. "The Soviet revisionist renegade clique . . . bullied all its neighboring countries . . . [and] flagrantly sent troops to occupy Czechoslovakia." As part of its irrepressible imperialist imperative, the Soviet Union was "stretching its sinister claws of aggression to socialist China."[48]

Maoist theoreticians had reproduced, in caricature, almost the entire rationale employed by Marxists in the late 1920s and 1930s to characterize fascism. The implications were transparent. Chinese Marxists identified the Soviet Union as a variant of "fascist dictatorship" under the "signboard of socialism."[49] For Maoist theoreticians, one of the major implications of the restoration of capitalism in the Soviet Union was the effort by those in authority to pretend that the dictatorship they had constructed really represented a "state of the whole people" in which classes and class conflict no longer occupied a significant place.[50] Maoists maintained that the Soviet notion of a "state of the whole people" sought to introduce the "class harmony" that underlay the fascist rationale for a state that served the nation by standing above class conflict and class interest. Any effort, Maoists argued, that "loses sight of the class struggle" effectively abandons the theoretical core of Marxism–Leninism and surrenders itself to the international forces of imperialism, the heirs of prewar fascism.[51]

In all of this, what the Maoists imagined themselves as doing was a "strictly scientific class analysis" of developments in the Soviet Union and what those developments implied for the "world revolution of the proletariat."[52] What was singular in the Maoist account was the argument that different, antagonistic classes persisted under socialism, a system that had abolished the private ownership of property. "Class" was defined as any body of individuals who enjoyed any advantage in any system. In effect, there could be "exploiting" classes in any system, and since fascism was identified with a system of exploitation, one could expect to find fascism anywhere.

Given these kinds of assessments, "bourgeois" classes were to be found in both the Soviet Union and Maoist China, where private property had long been eliminated and the means of production socialized.[53] As long as any inequality existed anywhere, class distinctions existed by entailment. Where there were classes, there one would find fascism. Given the nature of the argument, Maoists could argue that even after the establishment of the dictatorship of the proletariat, classes and "fierce" conflict of classes could be expected to persist "for a very long time," perhaps for as long as "100 million years."[54] Such a notion could only have very sobering implications for fascist studies, as well as for traditional Marxist eschatology.

In effect, Maoists had "creatively developed" Marxism–Leninism in their own unique fashion. Under the new dispensation, the Marxist "dictatorship of the proletariat" harbored within itself a threat of self-destruction. According to Maoist theoreticians, a "life-and-death struggle" would continue throughout the epoch of the dictatorship of the proletariat "between the two major antagonistic classes, the proletariat and the bourgeoisie." Even decades after the domestic victory of Marxism–Leninism, the bourgeoisie might usurp power, as they did under Khrushchev. Any time during the reign of the dictatorship of the proletariat, capitalism might be restored, and socialism might disintegrate into a variant of fascism.[55] All those threats would persist into the indeterminate future.

All those tortured conjectures were not the products of unknown Chinese Maoists. Two of the major theoreticians providing the rationale for the Maoist interpretation of fascism were Yao Wenyuan and Zhang Chunqiao, founding members of the now infamous "Gang of Four." They were the theoreticians of the Great Proletarian Cultural Revolution that held Maoist China in thrall for about a decade. Not only did the Cultural Revolution leave more than a million victims in its train, it reduced "Marxist theory" to a collection of singular stupidities.

What the "creative developments" of the theoreticians of the Cultural Revolution gave rise to was a major threat to the integrity of any socialist system predicated on the collective ownership of the means of production. The major theoreticians of China's Cultural Revolution argued that while the ownership of the means of production marked a major development in the transition from capitalism to socialism, it was the "ideological and political line" entertained by the Communist Party that determined "which class owns those [means of production] in actual fact."[56]

In the Soviet Union, after about four decades of collective ownership of the means of production, the "new bourgeoisie" in the bureaucracy had chosen to "restore capitalism." In Maoist China, no less a threat hung over socialism. If the leadership of the Chinese Communist Party chose to restore capitalism, all they would have to do is "change the line and policies of the Party." They would "hoist the flag of the dictatorship of the proletariat" over the masses, but in fact would impose a "fascist dictatorship."[57]

The theoreticians of the Gang of Four argued that since socialist society had only recently been born of capitalism, it would be, according to Marx, himself, "in every respect, economically, morally, and intellectually, still stamped with the birth marks of the old society from whose womb it emerges."[58] As a consequence, any failure to energetically defend socialism *ideologically* would inevitably lead to the restoration of capitalism and the inevitable advent of fascism.[59]

For the Maoist theoreticians of the Cultural Revolution, it was the "correctness or incorrectness of the ideological and political line" that determined whether socialism or fascism would prevail in any Marxist–Leninist society. It was not the economics of any particular period, but its intellectual "superstructure" that determined outcomes.[60] For Maoist theoreticians, "politics" was "the concentrated expression of economics" and was in command.[61] Marxism had been transformed from a system in which economics was the ultimate determinant of events to one in which "politics" and the entire ideological superstructure of society assumed "command."[62] For late Maoism, it was a "political line," an ideological disposition, that determined social, economic, and historic outcomes.

It was the "politics," the ideological orientation of some members of the Chinese Communist Party, that made them "capitalist roaders." Having failed to understand the essentials of socialist revolution, they sought the restoration of a market economy, with its insistence on efficiency measured in terms of profit and productivity calculated in terms of wages—all of which would "undermine the socialist planned economy."[63] This would contribute not only to the restoration of state monopoly capitalism, the "catering to the needs of imperialism," but, of necessity, to the creation of "fascist dictatorship."[64]

The entire collection of propositions that make up the substance of this "theory" was attributed to the "genius" of Mao Zedong. "Chairman Mao," the world was told,

> with the gifts of genius, creatively and comprehensively developed Marxism–Leninism. Basing himself on the fundamental theses of Marxism–Leninism, Chairman Mao has summed up the experience of the practice of the Chinese revolution and the world revolution, and the painful lesson of the usurpation of the leadership of the Party and the state of the Soviet Union by the modern revisionist clique, systematically put forward the theory concerning classes, class contradictions and class struggle that exist in socialist society, greatly enriched and developed the Marxist–Leninist theory on the dictatorship of the proletariat.[65]

The account concluded with the insistence that "every sentence by Chairman Mao is the truth, and carries more weight than ten thousand ordinary sentences." There was no doubt that the Marxist theorists of Mao's China took this entire "dialectical development" very seriously.

Armed with the insights of the incarnate "never-setting red sun," Zhou Enlai warned that "the criminal aim of counterrevolutionary revisionists" was not only to restore capitalism; it was to "turn the Marxist–Leninist Chinese Communist Party into a revisionist, fascist Party."[66] By implication, Mao Zedong's development of Marxism–Leninism was a "new" and "creatively developed" theory of fascism.

However methodologically impaired and intellectually impoverished Mao's new interpretation of fascism may have been, it was instructive. It demonstrated that as long as the international academic community was prepared to be content with a loosely framed catalog of descriptive traits as an adequate characterization of fascism, that characterization might be made to fit almost any political system. Fascism might make its appearance in capitalist or socialist environments equally well.

The interwar version of the Marxist–Leninist interpretation of fascism had held that the modern world had a choice between only fascism and socialism. The Maoist variant of the standard version held that even socialism could not fully protect humankind from fascism. Long after the abolition of private property and the suppression of all market activity, fascism might very well appear. Quite aside from the fact that this could only be depressing to Marxists everywhere, the reality was that the theoreticians of Maoism could provide very little help to Marxist–Leninists trying to decide whether or not a socialist community was taking the "sinister" road to state monopoly capitalism, collusion with imperialism, and the creation of a fascist dictatorship. Since private ownership of the means of production no longer existed in socialist society, it was impossible to identify the bourgeoisie, whether petty or grand, by virtue of their assets.

An alternative criterion for identifying "renegade cliques," of course, might be the degree of control over the means of production enjoyed by any segment of the population. As has been suggested, control over the means of production might serve as the functional equivalent of ownership. But even this could hardly serve, because Maoists insisted that not all "persons in authority" or those in control of the means of production were "renegades," "revisionists," "ghosts," "monsters", or potential fascists.[67] Only a "handful" among them constituted a threat to socialism. The problem was identifying that pernicious handful.

Even the genius of Mao Zedong failed to warn him that Liu Shaoqi and Lin Biao, his self-selected heirs, were revisionist monsters and members of a "renegade clique" threatening China with fascism. Mao, at different times, had chosen one or the other ranking party member as his immediate political heir only to belatedly discover that he or they were "capitalist roaders," "rightists," and potential fascists.

If even Mao had that kind of difficulty in identifying the renegades of revisionism, it is hard to imagine how the average Chinese Communist could be expected to do much better. Maoism's interpretation of fascism was expected to serve as a theoretical guide in all this apparent confusion. If the revisionists who threatened to restore capitalism in Maoist China were few in number and were not distinguished by their positions in authority or their possession or control of the means of production, then the great masses of the people might have problems in identifying them—even equipped with Mao's new theory of fascism.

In the effort to resolve this problem, Maoist theoreticians immediately proposed a supplementary "monster detector," or a "magic mirror" that would instantly reveal the presence of "capitalist roaders."[68] Mao Zedong's thought was proposed as the infallible guide in distinguishing the threatening "bourgeois line" from that of the "proletariat." We were informed that when the worker, peasant, and soldier masses "grasp Mao Zedong Thought . . . [they] have the highest criterion to distinguish right from wrong, they have the vantage ground from which to see far ahead, and they can discern the essence through the appearance. . . . No anti-Party, anti-socialist element can escape their notice."[69] All this would seem to be reasonably simple if there were any way to determine the specific content of Mao Zedong's thought with any assurance.

One of the major admonitions broadcast by Maoist theoreticians was that the "handful of Party persons in authority who were taking the capitalist road" were incredibly deceptive. They raised the red flag and the banner of revolution to combat the red flag and the revolution—and they simulated adherence to Mao Thought in order to oppose Mao's thought.[70] For years, capitalist roaders like Liu Shaoqi apparently succeeded in deceiving Mao Zedong himself.

In order to resolve all these issues, Mao's theoreticians recommended simple obedience to the masses of China. A list of exemplary "heroes" and "models" was supplied. These heroes expressed sentiments that were remarkably uniform. In one manner or another, they all affirmed, "I will do as Chairman Mao says." In one manner or another, they all insisted, "I am determined to act in accordance with Chairman Mao's instructions."[71] Maoists, in fact, had a standard response to the question of how one might recognize revisionist monsters and ghosts when they conceal themselves in Mao's thought and wave the red flag to oppose the red flag. The answer was "to read Chairman Mao's works, follow his teachings and act on his instructions."[72] It was all terribly simple. To be a true Maoist revolutionary, to thwart fascists, all one had to do was to obey the Chairman in an orgy of submission that many academicians, East and West, insisted was a defining trait of right-wing extremism.

For Maoists, the injunction was: "We must fulfill the instructions of Comrade Mao Zedong regardless of whether we have or have not yet understood them."[73] For Mao, the preoccupation with "understanding" and "knowing" was debilitating. He insisted that "in history it is always those with little learning who overthrow those with more learning"—and while he did not propose to close the schools of China, he did insist that "it is not absolutely necessary to attend school," for those who attend school may acquire learning, but lose the "Truth."

For Mao, it was "experience" that delivered real learning. As a consequence, he insisted that there was entirely "too much studying going on" in China. He deemed this "exceedingly harmful." It was evident to him that "to read too many books is harmful"—for "if you read too many books, they petrify your mind."[74]

One consequence of these notions was Mao's injunction: "We must drive actors, poets, dramatists and writers out of the cities, and pack them all off to the countryside," where they might abandon reading and writing and "experience reality."[75]

Maoism scorned intellectuals and intellectualism. It sought a kind of transcendent "wisdom" in youth and direct experience. It advocated the learning of the battlefield and the violence of revolution. For Maoists, obedience, experience, and "struggle" were advanced as essential to the creation of a "new world" and "new men." Displaying some of the major characteristics of "right-wing extremism," "left-wing" Maoism confounded some of the distinctions that have been classificatory folk wisdom in social science for almost the entire twentieth century.

Perhaps more significant than this is that for Maoism "struggle" meant many things, including that violence, and war contributed to the realization of political goals. Struggle, violence and war were advanced as solutions to problems both domestic and foreign. "Only by repeated and fierce struggles can the new thing grow in strength and rise to predominance, and only thus can the old thing be weakened and forced to perish."[76] Revisionists apparently failed to understand that the "dialectic of history" required "permanent struggle" if socialist momentum were not to be surrendered to fascism.

Mao was prepared to argue that international war was simply a necessary form of "struggle," and any suggestion "that capitalism may peacefully grow over to socialism . . . is a serious distortion of Marxism."[77] To "overthrow the enemy," domestic or foreign, "revolutionary violence" is not only a necessity, it "is a rule."[78] Socialism can be built only through civil or international war. "To see the ills of war but not its benefits is a one-sided view. It is of no use to the people's revolution to speak one-sidedly of the destructiveness of war."[79]

For Mao, violence was creative; it was an inescapable constituent of the revolutionary process. To deny its role in the process was to deny the revolution and the future of socialist society. The "philosophy of violence," traditionally conceived of as the "pathology" of right-wing extremism, seems to have had a place in the conjectures of the Left.

According to Maoist theoreticians, the revisionists failed to understand that it was fierce class conflict and all the violence that attended the Great Proletarian Cultural Revolution that provided the energy without which not only would socialism fail, but historical development would cease. Maoists anticipated many, many cultural revolutions that would be undertaken with all the conviction and attendant struggle of the first. Eternal "struggle" against the threat of revisionism and fascism was the price to be paid for socialism by the people of China.

Drawing on all these notions, Maoists worked for about a decade to put together a theory that would lift Marxism–Leninism "to a completely new stage."[80] What they delivered was clearly different from anything to be found in either classical Marxism or orthodox Leninism. Of all the curiosities they produced, the Maoist interpretation of fascism was perhaps the strangest.

It was most curious because, even before the close of the Maoist period, the Maoist theory of fascism had turned on itself. This theory represented little more than a distorted mirror image of the system created by the Chinese Communist Party. So obvious was the fact that, three months before Mao's death in 1976, a revolutionary Red Guard, Chen Erjin, produced a singularly doleful assessment of socialism in China. Chen, an avowed Marxist, concluded that Maoism itself was a variant of European fascism.[81]

When Chen submitted his work for publication, he was immediately arrested by the authorities as politically subversive. That he was arrested is hardly surprising. What is interesting is his analysis, which Chen considered Marxist in both spirit and letter.

Chen sought to understand the socialism of his country using the conceptual machinery of Marxism. His conclusions were quasi-deductive extensions of the Maoist theory of fascism itself. He began his account by identifying the economic base of the "predatory new system of exploitation" that clearly threatened to overwhelm the socialism of Maoist China. Since socialism is predicated on the abolition of private property, the state system that emerges in the wake of Marxist–Leninist revolution is one into whose hands all property is collected. All property becomes state property.

Those who administer state property become a "new class." This newly emergent class—"the bureaucrat-monopoly privileged class"—arrogates to itself "the twin powers of political leadership and economic control." Chen argued that the new privileged elite of the first postrevolutionary stage of socialism tends to construct a "bureaucratic-military machine" that resonates with the sound of "the gongs and drums of narrow-minded patriotism and nationalism." The masses are distracted by war and preparation for war. Confused by "deceitful propaganda," seduced by the rhetoric of revolutionary eschatology, labor is domesticated to the system. What had emerged out of the socialist revolution in China, according to this youthful critic, was unmistakenly a "fascist dictatorship."[82] Chen had turned the Maoist theory of fascism on itself.

Chen argued, with perhaps more coherence than the Marxists who preceded him, that the "root cause" of the emergence of fascism in a socialist state is to be located in the contradiction that rests at the very foundation of the postrevolutionary mode of production. That a small minority concentrates all coercive power in its hands, while controlling the highly organized means of social production, results in the creation of a hierarchical system potentially more despotic than the state monopoly capitalism of which it is an analog. The concentration of political power in the hands of the "new class" allows totalitarian "monopoly to be exerted over all spheres" of society.[83] The major overt features of the system are (1) nonelective appointments to positions of power at the discretion and pleasure of the party and its leader; (2) the hierarchical arrangement of authority; (3) the complete separation of state organs from any responsibility to the general population; and (4) the "sanctification of the Party."[84]

Chen argued that the prevailing circumstances ultimately require people "to prostrate themselves in adulation before the Party. . . . First of all, it is the Party leader who is canonized and idolized, and then eventually every level and each individual member of the Party organization." No opposition could prevail against such a "charismatic" system. "Proletarian dictatorship" is transformed into "social-fascist dictatorship by the bureaucrat-monopoly privileged class."[85]

By the end of 1980, when the People's Republic had entered into its long period of economic reform under Mao's successor, Deng Xiaoping, many of Communist China's dissidents no longer spoke the Aesopian language they had earlier employed to conceal their true intent. There was no longer talk of a foreign "revisionist system" or the proposed "right-wing" system of the opponents of Mao Zedong—that of "capitalist roaders." Mao Zedong was identified with the "socialist-fascist system" that had grown out of what had been spoken of as the "dictatorship of the proletariat." It was Mao who had captained the passage from one to the other. Mao had created the system that shared features with that crafted by Benito Mussolini half a century before. One Chinese dissident reminded us that Mussolini himself had been a leader of the "left-wing" Italian Socialist Party before he became the "right-wing" *Duce* of Fascism.[86]

In fact, Wang Xizhe, that same critic, suggested that Maoism shared species traits with Stalinism, Italian Fascism, and Hitler's National Socialism.[87] What he alluded to were the familiar properties shared by all these systems. What distinguished "Marxist" systems from those traditionally called "fascist" was the abolition and monopolization of private property by the state and their insistence on the significance and perpetuity of class warfare.[88] "Stalinism," Wang argued, was an appropriate designation for "Marxist" socialist-fascism, while "fascism" covered all similar non-Marxist systems. All these, he argued, were species variants of the same genus.

According to Wang, Maoism was a perverse form of Stalinism. Where Stalinism had been content to bureaucratize the system, Maoism sought direct and immediate control of the masses through interminable "campaigns" and "struggles." Mao was even prepared to attack his own party in order to impose his will directly on everyone. Out of the ruins of the Chinese Communist Party, largely destroyed in the long struggle of the Great Proletarian Cultural Revolution, Mao created what Wang chose to call "a Mao Zedong Fascist Party."[89]

By the end of the decade of the 1970s and the commencement of the 1980s, the Marxist–Leninist theory of fascism had concluded its trajectory in China. By the time of Mao's death in September 1976, the Marxist–Leninist theory of fascism had devolved into a loosely jointed collection of propositions that identified the bureaucratic strata of socialist communities as the functional equivalents of the various subclasses of the bourgeoisie in capitalist society. Without fundamental political reform, such stratified socialist systems would forever generate new bourgeois elements that would be the operational equivalents of the "big capitalists" and "finance capitalists" who were understood to have dominated Mussolini's Fascism. Like Mussolini's Fascism, "socialist-fascism" put "politics," not property, in command. Like Fascism, "socialist-fascism" was animated by a vision, not controlled by property.

As a function of those insights, during the final years of Mao's rule, the Marxist–Leninist theory of fascism had transformed itself into a searching critique of socialist rule itself. In the course of that transformation, many things became evident. It was clear that the categories that afforded apparent substance to the original schemata were, at best, ill defined.

In the course of the original analysis of fascism, for example, the Marxist concept *class* was made to refer to many different social aggregates—all ill defined. Ultimately, "classes" were understood to function in systems in which no private property existed. "Classes" were defined, not in terms of the property relations of persons to the means of production, but in terms of the potential enjoyed by any group in terms of exploitation. "Class" was defined in terms of real or fancied exploitation, by virtue of coercive state control, taking place where private property did not exist.

Beyond that, in the course of the analysis of fascism, many Marxists came to recognize that forced industrial development and economic growth, together with the exigencies of time and circumstance, made an interim period of authoritarian rule a necessity. If a less developed community sought to survive and prevail in the modern world, it required a broad, deep industrial base. To transform the essentially labor-intensive agrarian systems of the past into the revolutionary, developmental enterprises of the present might require an indeterminate period of minority control.[90]

That period was variously identified. In circumstances in which private property has been abolished and the productive system is governed by command, this period was called by some the "dictatorship of the most advanced vanguard of the proletariat." It was a party dictatorship. In a system in which private property is tolerated and the economy is governed by market signals, the period was identified by others as generic fascism.

What Marxist theory, in one or other of its forms, managed to produce during the years between the Sino–Soviet dispute and the death of Mao Zedong in 1976 was a reformulation of inherited notions about fascism. Fascism was no longer conceived of as simply the pathological product of the final crisis of industrial capitalism. It was a form of developmental dictatorship that could arise anywhere if an exiguous minority assumed the responsibilities of control and administration of the property of a community. In such a system, "class," defined in terms of the ownership of property, was no longer a significant social, political, or economic determinant. In fact, class was an artifact of monopoly political control. It was politics that determined the major features of the system— whether "socialist" or "fascist." Such a system characteristically comes into being in retrograde economic circumstances—in communities suffering retarded industrial development. The "socialism" of such a system is not a reflection of its economic base, but the product of political decision.

All these assessments were going on at the close of the Maoist era and at the commencement of the transition to the rule of Deng Xiaoping. Marxist efforts to understand fascism had produced a body of thought out of which a number of very critical questions would emerge. These questions would be significant during the entire period of reform entrained by Deng Xiaoping's accession to power as "Paramount Leader" of China. Madame Mao, the redoubtable Jiang Qing, provided what is perhaps the most appropriate epitaph to the long history of the Marxist theory of fascism in China by identifying Deng, Mao's successor, as a fascist and the system he inherited as one exquisitely fascist.[91]

The subsequent history of the Marxist–Leninist theory of fascism in the Soviet Union protracted the story of Marxism's relationship with fascism still further. Throughout the decade of the 1980s, until the disintegration of Marxism–Leninism as a political system, fascism was to haunt the intellectuals of the Soviet Union. In the end, fascism survived as Marxism–Leninism passed, unceremoniously, into history.

Fascism and the Devolution of Marxism in the Soviet Union

As distinct from the history of the Marxist–Leninist theory of fascism in Maoist China, the history of the Marxist–Leninist theory of fascism in the Soviet Union is singular in a number of ways. An account of the history of the Marxist–Leninist theory of fascism in the Soviet Union is not restricted to theory—it ultimately becomes directly concerned with fascist practice. In the course of time, as will be argued, Soviet intellectuals themselves became advocates of a clearly discernible form of generic fascism.

Correlative with those developments, the Marxist–Leninists of the Soviet Union became increasingly concerned with the devolution of Marxism–Leninism itself. This devolution began with the death of Josef Stalin in 1953. Throughout the interwar years, Soviet ideology had continued in its seeming imperturbability. With its defeat in the Second World War, fascism was thoroughly discredited. In the Soviet Union, in the years immediately following the war, the term *fascism* was employed as a simple term of derogation to identify Adolf Hitler's genocidal regime, and there was literally no one who pretended to find any merit whatsoever in such a system. Stalin's Marxism–Leninism was secure from any criticism from the "extreme right."

In the years that followed the Second World War, revolutionary China emerged as a revolutionary power on the Asian continent and took on all the major features of Stalinism. In both Communist China and the Soviet Union, the cult of the leader was the unifying center of all political life. It is understood now, in retrospect, that while the talk was of "Marxism" and "Marxism–Leninism," the reality was something vastly different.

With Stalin's death in March 1953, the Soviet Union went into almost immediate political and ideological decompression. Almost immediately, Marxism–Leninism was no longer a living faith for most of the leadership of the Communist Party of the Soviet Union. There was the suggestion that something had always been very wrong with the Marxism–Leninism of Josef Stalin, the "Father of Peoples." Stalin had created a political, social, and economic system that bore little resemblance to anything suggested in the theoretical works of Marx and Engels. There was, of course, something infinitely more objectionable in Stalinism than its intellectual failures, but those disabilities suggested the system's overall morbidity.

After his death, substantial parts of the creed made official by Stalin during his rule became suspect. This awareness probably affected the confidence with which the Soviet Union faced the increased resistance to communist rule that began to mount throughout its empire. Almost everywhere that the Soviet Union had exercised its influence, overt political resistance began to emerge.

Almost immediately after Stalin's death, there were uprisings in Berlin against the Soviet occupation and the Marxist–Leninist government.[1] The uprisings in East Germany and the subsequent unrest in Poland signaled the opening of a critical period in the history of the Soviet Union. In his struggle for the succession, Khrushchev intimated that the Soviet Union required a major review and reform of its most fundamental institutions. It was tacitly acknowledged that the integrity of the inherited doctrine had suffered grievously at the hands of the Soviet Union's recently deceased *Vozhd*.[2]

After the death of Stalin in March 1953 and the revelations of Khrushchev in February 1956, Marxist theoreticians in Moscow were confronted by a clutch of serious problems. While everyone seemed to feel the need to abandon Stalinism as the system's rationale, it was not evident how the political and moral legitimacy of the Soviet Union could be preserved in its absence.

Stalinism was to be forsaken, but an effort was made to preserve Marxism–Leninism as a constructive, meaningful creed for Soviet citizens. Stalin's heirs had inherited an arabesque political system, characterized by properties all but indistinguishable from generic fascism, yet legitimated by an ideology to which it bore no resemblance.

There was talk of a "return to Leninism" in the effort to reestablish regime legitimacy, but it soon became clear that Stalinism could not be so easily distinguished from Leninism. In retrospect, it is evident that Soviet ideology entered into crisis with Stalin's death and followed him in death only with the disintegration of the Soviet system itself. The crisis resolved itself in the 1980s only with the emergence of two opposed ideologies—one a variant of Western democracy, the other an unmistakable variant of fascism. Such a denouement, totally unexpected by Western scholars, tells us something about fascism and a great deal about Marxism–Leninism.

In retrospect, it is possible to trace the course of the decay of Marxist theory in the Soviet Union with reasonable accuracy. It began with the death of Stalin and the efforts at "de-Stalinization" that followed. There is considerable evidence suggesting that Khrushchev, in the years following the death of Stalin, attempted to recapture and implement some of the humanitarian and liberating tenets of the declaratory creed of the original Marxists that Stalin had pretended served as the legitimating rationale for the Soviet system. In a real sense, Khrushchev seems to have sought to have Marxism–Leninism, purged of Stalinism, conform to the romantic eschatology of the early Bolsheviks, who were caught up in the vision of a world revolution of workers that would bring peace, harmony, and material abundance in its wake.

In the immediate post-Stalinist years, legislation was passed, for example, that sought to preclude the further possibility of mass terror. Regulations were promulgated designed to curb police powers by reducing the secret police to a state committee under party control.[3] There seems to have been an intention to do something about the concentration camps that dotted the landscape.

However Marxist theoreticians chose to interpret the end of the Stalin era, there was little doubt that Marxism–Leninism had revealed itself to be anything but an inerrant guide to political leadership. The sense of malaise that followed was exacerbated by Khrushchev's penchant for calling up, once again, all the Marxist slogans that the first Bolsheviks had carried in their rucksacks. There was talk of the imminence of communism, of improved living standards, and of "classless democracy."[4] Khrushchev sought to reaffirm the romantic and Enlightenment values presumably harbored by the original makers of the Russian Revolution. In that sense, he anticipated much of the subsequent ideological "restructuring" by Mikhail Gorbachev, who, twenty years later, was to resolve the crisis begun with the death of Stalin by bringing down the Soviet system.

In the years between Khrushchev and Gorbachev, the Soviet Union went into a long somnolence—years of economic stagnation and gradual political decay. It was during those years that the entire issue of "fascism" reemerged both as theory and reality. It was an issue that was to shape the end of the Soviet Union and influence the future of the new, post-Soviet Russia.

By the mid-1960s, as we have seen, Chinese Marxists had condemned "de-Stalinization" as an abandonment of socialism and an embrace of "social-fascism." In some sense, that was true. It was Stalinism that had provided the ideological rationale for "socialism in one country." It was Stalinism that had identified "fascism" as a bourgeois excrescence of late capitalism. And it was Stalinism that gave institutional form and ideological legitimation to Mao's People's Republic of China. The abandonment of Stalinism signified, for the Marxists of China, a counterrevolutionary blow against socialism and the first step in the full restoration of state monopoly capitalism in the USSR.[5]

The extent of the ideological decay that took place under Stalin's ministrations was revealed only years later, in the intense introspection of Mikhail Gorbachev's *glasnost*. Only then could Soviet thinkers fully expand upon Stalin's "irrationality"—his "mental illness"—in an effort not only to explain the enormities committed in his name, but to account for the disintegration of Marxism–Leninism as an ideology.[6] By the end of his life, Stalin had so tortured Marxist theory that it no longer possessed credibility. The sense of cynicism that overwhelmed Soviet intellectuals was immensely damaging to regime legitimacy. If Stalin and those around him who professed to be Marxist theoreticians could be led so far astray for so many years, it was difficult to see the merits of Marxism as a prophylactic against error, still less as a legitimating rationale for the system.

Whatever effort was made to keep Khrushchev's revelations at the Twentieth Party Congress secret, they were almost immediately broadcast worldwide. The most dedicated Marxists could not fail to recognize the implications of Khrushchev's indictment of Stalin. For an entire epoch, Marxism–Leninism in the Soviet Union had "degenerated."[7]

The consequences of this "crisis of conscience" in the Soviet Union unleashed turmoil in Eastern Europe. A series of crises in Poland were followed by anticommunist revolution in Hungary, begun by Imre Nagy's attempt the rehabilitate his system's legitimating ideology. In 1956, Nagy, who had originally been brought to power on the bayonets of the Soviet army, insisted that if his nation were to survive, it would be necessary to abandon Marxist "dogmatism, and exegetic Talmudisms" for some more viable alternative. He sought to "modernize" Marxism, by abandoning the "old, sometimes antiquated scholastic theories" that had been imposed on the satellites of Stalin's Soviet Union.[8] He sought an alternative socialism. His efforts were suppressed only with the force of Soviet arms.

The unraveling of what had been the rationale of the Marxist world system created increasingly unmanageable tensions between the Soviet Union and the Marxists of the People's Republic of China. Major ideological and policy differences very soon created an abyss between the Kremlin and the Maoists of Beijing.[9] The Sino–Soviet conflict that emerged during the tenure of Khrushchev further bankrupted the notion of the universal inerrancy of Marxism–Leninism. The consequence was a predictable diminution of ideological legitimacy for both Moscow and Beijing. It became increasingly apparent that both Moscow and Beijing were responding, and appealing, to their respective national interests rather than to any internationalist Marxist ideological imperatives.

As many had long argued, the revolution in Russia and the system Stalin had created gave every appearance of being fundamentally national, not international, in form and in inspiration. No less could be said of the revolution in China. In the face of such considerations, there was increasing ideological ferment among Russian and Soviet intellectuals. Within that ferment, the first shoots of anti-regime dissidence made their appearance.

In a forlorn effort to revivify Marxism–Leninism in a relatively liberal contest of opinions, Khrushchev allowed the expression of modest protest. To that apparent end, he authorized the publication of some works critical of the Soviet system—among them a novella entitled *One Day in the Life of Ivan Denisovich* by a then little-known writer, Alexander Solzhenitsyn. It was a depressing depiction of the grim realities of Soviet life under Marxism–Leninism. It was to be followed by works by Solzhenitsyn and others that were increasingly critical not only of life, but also of thought, under the dominion of Marxism–Leninism.

At about the same time, the first significant religious protests against the persecution of the Orthodox Church by the Soviet authorities took place.[10] Along with all this, the first revolutionary anti-Marxist, Russian nationalist dissidents began to gather in clandestine organizations. In February 1964 an "underground liberation army" made its presence known in Leningrad. The All-Russian Social-Christian Union for the Liberation of the People, as it identified itself, continued to recruit members and generate anti-regime literature until its discovery and dissolution by the KGB in 1967.[11]

Not only was the All-Russian Union anti-Marxist, it was clearly nationalist in the most traditional sense of the word. It characterized its own ideology as "Social-Christian" and rejected Marxism as not only "deeply anti-moral," but "anti-national" as well. The "People's Revolutionary Charter" of the All-Russian Union affirmed that Communist rule had become possible in Russia only because Marxists had "uprooted" the "living soul of a people—its national tradition."[12] It thus picked up a theme that had been central to the convictions of anti-Bolshevism since the time of the revolution in 1917.

In the turmoil that attended the decomposition of Marxism as a legitimating rationale, some of the elements of traditional nationalism began to reappear. What was becoming increasingly apparent was that "Soviet patriotism," without roots in the history of Imperial Russia, would no longer serve as an effective surrogate for Russian nationalism.

During the 1920s and 1930s, Fascist theoreticians had identified "Soviet patriotism" as a functional substitute for Russian nationalism. It was clear that the substitution satisfied their anticipation of an inevitable abandonment of Marxist internationalism by Marxists themselves. For the Fascist thinkers of the interwar years, Soviet patriotism, with Great Russians at its heart, satisfied their theoretical expectations.[13]

By the mid-1960s in the Soviet Union, the issue of "Soviet patriotism," as distinct from "Russian nationalism," became increasingly acrimonious. Many Soviet intellectuals simply spoke of "patriotism" and the "Motherland," leaving unclear whether the referent was Russia or the Soviet Union. Regardless of the confusion, dissident intellectuals made increasing reference to "national traditions" and the "spirit of the nation," with "Russia" as a specific referent. At times, there was a conscious rejection of what was seen as an artificial Soviet patriotism, in order to embrace a genuine Russian nationalism.[14] The All-Russian Union was among the first and better known of those dissident nationalist groups that opted for Russian nationalism as distinct from Soviet patriotism.

Below the level of ideological reflection, student groups of the 1960s organized themselves in a spontaneous effort to protect Russia's artistic and cultural heritage—evidence of the nation's past glories, sometimes neglected and almost always deplored by the Soviet regime. There were voluntary societies for the collection and display of traditional artifacts. Touring groups were formed to visit old monuments and religious shrines. There was a preoccupation with the pre-Soviet history of Imperial Russia, with its accomplishments, sacrifices, and meaning in the world.

Of greater interest for the present discussion is the occurrence among the diverse elements that provided the substance of the ideology of the new/old Russian nationalism that appeared at that time of unmistakable fascist components. The All-Russian Social-Christian Union, for example, anticipated an anti-Marxist "corporative order"—the functional organization of all productive components—that would operate under the overarching, interventionist auspices of a nationalist, "theocratic" state.[15]

While the clear intention of the All-Russian Union was politically liberal, in the classic sense of "liberal," the intellectual leadership was under the doctrinal influence of, among others, Nikolai Berdiaev, who had some evident, if relatively minor, fascist sympathies.[16] The similarities and sympathies were relatively insubstantial, but the emerging nationalism was tendentially anti-Western, ill disposed toward "inorganic" political democracy, vaguely anti-capitalist, but supportive of private property and relatively free market economics—sentiments clearly reminiscent of the first Fascism.[17] Marxism in the Soviet Union of Nikita Khrushchev and Leonid Brezhnev was being gradually hollowed out by the first efforts of an anti-regime nationalism that saw itself, in a substantial sense, as a "third way" between Western capitalism and Bolshevism.

By the middle of the 1960s, Marxism in the Soviet Union had entered into a protracted ideological crisis from which it was not destined to emerge. Together with the rise of an Orthodox Christian Russian nationalism, a popular, conciliatory nationalism made its first clear appearance among the establishment intelligentsia.[18] Specialists have simply noted that "a patriotic revival was only to be expected in view of the decline of Marxist–Leninist ideology," but something more was transpiring.[19]

In the mid-1960s, Khrushchev was overwhelmed by his opponents in the Party who charged him with having weakened the Soviet Union with his programs of reform and liberalization. Leonid Brezhnev, who succeeded him, sought to offset the corrosive influence of political liberalism on the Soviet dictatorship. Some effort was made to control the underground *samizdat*, and dissidents like Solzhenitsyn and Andrei Sakharov were increasingly subject to obstruction and censure. Nonetheless, during the late 1960s, non-orthodox themes surfaced more and more frequently in the establishment literature of the Soviet Union.

A great many tributaries flowed into an emerging "establishment nationalism." There was the Slavophile tradition of the nineteenth century, which carried along with it the influence of all its notables, ranging from Nikolai Danilevsky to Fyodor Dostoyevsky. And there were the authors of the early National Bolshevik tradition who had combined neo-Slavophilism and Stalinism in such a way that it was difficult to disentangle the two.

The nationalist revival among establishment intellectuals took many forms and fielded many arguments. Spokesmen for the revival articulated their arguments in literary journals like *Voprosy literaturi* and political magazines like *Molodaya gvardiya* and *Nash sovremennik*. Not only did such works contain a rediscovery of the Slavophile thinkers of the nineteeth century; there was the occasional call for an entire reassessment of Russia's long history from an independent—that is to say, a non-Marxist—perspective.

In 1968, for example, Viktor Chalmaev published a long article entitled "Inevitability," in which he argued that the history of Russia was to be understood in terms of the development and maturation of its "national spirit," rather than of social revolution and class warfare.[20] Invoking a historicism fundamentally more Hegelian and nationalist than Marxist and internationalist, Chalmaev conceived of Bolshevism simply as one of many manifestations of the Russian national spirit. Chalmaev conjured up one of the favorite images of those Russian nationalists of the 1920s who attempted to find some redeeming nationalist message in the apparent internationalism of Bolshevism.

Chalmaev argued that Russia, at the heart of the Soviet Union, required renewal. The Soviet Union had allowed itself to become bereft of soul and spirit. It had become materialistic, devoid of purpose, and uninspired. Its population had become corrupt and careerist, selfish and grasping. The argument had manifest relevance. It offered some sort of explanation of the measurable contraction of the Soviet Union's output, the declining productivity of labor, the inefficiency of enterprise, the stagnation in technological innovation, and the catastrophic waste of resources.[21]

The enthusiasts of reemergent Russian nationalism sought to restore enterprise and vitality to what have since been identified as years of stagnation under Brezhnev. They sought to reawaken dedication and a willingness for self-sacrifice among all sectors of society. To do that, they conjured up the familiar images of external threat. The Soviet Union was involved in a struggle for its very existence. The new/old nationalists contrasted the decadent, materialistic West and a confused, but still vital Russia, making a distinction and broadcasting an invocation familiar to anyone at all knowledgeable about the concerns of Slavophiles in the nineteenth century and National Bolsheviks in the twentieth.

The revived nationalism was energized by a pervasive sense of impending catastrophe. There was allusion to an imminent apocalyptic clash of cultures in which the Soviet, or Russian, state and society might succumb to the threats, importunings, and violence of the spiritually bankrupt West.

Among many of the increasing number of nationalists and patriots, there was a growing rehabilitation of Orthodox Christianity and a heralding of a romantic return to the "Motherland." At the center of the historic vision was neither confession, class, nor race. It was the nation that was key—and it was the commitment to the survival and prevalence of the nation, however conceived, that animated the entire enterprise.

Marxism had begun unraveling even before the rise of Russian nationalism and non-Marxist patriotism. By the beginning of the 1980s, there were few intellectuals in the Soviet Union who were prepared to undertake the unqualified defense of Marxism in any of its variants. More and more found political inspiration in the new/old Russian nationalism that had assumed increasingly concrete form in the 1970s. By the end of the 1980s, the political and economic situation in the Soviet Union had deteriorated to the point where even the intellectuals of the Communist Party itself were attempting to formulate alternatives to the Marxism–Leninism that nominally still prevailed.[22] They had witnessed the Polish proletariat rise up against their oppressors—the Marxist–Leninist oligarchy of Poland. They fully understood that the Polish uprising of August 1980 had been a working-class revolution against a new class of bureaucratic oppressors who pretended to be "proletarians," animated by what pretended to be the "proletarian" ideology of Marx, Lenin, and Stalin. It had been a replay, on a far grander scale, of the Berlin uprisings of 1953, the Hungarian rebellion of 1956, and the "Prague Spring" of 1968.

The "new thinking" of Mikhail Gorbachev did very little to redeem the old doctrines.[23] In 1970 Alexander Solzhenitsyn had counselled the leaders of the Soviet Union to persist in their authoritarianism if they must, but urged them to abandon the ideology that gave lie to the system. Gorbachev succeeded in doing just the opposite. He insisted on Marxist–Leninist inspiration for his reforms and proceeded to attempt the dismantling of the authoritarian state.

The consequences were not long in coming. After some initial hesitation, by 1986 and 1987 the most distinguished members of the Kremlin elite were savagely criticizing the administrative command system that had been the core of the Soviet economy for more than half a century.[24] That inevitably led to the merciless criticism of Stalin and Stalinism, divesting the inherited ideology of any coherence it might still have retained. The people of the Soviet Union no longer found inspiration in ideological truths or the political imperatives of a "proletarian" ideological mission. Without doctrinal legitimation and inspiration, there was no assurance that the system could maintain its integrity under stress.

By the end of the decade, the Soviet Union was left with a hegemonic party no longer convinced of its own mission, a hobbled security apparatus no longer capable of controlling events, a population that had long since lost patience with food and commodity shortages, a military that was demoralized, and more and more intellectuals who sought to separate the future of their nation from the fate of Marxism–Leninism. By the end of the 1980s, many intellectuals were concerning themselves with the survival of a Greater Russia, independent of Marxism in any form.

By that time, there were despairing intellectuals who were prepared to argue that only an emergency regime—Marxist, non-Marxist, or anti-Marxist—could salvage the situation. Only a strong state could save Russia and protect the integrity of the Soviet Union. Dissociating itself from the discredited inherited ideology, such a state could establish a new legitimacy by invoking the emergency powers necessary to meet prevailing exigencies.[25] One of the most interesting and important of the intellectuals initially putting forward those arguments was Sergei Kurginian.[26]

By the end of the 1980s, Kurginian, an informed Marxist and a member of the Communist Party of the Soviet Union, was seeking "national salvation" in a program dictated not by the inherited ideology, but by what he considered the political and economic reality then prevailing in the Soviet Union.[27] Fragmentary in delivery and sometimes loosely argued, that program had an implicit and explicit logic that found expression in familiar themes.

What Kurginian and those who sympathized with him recommended to the leadership of the Soviet Union was abandonment of most of the fictions that had collected around the Marxist–Leninist state. Most of those fictions had become, at best, transparently ineffectual—at worst, they contributed to the decay of the entire system.

Kurginian's arguments addressed an issue on which the Soviet Union was to founder. At the time of Stalin's death, Khrushchev had sought to divest the Soviet Union of all the pretenses that had been used to justify terror, political violence, and mass murder. Khrushchev sought a half-hearted return to the Enlightenment and democratic values of the classical Marxism of the nineteenth century. There was even talk of political diversity and improved living conditions, and the promised abundance of communism.

Kurginian's recommendation, like Solzhenitsyn's, was that the leadership of the Soviet Union would be wiser to abandon the "values of the Enlightenment," with all their associated passivity and political pluralities, and reinforce the more traditional "Eastern" values of commitment, dedication, and sacrifice. For a nation in crisis, democratic and consumerist values detracted from collective survival potential.

Kurginian candidly admitted that no one in the Soviet Union believed in the supposed "democracy" of the Soviet system. It would be hard to conceive of how the prevailing system could "democratize" itself without self-destruction. Certainly no one believed that the essentially nonmarket economy of the Soviet Union could provide the quality and quantity of consumer goods made available in the West.[28] To indiscriminately "marketize" the Soviet economy would be to court disaster.

Kurginian urged the abandonment of any appeal to such "Enlightenment" values in the effort to preserve the Soviet Union in the face of cataclysmic threats to its survival. What he advocated was an unambiguous appeal to those "indigenous" values that had lifted the people of Russia and the Soviet Union from agrarianism to industrial modernity, from defeat and humiliation in the First World War to victory in the Second.

However Kurginian and those who shared his convictions were identified by others, or whatever they called themselves, it was clear that he and those around him were prepared to dismiss all the arabesque reasoning of inherited doctrine in the search for solutions.[29] They all prided themselves on being recognized as activists and pragmatists, more concerned with the salvation of their nation than with ideological orthodoxy.

Given this disposition, Kurginian made eminently clear that he was convinced that only a strong state, informed by a strong leadership, could solve the problems that had overwhelmed the Soviet Union.[30] He dismissed those thinkers who pretended that the state was not really essential to the maintenance, protection, and enhancement of the nation, and which, in some communist future, would no longer be necessary. Kurginian was an unabashed statist and was absolutely convinced that a strong state is necessary in any society.[31]

Everything Kurginian wrote clearly conveyed his conviction that the state was at the core of his program. Equally clear was his general assessment of Stalin. Stalin had created a powerful state, a state necessary to the extensive industrial growth that provided the Soviet Union with the strengths that assured its place in the world—not because of Marxist doctrine, but in spite of it.

Stalin ruled a hierarchically structured, authoritarian state, inflexibly controlled by a declassed, self-selected, bureaucratic elite committed to an arduous program of industrialization that required the relentless enterprise of the Soviet people. Kurginian recognized that while the cost in human lives had been devastating, and was to be deplored, Stalin had created an industrial base that could withstand the shock of the German invasion, absorb the tremendous losses this entailed, and still provide the wherewithal to supply the Soviet forces with the weapons that ultimately brought victory.[32] For Kurginian, whatever fictions surrounded the Stalin Constitution of 1936, the truth was that Stalin administered an inflexibly authoritarian and highly centralized state. And the Soviet Union had prospered and prevailed.

Implicit in Kurginian's account is the recognition that Stalin was fully prepared to exploit ideological fictions to elicit the compliant submission of the people of the Soviet Union and to win the passive and active support of a substantial portion of the world's academics. Domestic and foreign audiences were told that in the Union of Soviet Socialist Republics, the *Vozhd*, the "Leader," ruled by public acclamation—and that the directors of enterprise and stewards of labor organizations were all democratically chosen by their constituencies and served at their pleasure. And, of course, there was the insistence that the Soviet Union was an egalitarian "classless society" in which a "proletarian leadership" governed a "workers' state."

Kurginian clearly recognized all that as unselfconscious fiction. He maintained that the original Soviet system had been constructed by Stalin not as an egalitarian democracy devoted to consumer satisfaction, but as an authoritarian enterprise to specifically service the demanding requirements of extensive industrialization, economic expansion, and the enhancement of the nation-state. Command and control were aggressive, determined, and centralized in a powerful state machine. Whatever legitimating fictions Stalin invoked, for whatever reason, he never deluded himself that they had any implications for conduct.

Stalin had constructed an authoritarian, hierarchical state to defend the nation, to assure its survival and continuity, to combat foreign "imperialism," and to make the Soviet Union a world hegemon. Stalin designed the system for war, for combat, and for victory. He intended to forge the Soviet people into a weapon in the service of a world mission. Neither Stalin nor anyone around him was deluded by the democratic, liberal fictions with which the system was camouflaged.

For Kurginian, whatever disabilities began to afflict Stalinism in the last years of the *Vozhd*, the contaminants that were ultimately to threaten the survival of that vigorous system were introduced with the anti-Stalinist reforms attempted by Khrushchev. It was Khrushchev who spoke of economic decentralization, and it was he who attempted to insinuate into an unaccommodating system the elements of a "consumer society." Under Khrushchev, there was talk of political and economic liberalization in a search for system "responsiveness." There was even the suggestion that the then living generation of Soviet citizens would enjoy all the material abundance of the utopian communist society anticipated by Marx. Khrushchev had apparently begun to believe the myths that had been employed by Stalin to legitimate his dictatorship.

Following Khrushchev, the system continued its gradual, slowly accelerating decline. Those who attempted to "re-Stalinize" the Soviet Union largely failed in their attempts to arrest the descent. By the mid-1980s, so much confusion had collected around the ideological rationale for governance that Soviet intellectuals divided themselves, whatever the qualifications, into two camps: those who sought to satisfy the expectations that the myths of the system had aroused and those who advocated both an abandonment of the myths and major reforms of the system, under the authoritarian control of a strengthened state. Kurginian was clearly in the latter camp.[33]

Among those who sought to satisfy the expectations generated by the myths of democracy and material abundance were Mikhail Gorbachev's "radical reformers." They tried to make the USSR more responsive to the civil and human rights demands of its citizens. They spoke seriously of "democratic elections" and of a market economy that would satisfy the material desires of consumers. They sought to fulfill the democratic and welfare outcomes that Marxism seemed forever to have promised but never delivered. As a consequence, radical reform was both implicitly and explicitly anti-Stalinist, committed to an uncertain, vague, half-articulated "humane Marxism."[34]

Kurginian's response was fundamentally different. For Kurginian, what was required was perfectly clear. Gorbachev and his radical reformers had allowed themselves to become captive to a whole series of insubstantial myths and stultifying fictions. Unable to understand their own history and confused by their own fictions, the "radical reform" leadership of the Soviet Union was attempting to satisfy mythic expectations. What that leadership failed to appreciate, in Kurginian's judgment, was that the effort would fatally compromise not only the economic system, but the state as well.

Confused by their own liberal and pseudo-humanitarian notions, Gorbachev and his reformers had allowed the power of the Soviet state to dissipate in a welter of slogans. Unlike Stalin and his entourage, they had begun to believe the fictions that had collected around the Soviet system from its inception.

Kurginian urged that real reform required not an attempt to satisfy the demands of the myths, but a candid recognition of the realities facing the Soviet Union behind the fog of fictions. He advocated abandoning the "Marxism" the radical reformers sought to implement. In general, he spoke of their Marxism as "irreparably anachronistic and stultifying."[35] What he meant by that was not difficult to discern.

Kurginian wanted to sweep away all the comfortable fictions with which several generations of Marxists in the Soviet Union had deluded themselves and disappointed others. He objected to the prevailing disposition of Gorbachev's liberal reformers to continue to mislead the suffering people of the Soviet Union with talk of "equality," "representative pluralism," and an "economy of consumer abundance."[36] In doing so, "humane Marxism–Leninism" was betraying the most fundamental interests of the Soviet Union and its people.

Kurginian argued that the world was a very dangerous place. All its denizens were driven by an irrepressible desire for power. Power in all its forms, as suasion, appeal, command, and domination, was central to Kurginian's thought. For him, it was the drive for power that created the distinctions between the ruled and the rulers to be observed in all and any organized aggregate of human beings. For Kurginian, all this was as true for the international, as for any local, community.[37]

It was in this context that Kurginian saw the modern world system arranging itself in a hierarchy of states. Possessed of all the qualitative and quantitative advantages to be purchased by sophisticated science, advanced technology, and the control of information, the most mature capitalist economies enjoy almost absolute control over the life circumstances of those less advantaged. Science and technology provide some states and some configurations of states with the material power to rule others. Dependent states are exploited, overtly or by indirection, reducing them to no more than repositories of raw materials and cheap labor for their technologically advanced oppressors.

In Kurginian's view, the privileged of the modern world have created an international system that has become increasingly "ossified," one that denies the less developed countries any opportunity to escape their predicament, condemning them, in effect, to perpetual subordination.[38] Fortunately, Kurginian argued, until the advent of Gorbachev and his reformers, the Soviet Union remained outside the fabricated hierarchy of contemporary international privilege. The Soviet Union had refused to submit to the requirements of the international system, and it possessed sufficient conventional and unconventional military capabilities to preclude having the system imposed upon it. As a consequence, only the Soviet Union remained in a position to save the world community from perpetual servitude to the "technocratic" imperialists.

What Gorbachev and his "humanitarian liberals" threatened to do, by pursuing their "democratic" reforms, was to render the Soviet Union vulnerable to that prevailing exploitative international arrangement.[39] In their passion to "democratically" reform the Soviet Union, they were prepared to conform to the international rules of the game dictated by the advanced imperialist powers. They had, in effect, accepted "human rights," "democracy," and material well-being as measures of national legitimacy. Gorbachev was prepared to allow the Soviet Union to be measured against criteria that favored Western imperialists.

Instead of holding firm to the independence of the Soviet Union, Gorbachev's liberals attempted to compete with the West in terms of crass materialism, self-interest, individualism, a profane preoccupation with personal pleasure, and a diminished concern for others.[40] The leaders of the Soviet Union had abandoned heroism, virtue, and concern for the collectivity, in an attempt to be more liberal than their opponents. The consequence, in Kurginian's view, could very well be the collapse of the Soviet Union and its reduction to a servile nation, forever inferior to the industrialized democracies of the West.

In its effort to conform to the norms of the imperialist powers, the Soviet Union's "humanitarian intelligentsia" had opened the gates of the Soviet Union to a flood of Western influences—the mass culture of nihilism and spiritual corruption. The "humane Marxists" of Mikhail Gorbachev were prepared to "democratize" the state and "marketize" the economy, thereby weakening both and sacrificing the nation's most fundamental interests in the effort to purchase the temporary approval of foreigners.[41]

For Kurginian, all this signified a "spiritual weakness" that carried ominous consequences in its train. The strong state that had in the past protected the Soviet people from foreign exploitation was being undermined. The genius of Soviet science and the competence of its technicians were being lost by the failure of the state to provide succor and protection. Stalin, Kurginian reminded his readers, had left the Soviet Union one of the world's great powers. Gorbachev and his reformers were supervising its dismantling. What reality demanded was the survival, independence, and development of the Soviet state, the principal agent assuring the survival, independence, and development of the national community in an international contest more threatening than armed conflict.

In order to restore the Soviet Union to its former station, Kurginian argued that patriotism must, once again, serve to seamlessly unite all Soviet citizens in a renovative program of national development implemented by a strong state and supervised by an intelligent, heroic, spiritual elite. Under such guidance, the people of the Soviet Union would root out the elements of a "criminal bourgeoisie" that had collected around the profits to be made by the liberalization of the nation's economy.[42] A patriotic people would rekindle the dedication of a party and a bureaucracy that had become unresponsive and corrupt.[43] Once again, Soviet science, with its gifted engineers, managers, inventors, and technicians, would be without peer in the modern world.

Kurginian anticipated that Soviet military and industrial enterprise could effectively compete with the dominant Western democracies only through the creation of state-sponsored "megastructures," combinations of talent and enterprise that could discharge functions that clearly exceeded the capacity of the Soviet Union's existing institutions. Within an economy in which the price structure would be significantly influenced by market signals, Kurginian urged that Soviet workers, managers, and representatives of the state be collected in productive organizations sustained, influenced, and supervised by corporative bodies that would assure political control, unanimity of response, and integration of effort.[44]

The subsequent salvation of the Soviet "Motherland" would proceed in an atmosphere of high moral tension—assured by the inculcation of an evocative "Red religion" that would enjoin patriotism, "communalism," application in labor, self-sacrifice, morality, and heroism.[45] The leaders and the led would unite in a sense of dedication to the national community.

The "white communism" advocated by Kurginian was an authoritarian, elitist, national socialism that had discovered the "religious roots" of the Russian state. It was a non-Marxist communism that would encourage its citizens to "strive for a life that is rewarding and enriching in the spiritual, rather than the material, sense."[46] It was a communism that saw Bolshevism not as a "proletarian revolution," but as a stage in the evolution of Greater Russia.

It is difficult not to recognize the thought and sentiment of other times and other places in Kurginian's notions. In his thought one finds a suggestion of Friedrich Nietzsche's "will to power," Vilfredo Pareto's conceptions of the elite and the subordinate non-elite, as well as Roberto Michels and Gaetano Mosca's distinctions between the rulers and the ruled. There is something of Georges Sorel in the political moralizing, and in Kurginian's passion, there is an echo of the nationalism of Enrico Corradini and Alfredo Rocco—intellectuals who gave the light of their doctrines to Mussolini's Fascism.

For Kurginian, the will to power was an inexpungeable and unalterable human disposition. It found expression in the creation of elites and in their rotation. For Kurginian, the evidence of history confirmed that all known systems have been characterized by expressions of power in the hierarchical arrangement of a minority of rulers and a ruled majority.

From Kurginian's account, it is clear that he was convinced that, in the effort

to perpetuate their dominance, elites employ "derivations," conscious or uncon-
scious fictions, that serve as ideological legitimations for their rule.[47] When an
elite fails, its ideology fails as well. Pareto, Michels, and Mosca said nothing less.

There is in Kurginian's conception the image of cultures in conflict, of
nations rising to meet moral challenge, and of other nations falling into decay.
Moreover, there is a sense of urgency in Kurganian's program for the renewal of
the Motherland—the restoration of its moral strength in the face of decadence.
Sorel, Corradini, and Rocco said nothing less.

More than proto-fascist thought, there is the unmistakable conceptual language of Fascism in Kurginian's exposition. Not only is the union of "organizations of producers" in a state-dominant corporative structure a reflection of
Fascist thought and institutions; even those aspects of Kurginian's thought that
appear innovative have clear Fascist precedents.[48] Kurginian speaks of technical
committees and state-sponsored corporations that would marshal and supervise
all the nation's talents in its uneven competition with those foreign systems that
have the advantage of being intensively developed and extraordinarily productive. The affinities with Fascism are transparent.

From its very commencement, Fascist developmentalism anticipated a role
for "committees of competence" that would ensure rapid technological development for a comparatively retrograde Italian economy.[49] As Fascism matured, the
system that had initially been economically liberal became increasingly dominated by the state. In the course of the economy's etatization, Fascism developed
very large para-state organizations, putatively to serve the nation's critical needs
in its competition with the advanced "plutocratic" economies of the industrial
democracies.[50]

In Kurginian's prose, all the trappings of classical Marxism fall away. Kurginian advocates a consuming nationalism, an abiding elitism that provides the
form and structure of an authoritarian state, in a mixed economy influenced and
fueled by a market.[51] He is, in a deep and philosophical sense, anti-egalitarian, as
well as fundamentally and unalterably anti-democratic, and has so conceived the
Soviet system since its foundation.

It is very clear that, for Kurginian, the Bolshevik revolution was a manifestation of vital energy on the part of a people who sought to not only survive, but
prevail. Kurginian saw the Bolshevik revolution as a combination of tradition
and progress that offered the promise of securing a place in the sun for a people
whose history is as old as civilization. For Kurginian, the Marxist myths that
attended the revolution were of little consequence. They were simply its legitimating "derivations."[52]

What was real for Kurginian was the strong nationalist state, the burgeoning
industry, the military might, and the victory in war that gave meaning to the

sacrifice, the heroism, and the labor of the Soviet people. Whatever else it was, Bolshevism gave rise to the state that sought the renewal and restoration of the Motherland. What Kurginian found of merit in Bolshevism was the protection it afforded the people and the culture of the Eastern nation, united in a common destiny and mission, in its conflict with the decadent West.[53] Kurginian recognizes the nation in the state, and sees merit in Bolshevism only insofar as its state served the ultimate interests of the nation.

In Kurginian, there is talk of the rising threat of the "materialist West" and the vulnerability to that threat of the "traditional East." He alludes to the instinctive response of a healthy community to the threat of extinction. He refers to the humiliation suffered by the people of Russia and the Soviet Union at the hands of overbearing foreigners. And he condemns those who would betray the Motherland for the pottage of personal profit.

There are many things to be found in Kurginian, including the best traditions of Russian nationalism and the anti-Marxism of the Russian emigrés of the 1920s. What one finds too is an expression of a doctrine that contains the shadow of some of the most coherent convictions of Mussolini's Fascism.[54] There is generic fascism in the appeal to a strong state led by elites composed of "heroes" and "saints." There is generic fascism in the express rejection of pluralist democracy and Western liberalism. There is fascism in the conception of the nation as the union of all those sharing a common destiny and pursuing a common mission. There is fascism in the conviction that "the only possible type of state is a corporatist one."[55] There is fascism in the appeal to a religion of patriotism as the solvent that reduces class and category differences to one vital unity. And there is fascism in the rhetoric of power, war, and the healing of the pain of national humiliation through prevalence in deadly competition.

The fact that Marxist theoreticians were unable to forestall the appearance of a variant of fascism among their own members, providing its protagonists instead with status and privilege, is a commentary not only on their incompetence, but on the quality of their "theory" and the commonplace distinctions between "left" and "right" political persuasions.[56] More important still, perhaps, Marxist–Leninists had not understood their own political, social, and economic arrangements sufficiently well to preclude their ultimate collapse. They were to be passively overwhelmed by events. The final certification of Marxism's intellectual destitution and the transparent inadequacy of its understanding of fascism was the failure of its theoreticians to recognize the signs of ideological alienation and the rise of the fascist impulse that accompanied the end of their system.[57]

Sergei Kurginian is important in all this. In the period immediately before the final collapse, he had already articulated the first outlines of a new ideology for the salvation of Russia. It was an ideology sharing critical features with

Fascism. With that ideology, Kurginian was to influence Alexander Prokhanov, and through Prokhanov the leader of the Communist Party of the Russian Federation. There is a direct line of descent from the proto-fascism of Sergei Kurginian to the present convictions of one of the Soviet Union's foremost Marxist–Leninists, Gennadi Ziuganov.

There is no little irony in the fact that some kind of fascism should grow out of the decay of Marxism–Leninism and that its principal advocate should be the leader of the Communist Party of the Russian Federation. By the time of the disappearance of the Soviet Union in December 1991, it had become evident to many Russian intellectuals, and no fewer foreigners, that Marxism–Leninism had never really understood either itself or Fascism.

6

Fascism and Post-Soviet Russia

That a form of fascism made its appearance in the Soviet Union with the first signs of systemic deterioration has been difficult for most academicians to understand. More than half a century ago, the Soviet Union had been one of the major protagonists in the "war against fascism." More than twenty million Russians died in its course. Given this fact alone, there were very few in the West who anticipated the emergence of any ideology approximating fascism on Soviet soil.[1]

What seems to have transpired is instructive. In the first instance, the fascism that emerged as a consequence of the collapse of the old system was not mimetic. Intellectuals in the Soviet Union did not read fascist literature and decide that the doctrine expressed fitted their evolving circumstances. The appearance of fascist elements in Soviet thought was not the result of intellectuals discovering the fascist literature of the 1920s and 1930s. The Soviet proto-fascism that emerged in the Gorbachev era was the spontaneous and reactive response on the part of Soviet intellectuals to a developing ideological crisis. It was a reaction to domestic circumstances and perceived external perils.

As has been suggested, this was all but totally unanticipated by Marxist–Leninist theoreticians themselves. In fact, the disintegration of the Soviet Union and the ideological collapse of Marxism–Leninism in Eastern Europe were all but totally unexpected by Western scholars as well.[2] With the perspective of hindsight, of course, everyone should have realized that by the mid-1980s the Soviet Union had entered a critical, penultimate phase of its history. Since the mid-1970s, there had been a gradually accelerating decline in the levels of Soviet production.[3] By the end of 1986, it was clear that the Soviet economy would require an enormous improvement in total factor productivity if it were to survive until the end of the century. There was widespread consensus among the leadership of the Soviet Union concerning the necessity for substantial, if not systemic, change in the economic system.

Partially as a consequence of that realization, coupled with multiple system failures, the legitimating ideological rationale of Marxist–Leninist rule became increasingly irrelevant. At first, the irrelevance was concealed by making ritual appeal to inherited doctrines. The Twenty-Seventh Party Congress Program of the Communist Party of the Soviet Union in 1986 still insisted that as a consequence of the "worsening of the general crisis of capitalism. . . . the advance of humanity towards socialism and communism . . . is inevitable." It was affirmed, with perfect orthodoxy and apparent conviction, that "history. . . . has entrusted the working class with the mission of the revolutionary transformation of the old society and the creation of the new one."[4]

Even Mikhail Gorbachev, responsible for the "new thinking" that increasingly challenged the "old," still insisted that the "class-motivated approach to all phenomena of social life is the ABC of Marxism," and that Marxists were expected to employ that approach in the assessment of contemporary social and political issues.[5] References to "class analysis" and "proletarian revolution," as well as appeals to Leninism and the heritage of "Bolshevism," were iterated and reiterated in the political rhetoric of a system in evident ideological disarray.[6]

For all that, some of the principal "Marxist" spokesmen for the Gorbachev reforms began to make increasingly frequent references to universal "bourgeois" values and decreasing references to Marxist class ones. Gorbachev himself specifically renounced the "use of force and the threat of force" as instruments of class warfare or international policy. International relations were no longer to be interpreted as "class struggle" on a world scale. Gorbachev seemed to want to make "international peace" something of a primary, class-transcendent, value.[7]

At the Twenty-Seventh Party Congress, Gorbachev had already urged that Marxist–Leninists "shed once and for all, resolutely and irrevocably," all ideas about the "acceptability and permissibility of wars and armed conflict."[8] In his major work, Gorbachev attempted to separate the notions of "socialist revolution," Marxist values, and mass violence.[9]

Few Marxist theoreticians had ever before been prepared to explicitly reject "revolutionary" war, armed conflict, or broad-based violence as the price of universal peace. Neither Marx nor Lenin were pacifists. International wars and revolutionary armed conflict were understood to be class struggles employing military means, and they were to be won through violence. Marxist–Leninist prose had always been alive with military metaphors, an insistence on class warfare, and allusions to "just wars."

What appears clear in retrospect is that the failure of the Soviet economy had undermined the confidence of the leadership in the Soviet Union. More and more members of the military and political elites no longer believed that Marxist–Leninists could emerge victorious from any armed conflict with the advanced industrial democracies.[10] Gorbachev himself was frank in inextricably relating the "country's defense" to its economic performance.[11] As its economy failed, it became manifestly evident that the Soviet Union would be increasingly at risk in the event of armed conflict.[12]

The overall decline in the Soviet Union's productivity not only produced domestic problems of almost unmanageable proportions, it also made it impossible to keep pace with the United States in the increasingly demanding arms race. Everything pointed to the inability of the Soviet Union to survive in a protracted technological, economic, or military contest with the industrial democracies.

At the more immediate level of foreign affairs, it seemed evident that Marxist–Leninist revolution in less developed environments did nothing to enhance the future prospects of the Soviet Union. Armed revolution on the periphery of the industrially advanced economies apparently did nothing to impair their survivability. Such revolutions resulted only in the creation of Soviet dependencies at a time when Moscow could ill afford the expenditures required to sustain them. There was even talk about the satellite nations of Eastern Europe having become more burdens than assets to the Soviet Union.

Given the prevailing circumstances, the appeal to the universal values of peace and compromise takes on the appearance of a cynical response to inescapable reality. Many students of Soviet affairs, however, have rejected such an interpretation. Mikhail Gorbachev seems to have been a person of conviction, and his appeal to leftist universalistic values genuine. The nations of the world, Gorbachev argued, had become increasingly one and interdependent.[13] Beset by the threat of nuclear destruction, resource depletion, ecological catastrophe, and overcrowding, it was necessary for nations to come together in the spirit of compromise, cooperation, and goodwill to protect the future of humankind.

However one chooses to interpret Gorbachev's "new thinking," by the end of the 1980s, Soviet spokesmen insisted that the foreign policy of the USSR proceeded from "a vision of the world as a supreme value."[14] Instrumental to this supreme value were the Western liberal values of "freedom, justice, tolerance, and pluralism in the defense of the principles of democracy."[15] Some of the major intellectuals of the Soviet Union even went so far as to trace all those newly acknowledged "Marxist–Leninist" values to "Voltaire and Rousseau, Montesquieu and Hugo Grotius, [Thomas] Jefferson and [Tom] Paine."[16] In effect, Gorbachev had committed the Soviet Union to all the political and moral values of the industrialized West. As the Soviet Union gradually lapsed into economic catastrophe, the Gorbachev reforms provided an entirely new interpretation of the the traditional ideology of the Soviet Union.[17]

Even before the advent of Gorbachev, regime intellectuals were advocating an abandonment of some of the critical directives of Marxism–Leninism. As early as 1985, B. P. Kurashvili proposed a "new and desirable system" in which the socialist economy would be "guided by the regulating power of the market."[18] There was increasing talk of introducing "commodity–money relations" into the economy, in an effort to generate a rational price structure that would contribute to a reduction of intersectoral imbalances and wastage. Only a few years earlier, such ideas had been denounced as "incompatible with the production relations of socialism."[19]

By the end of the 1980s, socialist economists were making frank allusion to the necessity of initiating changes in resource ownership within the Soviet economy. State ownership of the means of production had come to be seen as an obstruction to the effective employment of national resources. Many argued that state property, in terms of productive goods and resources, was treated as though it belonged to no one. Since property belonged to the state, individuals purloined, neglected, and employed it without regard to cost or potential benefit. Only private ownership, it was argued, would provide protection for property in general and supply the necessary incentives to control costs, assure rational use, and ultimately supply competitive products for end users. More and more Soviet economists became convinced that it was only the threat of personal loss that could assure individual and collective compliance with sound economic practice.[20]

In the midst of all this ideological and policy soul searching, Mikhail Gorbachev made more and more frequent appeal to humankind's "universally shared values."[21] In an interdependent world, he maintained, capitalist and socialist systems could cooperate because of the prevalence of just such shared values. Marxists, Gorbachev insisted, were prepared to combine "class and universal human principles in real world development" in order to work with systems that had hitherto been considered irremediably exploitative, warmongering, and imperialist.[22]

By the end of the 1980s, Gorbachev's policies attested to the irrelevance of Marxism in whatever form. Gorbachev was prepared to work with any foreign power, "socialist" or "imperialist," in the pursuit of universal peace. His declaratory policy went far beyond "peaceful coexistence." Lenin's advocacy of such coexistence was entirely pragmatic, invoked at a time when the Soviet Union required an interval for recuperation and rehabilitation. It is clear that Lenin, in his revolutionary fervor, anticipated that the Soviet Union's economic disabilities would be rapidly offset. "Peaceful coexistence" was to be the brief interlude before the final world victory of revolutionary Marxism. Lenin never envisioned that the economic shortcomings of the Soviet Union would compel Moscow to forever compromise the future of the universal "proletarian revolution" in order to survive.

Gorbachev, by contrast, gave every indication of a readiness to do precisely that. He advocated a foreign policy based on the conviction that the Soviet Union and its "imperialist" opponents could unite in the pursuit of "global values." Whatever talk there was of Marxist theory, there was very little, if any, concern with the future of "class struggle" or "world revolution." For Gorbachev, the Soviet Union had cleansed itself of "Stalinism and all other filth" and was prepared to collaborate with the "imperialist powers" on the basis of shared human values.[23] In some sense or other, Gorbachev had become convinced that "imperialism" and Marxism–Leninism could cooperate, because all human beings, capitalist or socialist, were animated by "progressive general human values." For Gorbachev, those "progressive general human values" were clearly not "class-based." They included "truth and conscience, justice and freedom, morality and humanism."[24]

By the beginning of the 1990s, the Soviet Union found itself afflicted with a devastated economy, policy uncertainty, and ideological confusion. In terms of domestic economic policy there was talk of private property, cost account- ing, market adjuncts, and economic incentives. There was talk of "freedom of choice" and of the "popular selection" of the leadership of the Soviet Union.[25] Gorbachev and those around him appeared prepared to embrace the values of a consumer-oriented representative democracy. In foreign policy, the leadership of the Communist Party of the Soviet Union, in principle, seemed committed to a form of what both Marx and Lenin identified as "bourgeois" universalism.

The opposition to Gorbachev coalesced around Marxist–Leninist intellec- tuals and party spokesmen. There were those in the highest ranks of the party who resisted market economics, consumerism, classless humanism, and pacific universalism. Together with the significant party opposition, a surly military complained that Gorbachev's "new thinking" made the armed forces of the Soviet Union something of a "social evil."[26]

Intellectuals like Sergei Kurginian served as spokesmen for the mounting opposition to Gorbachev. The "myths" and "fictions" that Kurginian so emphat- ically rejected constituted the ideological foundation of Mikhail Gorbachev's reforms. There is every indication that the work of intellectuals like Kurginian was supported by elements within the highest leadership ranks of the Commu- nist Party of the Soviet Union.[27] Kurginian was the favorite of high party offi- cials, and his intellectual center in Moscow was financially underwritten by party funds.[28]

The first intimations of an uncertain Russian proto-fascism, contained in the incoherent programmatic suggestions of the All-Russian Social-Christian Union for the Liberation of the People during the 1960s, gradually came together with the half-articulated nationalism of student groups and the Orthodox Church to lend inspiration to a growing anti-Gorbachev opposition within the Communist Party itself.[29] By the beginning of the 1990s, proto-fascism had been marshaled to the defense of a Marxist–Leninist system in its final stages of morbidity.

Suddenly, out of all this, with the increasing irrelevance of Marxism and Marxism–Leninism, "Eurasianism," "Russophilism," statism, elitism, irredentism, empire, and authoritarianism all became ideologically relevant again in the Soviet Union.[30] Once again, as in the time before the Bolshevik revolution, intellectual journals were filled with discussions of authoritarianism, nationalism, and empire, of cosmic destiny, and of human will and human heroism. There were increasing appeals to the "traditional Russian constants" of *narodnost, sobornost, dukhovnost*, and *derzhavnost*—conjuring up visions of the historic *Volk*, united in organic communion, undergoing transfiguration through conflict under the governance of a transformative "magnificent State."

Just as "de-Stalinization" afforded the first occasion for the emergence of anti-regime dissidence, so the collapse of the Soviet empire opened space for a proliferation of Russian nationalist sentiment. Russian nationalism, in all its pluriform distinctiveness, reappeared. Statism, elitism, "organic collectivism," and a special sense of national mission, became the intellectual stock-in-trade of a veritable multitude of "social patriots."

Even as Gorbachev's reforms wound down, for example, there were at least ten major *Pamiat* organizations operating in the Soviet Union, each with its own distinctive nationalist and statist program.[31] Each was the product of disillusionment and a sense of national betrayal. Each gave expression to the profound feelings of humiliation that Russians suffered as their empire collapsed in confrontation with the Western world.

The ideologues of *Pamiat* sought to account for the tragic history of Russia, the Bolshevik revolution as well as the collapse of the Soviet state, in terms of Jewish–Masonic conspiracies. All the *Pamiat* organizations were comfortable with their identification as heirs to the mantle of the anti-Semitic "Black Hundred" of pre-revolutionary Imperial Russia.[32]

They were not alone. Anti-Semitism has long been a feature of Russian political thought. In the crisis of the 1980s and the early 1990s its reappearance was not unexpected. Thus, it is not surprising that groups like that of Victor Yakushev's National-Social Union grew up alongside *Pamiat*. Equally convinced that "Zionists" were pursuing a plot to establish world hegemony, Yakushev advocated arraying a strong state, committed to the establishment and furtherance of "Aryan values," against them.

Alexander Barkashov's Russian National Union gave expression to a more sophisticated para-fascist political program, which was statist in orientation, authoritarian in principle, elitist by conviction, and voluntaristic by disposition. Given to the organization of paramilitary groups and a disciplined, hierarchically structured party, Barkashov was anti-Marxist–Leninist as well as anti-democratic.[33] He was also racist.[34]

Less grotesque, perhaps, was the reactive nationalism of Nikolai Lysenko. During the final days of the Soviet Union, Lysenko organized the Republican People's Party of Russia—almost immediately to become the National Republican Party of Russia. Lysenko was to be part of the coalition that sought to unite "all patriotic forces," whether left or right, in a National Salvation Front intended to halt the disintegration of the Motherland. He was to insist that the salvation of the Motherland overrode the partisanship of the Left and Right. While essentially anti-Bolshevik, Lysenko argued that the future of Russia required the mobilization of all, whatever their political persuasion, in the service of the imperial state.

In the thought of Nikolai Lysenko, the imperial state is the linchpin of Russian salvation. For Lysenko, it is the state that forges a nation out of people. It is the state that imparts will and resolve to what would otherwise be a mere aggregate of persons. It is the state that articulates the mission that defines the responsibilities of the ruling elite, inspires the administration, tempers the courage of the armed forces, and animates the thinking of every patriotic citizen.

Lysenko argued that inspired nations—like the Rome of antiquity—create empires that bring civilization and culture to their peripheries. For Lysenko, a Russia freed from the trammels of Marxism was uniquely suited to the performance of such a world-historical function.

While ready to marshal the forces of both Left and Right, Lysenko remains explicitly anti-Marxist–Leninist. Militantly anti-socialist and anti-liberal, Lysenko has no tolerance for what he takes to be Marxist and liberal Jewish machinations against the integrity of Russia and its empire. In fact, racism forms a major theme in Lysenko's doctrines. Besides references to the Jews, there are allusions to a Slavic "gene pool" that requires protection and an appeal to "Slavic unity" as instrumental to that purpose.

Lysenko's objections to Gorbachev, and to the liberal system that followed the collapse of the Soviet Union, turn on their putative pacifism and universal altruism—myths employed by transnational capitalism to undermine the uniqueness and survivability of Russia. Lysenko conceives of Russia as locked in an apocalyptic conflict with Western imperialism. He perceives the world as an arena in which an eternal struggle for survival takes place, with defeat meaning either extinction or enslavement. Those nations that fail to respond effectively to the clarion call to battle are defeated, to become the exploited, less developed communities dominated by those more technologically advanced.

For Lysenko, Francisco Franco and Charles de Gaulle represented variants of a "third way" between the devastation of Marxism–Leninism and the decadence of advanced industrial capitalism. In his judgment, Hitler's National Socialism was a pathological expression of that alternative.

What all this indicates is that in the immediate aftermath of the disintegration of the Soviet Union, there was an explosion of Russian nationalisms, each with its own "statist" and "patriotic" program intended to secure the salvation of the nation.[35] Among them were Slavophiles, post-Soviet centrists, anti-Westerners, developmentalists, racists, imperialists, national communists, anti-Semites, and Russophile mystics.[36] Almost all were, and remain, peripheral to the main political developments in post-Soviet Russia.

Some political groups were a little bit of everything and enjoyed a brief moment of vast popularity and seeming influence. Vladimir Zhirinovsky and his Liberal Democratic Party, as a case in point, enjoyed their passing popularity and seeming influence during the first years of post-Soviet Russia. However unimpressive Zhirinovsky and his party have been, they have engaged the interest of the West in a singular fashion. In the West, Zhirinovsky was spoken of as a possible "Rising Czar" and was thought of as a potential dictator of a future "Russian fascism."[37]

In what sense Zhirinovsky is a fascist is difficult to say with any intellectual conviction. He has successfully fought that characterization in Russian courts, and his ideas, while sharing many of the features of the anti-democratic, nationalist groups that have flourished in the chaos of post-Soviet Russia, are sufficiently inconsistent to leave one confused about their actual character.[38]

Zhirinovsky speaks of "lifting Russia from her knees." He speaks of restoring Russia's pride and undoing its humiliation.[39] His passion is that Russia should not be a mendicant among advantaged states. Russia should not beg at the table of the industrial democracies. For Zhirinovsky, Russia's great power status must be reaffirmed and reestablished. More than that, in its own defense and in defense of world civilization, Zhirinovsky argues that Russia must expand, not only to establish a defense perimeter around the Motherland, but to protect the international community from the West's "new world order," which could only bring increasing decadence and ultimate chaos in its train.

Zhirinovsky has argued in favor of an emergency regime that not only would restore stability and order to the Russian federation, but would provide a stimulus for the economy, reconstruct the nation's infrastructure, and provide for military capabilities that would see Russian forces "abut the Arctic Ocean on the North, the Pacific on the East, the Atlantic via the Black Sea, the Mediterranean

Sea and the Baltic Sea, and finally, in the South, [the Russian military] will wash up against the shore of the Indian Ocean."[40]

Zhirinovsky gives expression to the kind of reactive, authoritarian nationalism that, throughout the history of the twentieth century, has regularly given rise to one or another variant of fascism. Anti-Marxist and anti-liberal, in principle, Zhirinovsky charges Marxism with having failed Russia in at least two ways: (1) by imposing a dysfunctional command economy on a creative and productive people who otherwise would have established, fostered, and sustained an economic base suffcent to support a great nation; and (2) by insisting upon a "revolutionary internationalism" that never fully engaged the nationalism latent in the Russian people. He charges liberals with failing to understand the history and mission of that people.

In December 1993, a poll by *Nezavisimaya Gazeta* put Zhirinovsky's national approval rating at about 25 percent. In the elections of that year, his Liberal Democratic Party polled 22.8 percent of the votes cast. Zhirinovsky was riding the crest of the Russian nationalism that he considered critical to the mobilization of support for his renovative program.

Like fascists and proto-fascists everywhere, Zhirinovsky advocates an economic system guided by market signals, but subject, in principle, to substantial intervention by the state. While market forces would influence the growth, modernization, and presumed efficiency of the economy, the political system would be unqualifiedly authoritarian. Zhirinovsky rules his political party autocratically, and there is every reason to believe that political authoritarianism is central to his political convictions.[41]

Zhirinovsky maintains that his party will restore national discipline through the employment of action "squads," equipped with emergency powers, which would ruthlessly suppress all criminal activity and deport all non-Russians living illegally within the confines of the Russian federation. He advocates the creation of a politically centralized and authoritarian regime that would serve as a magnet around which all the non-Russian republics and ethnic enclaves of the former Soviet Union would once more collect themselves. Those regions would be reincorporated into a Greater Russian sphere of influence not as political equals, but as protectorates.[42] Zhirinovsky has made clear that he anticipates the irredentist re-creation of empire.

Zhirinovsky argues that there is an urgency to his program because he is convinced that mortal threats emanate from the East and the South—from a potentially aggressive and expansionist China, whose population already exceeds the carrying capacity of its soil, and from fanatical Muslim fundamentalists who seek to provoke their coreligionists in the Russian federation to rebellion. He argues that only an ardent nationalism can save Russia from such dangers.

There is some evidence that Zhirinovsky's program has attracted the support of a substantial minority of workers and soldiers. In fact, Zhirinovsky has made his appeal directly to the military, and it seems that there has been some resonance. More than that, Zhirinovsky recommends assigning state funds to the military, and for military science and research, and aggressively supporting the export of arms to those nations not opposed to the restoration of a Greater Russia. Zhirinovsky expects such policies, in the near and the long term, to contribute to the stabilization of the Russian domestic economy. Deficit spending, in the form of Keynesian pump priming, together with political stabilization, are intended to restart the Russian economy by providing meaningful employment to members of the military and workers in the civilian sector.

During the years between the disintegration of the former Soviet Union and the elections of 1996, Zhirinovsky seems to have attracted substantial popular support. It is also reasonably certain that during that period his appeal peaked. In the Duma elections of 1995, Zhirinovsky's Liberal Democratic Party garnered about 12 percent of the popular vote, down more than ten full percentage points from the elections in 1993. By the time of the presidential elections of June 1996, that support had diminished still further.

Like most of the proto-fascist political movements in the Russian Federation, Zhirinovsky's Liberal Democratic Party seems to have little prospect of sustained growth, durability, or ultimate political success. The party appears to have transient membership, volatile support, and uncertain institutional integrity. Zhirinovsky's own bizarre antics, dubious life-style, and eccentricities seem to have condemned him and his party to ultimate extinction.

All this suggests that the prospects of a domestic fascism in the former Soviet Union really turn on the political convictions and mobilizational efficacy of the "social patriots" who have collected around the political vision of ideologues like Sergei Kurginian and Alexander Prokhanov. It is they who have generated the sociopolitical ideas that seem to have survival potential in the strained ideological environment of Russia at the end of the twentieth century.

By the end of the 1980s, Kurginian had attracted the support of Alexander Prokhanov to his ideas—and it was Prokhanov who was to transfer much of their ideological substance to Gennadi Ziuganov, leader of the Communist Party of the Russian Federation. As the Soviet Union entered into its final stages of disintegration in July 1991, Ziuganov, together with eleven others, issued a manifesto entitled "A Word to the People," in which the citizens of the Soviet Union were told that a catastrophe of unparalleled magnitude had overwhelmed their "beloved Motherland" and its "majestic state."[43] The Soviet Union, victor of the war against fascism, a leader in world technology and cultural accomplishment, had been betrayed by a conspiracy of suborned leaders, who, in the treasonous search for personal wealth and aggrandizement, had betrayed the national beliefs, hopes, and aspirations of the people.

The signatories of the "Word to the People" called upon the military, as the "glorious defenders" of the state, not to allow the "destruction of the Fatherland." There was an appeal to the Russian Orthodox Church and to the Communist Party to defend the Motherland. "Russia, the most unique and the most beloved," was to be defended by those prepared to make a selfless commitment to an "all-national ideal."

The "Word to the People" was largely the work of Prokhanov, who by that time had become a major adviser to Ziuganov. Both these men were to exercise special influence in the post-Soviet Russian Federation.[44] The "Word to the People" was immediately seen as a direct attack on Gorbachev, leader of the Communist Party of the Soviet Union.[45] It was an attack on all the universal and liberal values Gorbachev espoused. It was an attack on the notion of a benign international system which accommodated nations and cultures without cost. It was an explicit rejection of the conviction that all human beings shared compatible and mutually supportive values that would sustain an interdependent community of nations. The "Word to the People" captured the full sense of the national humiliation that outraged the anti-Gorbachev elements within the Communist Party and the military, as well as the general citizenry of the Soviet Union, all of whom had witnessed the decline and disintegration of their native land.

Like Kurginian before him, Prokhanov was prepared to jettison the notion that the world was composed of peoples each longing to be united in either proletarian harmony or humane, politically liberal, and ecologically sensitive enterprise. Like Kurginian, Prokhanov saw the world as an arena for competitive confrontation, with the industrialized democracies seeking the subordination of the Soviet Union—to impose upon it an "American future."[46] For Prokhanov, the disintegration of the Soviet Union into the Confederation of Independent States was the final outcome of the "new thinking" of Mikhail Gorbachev.

Prokhanov, like Kurginian, was caught up in the trauma of the decay of the Soviet Union. For him, the Soviet Union was threatened with extinction because it had devolved into a shabby collection of ineffectual central structures that no longer represented the interests of the community. More than that, Gorbachev had committed the empire to a collection of "alien" values that gave every advantage to the privileged industrial democracies.

Like Kurginian, Prokhanov called upon the citizens of the Soviet Union to accept the moral and material responsibility for saving the "crumbling, dying" community that had once been Great Russia. Like Kurginian, Prokhanov invoked the image of strong men of principle and conviction calling on the masses to resist the importunings and stratagems of that "powerful, well-fed stratum," within both the party and Soviet society, that had betrayed the Soviet Union.[47] He sought to unite all the vital elements of the community in its defense. He sought to marshal the veterans, who had "gained real combat experience and demonstrated an ability to fight and shed blood for the state, this last contingent of 'statists' who died in the name of its idea in the canyons and wastelands of Asia."[48]

Like Kurginian, Prokhanov anticipated that those whose interests were linked with state industries in general and defense industries in particular would unite with the veterans of wars fought in the service of Imperial Russia—however Imperial Russia chose to identify itself. The combat veterans and selected entrepreneurial elements could provide the elite constituents for a renovative response to the imminent collapse of the system. Prokhanov was convinced that the general population could not possibly be secure in the vagaries of a proposed universalistic, market-governed system and would have recourse to the leadership of a determined elite. Together, the war veterans, the aggressive entrepreneurs, and the mobilized people, would fuel the rebirth of empire.

Among the signatories of Prokhanov's "Word to the People" of July 1991 were ranking leaders of the Soviet military and the Communist Party. Some (Vasili Starodubtsev and Alexander Tizyakov) were to become directly involved in the attempted *coup* against Mikhail Gorbachev. When the coup attempt was mounted in August 1991, its rationale shared substantial affinities with the expressed concerns of the "Word to the People."[49] In their "Message to the People," the leaders of the coup attempt made no recourse to Marxist appeals or class analysis. They spoke not of class or world revolution, but only of threats to the historic Motherland and its state. The ultimate defenders of the Marxist–Leninist system had abandoned all the tortured "dialectic" of Marxism and spoke the language of national, etatist resurgence.

With the final disintegration of the Soviet Union at the end of 1991, Prokhanov proceeded to identify Boris Yeltsin, president of its successor state, with the liberal, cosmopolitan, and "bourgeois" convictions of Mikhail Gorbachev and the domestic "left." For Prokhanov, both Gorbachev and Yeltsin had committed themselves to the values of Western liberalism, to a generic "democracy," and to a catalog of universalistic "human rights" that surrendered Russian distinctiveness to a kind of "mondialist" uniformity. In his view, both Gorbachev and Yeltsin had betrayed the future of Russia and its empire.

For Prokhanov, honor demanded that the survivors of the debacle that had settled on the nation commit themselves to the restoration of a Russian empire capable of performing the mission assigned to it by history and by destiny.[50] More than that, the restoration of empire would constitute a defense of vital "healthy" and "heroic" forces in a world threatened by an apocalyptic descent into absolute decadence.

Both Kurginian and Prokhanov are statists. Both advocate the re-creation of a strong, central state, staffed by an elite with competence, military spirit, and traditional disposition. Both are developmentalist, committed to a program of technological enhancement and economic growth as the necessary foundation for the power projection capabilities required for victory in a world of intense geostrategic competition. Both anticipate the re-creation of empire, the irredentist expansion of Russia to its historically established boundaries.

Prokhanov, like Kurginian, conceives of the world as the arena of "unending struggle, of a huge, gigantic conflict incorporating thousands of other conflicts." He sees Russia, at the moment, "toppled, vanquished and captive . . . in a noose fashioned by an alien civilization; hunter's whistles have led [the nation] into a punji trap."[51]

What makes Prokhanov unique, perhaps, is his candor. He has proclaimed himself an "anti-communist" at the same time that he has identified himself as a Stalinist. He has affirmed that he would support any political strategy, "white, red, Stalinist or fascist," if it contributes to the restoration of the Russian empire. In fact, Prokhanov appears to have expressed an admiration for Stalinism for the same reasons that he finds "Mussolini's historic program" appealing.[52]

The "strange attraction" which the "figure of Mussolini" holds for Prokhanov seems shared by Kurginian.[53] When Kurginian speaks of the reconstruction of the Russian state in a manner fundamentally different from that of the "Anglo-Saxons," he alludes to its erection on the foundation of a "corporative-syndicalist society" in which the interventionist state "carefully balances" all the elements of an "estate-based" economy.[54] This seems to be the substance of Prokhanov's "corporate imperial nationalism" which commentators have found so reminiscent of Italian Fascism.[55]

The intellectual relationship between Kurginian and Prokhanov during the first few years of the post-Soviet republic was intense. Kurginian, more the intellectual, seems to have supplied many of the basic ideas of Prokhanov's "corporate imperial nationalism." It was during the period of substantial intellectual collaboration that Prokhanov wrote the "Word to the People."

It was this document that sealed the union of "all patriotic forces," members of the Communist Party of the Russian Federation and a host of statists, imperialists, and nationalists, in an enterprise intended to defend the "national idea," restore Russia's "spiritual integrity," resist the "dismemberment" of its "body," and burnish the "majesty" of its state. The entire thrust of Prokhanov's "Word to the People" was nationalist, statist, voluntarist, developmental, and redemptionist. There was an appeal to tradition, to "cherished values," to the Orthodox Church, to the soldiers who had served their Motherland, to heroism, to courage, to labor, and to the "minstrels of the national idea." There was no talk of the truths of Marxism, of "class struggle," of "international proletarian revolution," of "capitalist exploitation," or of the "dictatorship of the proletariat." The "Word to the People" was written in the language of fascism, familiar to anyone at all knowledgeable about the political thought of the twentieth century.[56]

By the first years of the 1990s, it had become obvious that some form of fascism was maturing in post-Soviet Russia. To some among the national-statist leadership, this recognition generated increasing distress. In 1993, Kurginian raised the issue as a matter of conscience. In that year, Kurginian and Prokhanov tried to settle the issue of what role "fascist ideas" would play in the ideological rationale of Russia's "national-patriotic forces." Finding themselves caught between the discredited convictions of Marxism—Leninism and those of a form of Western capitalism they found repugnant, the leaders of the anti-Yeltsin opposition attempted to define their ideological position. On that occasion, Kurginian insisted that, whatever his interest in the political ideas of Mussolini, he had "never considered," and did not then consider, that the Russian "popular movement [or] the national idea . . . correlated in any way with anything that might fully claim to belong to fascist ideology."[57] What appears evident from his discussion at the time, as well as in earlier writings, was his conviction that "fascism" referred exclusively to the genocidal ideology of Adolf Hitler.

Thus Kurginian went on to lament the appearance of the symbols of the National Socialist SS in the pages of some of the major nationalist publications. He was scandalized by the imposition of Barkashov's swastika over the banner of the former Soviet Union and the "detached" and "objective" treatment meted out to the monsters of National Socialism in the pages of nationalist journals. He complained that many in the ranks of the national patriotic forces showed evidence of contamination by the "virus" of fascism.

He went on to warn that fascism was a "pathological response" to national humiliation against which patriots were advised to inoculate themselves. Patriots were warned that the anti-communism and unfettered greed of the free market enthusiasts of the Yeltsin administration had opened the "floodgates" to the baleful influence of "fascist ideology."

Prokhanov's response to Kurginian's concerns was carefully crafted and is instructive. He responded that, for more than seventy years, the censorship of the Marxist—Leninist government had denied Russians the right to explore non-Marxist, much less anti-Marxist, ideas. Russian intellectuals had been denied the opportunity to make their own informed judgment about any "unorthodox" collection of ideas. In the intellectual chaos of the post-Soviet present, Prokhanov went on, Russians had not only the right, but the obligation, to consider all political and social ideas, however much any of those ideas were deplored by those who considered themselves "proper."[58]

He went on to remind his audience that while it was true that fascism was associated with mass violence and brutality, no less could be said of Marxism–Leninism, which in the 1920s alone destroyed "four flourishing classes" of Russian society and in the 1930s consumed millions of Russians in the Great Purge.[59]

Prokhanov went on to suggest that if Kurginian's objection to fascism arose from the fact that it was a "pathological response" to national humiliation, it would be hard to imagine what a "nonpathological response" might be to the destruction of everything a nation held sacred. How, he asked, could one respond nonpathologically to the "eradication of national pride" and to the treachery that abandoned Russian women and children to starvation and exposed the nation to foreign pillage?

Later, in a published interview, Prokhanov acknowledged that he himself had been regularly identified as a "fascist." He went on to say that he had never taken umbrage at the use of the term to describe him or his work, since he had no clear idea as to what the term *fascism* meant to his critics. He understood full well that it was meant to demonize him, but other than that, the term was generally given no specific reference.[60] He spoke without difficulty of the emigré version of Russian fascism that enjoyed some prominence in the 1930s, as well as the "Italian version," suggesting that neither seemed to be an unmitigated evil and clearly distinguishing both from the overwhelmingly negative properties attributable to Hitler's National Socialism.[61]

Prokhanov has publicly recognized that the term *fascism* has been applied to a variety of political ideologies, movements, and regimes. He is prepared to admit that the national patriotic movement in post-Soviet Russia shares many affinities with the Fascism of Benito Mussolini, the authoritarianism of Francisco Franco, the mass-mobilizing anti-liberal developmentalism of Juan Peron, and the military conservatism of Augusto Pinochet—as well as the authoritarian national developmentalism of Josef Stalin.

Most politically aware Russians knew that the emigré fascists of Harbin associated Stalinism with an evolving "communo-fascism," and that ultimately they had decided that "Stalinism is exactly what we mistakenly called 'Russian Fascism.'"[62] None of this was lost on Prokhanov. He appears little concerned about how one characterizes the national patriotic movement in post-Soviet Russia. He is committed only to its success.

In that specific regard Prokhanov is among the most politically and intellectually interesting figures in the anti-liberal, anti-democratic opposition to the post-Soviet Yeltsin administration. He is particularly significant because he has supplied the intellectual substance for Gennadi Ziuganov's drive for leadership of the Russian Federation.[63]

As early as the publication of the "Word to the People," Ziuganov appealed to Prokhanov to formulate a program for the anti-Yeltsin opposition. It was a program to which he would commit the Communist Party of the Russian Federation. Since that time, employing that program, Ziuganov has distinguished his party from the Communist Party of the Soviet Union.[64]

As the Communist Party of the Soviet Union imploded, Ziuganov emerged as one of the most important political leaders in post-Soviet Russia. His party has not only retained its very substantial membership; it has attracted enough voters to make the Communist Party of the Russian Federation a very serious contender for power.

Ziuganov is a self-avowed communist who, while he speaks of "developing Marxism–Leninism," rarely employs the theoretical machinery of classical Marxism or the language of traditional Leninism.[65] Whereas Sergei Skvortsov, one of the leaders of the Communist Party of the Soviet Union, continues to invoke the conceptual language and imagery of Marxism—the necessities of the "dictatorship of the proletariat" and continued "class warfare"—Ziuganov has led his Communist Party of the Russian Federation away from all that.[66] There are fundamental distinctions between the Communist Party of the Soviet Union and that of the Russian Federation under Ziuganov.

Ziuganov rarely, if ever, appeals to the Marxist–Leninist ideological orthodoxy of the past. Rather, he often speaks of the "dogmatic teachings" of that time that were "patently out of date" and that contributed to the "national disgrace and the humiliation of the Russian state."[67] He appears remarkably unconcerned with Marxist–Leninist orthodoxy. His unequivocal purpose is clearly the rehabilitation of the Russian empire, at the core of which is "that ethno-political and spiritual-ideological community that is known to the world as the 'Russian people.'"[68]

Both Ziuganov's major works, *Beyond the Horizon* and *I Believe in Russia* "exude a sort of mystical nationalism. . . . Neither Red nor Pink, Mr Ziuganov is White—the latest incarnation of a centuries-long tradition of Russian nationalists who celebrate Orthodox Christianity, Slavic unity and imperial expansion."[69] Ziuganov's "Marxist" ideology is far less Marxist than it is nationalist, statist, and imperialist.

Ziuganov speaks with passion of the neglect in the former Soviet Union of the "immense and fundamentally important inner sphere of spiritual, cultural, and religious moral national existence" that constitutes the essence of the "idealist . . . dreamer . . . and ascetic people" of Russia. He speaks not of the "proletariat," but of Russians. He talks of "gathering on its land, under its own roof, under the protection of a single powerful state, all Russian people, all who consider Russia their Motherland."

There is more than irredentism in his enjoinments. There is a call to empire. Ziuganov insists that "Moscow does not have the right to abandon [its] traditional role of 'gatherer of the lands.'" Russia and its core of "idealistic" and "ascetic" creators are destined to attract lesser powers and less developed peoples to its civilizing enterprise. Russia cannot escape its role as an imperial power.[70] Russia, Ziuganov warns the rest of the world, cannot and "will not accept the humiliating role being imposed on it and will restore its natural position of great world power."[71] History demands that Russia be accorded its rightful place in the sun.

The world, for Ziuganov—as for Kurginian, Prokhanov, and most of the statists and nationalists produced in such great abundance in post-Soviet Russia—is a world of conflict in which major powers pursue "messianic, eschatological . . . projects." The mission of the United States and its allies is to establish a "global dictatorship." This dictatorship would occupy "the Atlantic Great Space," the main "territorial support" for a "world colonial empire," in which the former Soviet Union would be assigned a subordinate and subservient role. The dominant West, like an "insatiable octopus or gigantic whirlpool," seeks to extract minerals and cheap labor from the dependent countries in a process of exploitation that would condemn the major portions of the globe and the majority of the world's population to perpetual inferiority. Only Russia is capable of developing the national strength to resist the impostures of the Western colossus. Only Russia, having reconstructed "its own state system and its own ideological, political, economic, and military self-sufficiency," can provide a defense against the West. Only Russia can assure a "balanced world" in the "geopolitical equilibrium of . . . Great Spaces, civilizations, and ethno-religious 'centers of force.'"[72]

For Ziuganov, Russia is the vital center of a "Slavic core," and that core is the strength of a "Eurasian bloc" that serves as a geostrategic "counterweight to the hegemonic tendencies of the United States and the Atlantic Great Space." Russia is the "mononational" center of the resistance to Western decadence. It is the "main bearer of an ancient spiritual tradition whose fundamental values are . . . 'celestial.'"[73]

More surprising than the realization that all this has little, if anything, to do with Marxism, is the fact that it is clearly "Eurasian" in inspiration. Ziuganov speaks of Russia as the "core and main foundation of the Eurasian bloc," destined to occupy the "Great Space" between Murmansk and Vladivostok.[74] That "Eurasian bloc" will serve as the line of defense against Western hegemony.

These notions come out of the work of Prokhanov. More than that, their origins lie in the writings of the Eurasians of the 1920s, a group of anti-Marxist Russian emigrés who sought to put together a "new Russian ideology" that would "supplant" Marxism–Leninism and "lead a new Russia to a glorious future."[75]

The Eurasians perceived the Bolshevik experiment as part of the historic destiny of Russia. Like the Fascist theoreticians of the same period, the Eurasians expected Marxism–Leninism to be transformed by the realities of the modern world into a supremely nationalist ideology that would lead Russians to the creation of a "Great Political Space" in which national "authenticity" would resist the decadence of the modern world.[76]

More than that, the Eurasians were totalitarians and authoritarians by disposition and anticipated the eventual transformation of Stalinism into a more orthodox fascism.[77] The Eurasians were, and remain, elitists, rejecting with special vehemence all universalistic notions of humankind as empty abstractions. They rejected liberalism and "quantitative" democracy and perceived special merit in "meaningful cultural units," among which Eurasia, with Russia at its core, was historically most important.

Geopolitical Eurasianism today occupies a major place in Russian nationalist thought, as does a peculiar kind of "biological" Eurasianism, represented by the work of Lev Gumilev.[78] In general, it is clear that, to a surprising degree, Eurasianism has shaped the ideology of the man who today serves as leader of Russia's Communists and chairman of the National Patriotic Union. Ziuganov speaks candidly of Russia as "our Eurasian country" and has identified himself with the founders of Eurasianism, who represented the "creative response of the Russian national consciousness" to the Bolshevik revolution—and who gradually came to realize that the "Soviet system, freed from an ideological doctrinaire attitude [would be] the best state form" for a nationalist Russia struggling to defend itself against the decadence of the West.[79]

Of the Eurasianist intellectuals, Ziuganov regularly refers to Peter Nikolaevich Savitsky and Nikolai S. Trubetskoi, both fundamentally anti-democratic and anti-Western.[80] Both conceived of some form of totalitarianism as best suited to Russia. It was Trubetskoi who, in 1935, argued that "one of the fundamental theses of Eurasians [is] that modern democracy must give way to ideocracy."[81]

For Trubetskoi, what that meant was that the ideal nation must be ruled by a political elite, selected "for its faithfulness to a single common governing idea." This elite must be "united in a single ideological state organization," which must, in turn, "organize and control all aspects of life." Such an organization and control would inculcate in the citizens of the ideocratic state an ethic of sacrifice, with such sacrifice "viewed by all citizens as a morally valuable act."[82]

It is difficult not to see fascism in these enjoinments. Whatever qualifications

Eurasianists typically appended to their judgments, it seems evident that they entertained a broad-gauged sympathy for Italian Fascism. As much could be said for many of the other thinkers regularly cited in Ziuganov's writings and speeches. Ivan Alexandrovich Ilin, cited by Ziuganov on many occasions, spoke of Fascism after the Second World War as a "healthy, irresistible and inevitable phenomenon" that emerges to protect the state when the state is threatened.[83] In the "hour of national danger," the people will give themselves over to "dictator-ship" in order to assure the survival of the nation and its embodiment in the state.[84]

Ilin argued that fascism would reappear again when circumstances de-manded "high patriotic pride and national self-esteem." He advised, however, that for "future social and political movements of that kind another term rather than 'fascist' be selected" to identify themselves, since "fascism's enemies" had rendered the name odious.[85]

There can be little doubt as to what has transpired, and is continuing to transpire, in post-Soviet Russia. The leader of a Marxist–Leninist party has assumed the leadership of the nation's "national-patriotic" forces. In the process of assuming that leadership, all the ideological trappings of Marxism–Leninism have been abandoned. In their place is found the belief system of reactive and developmental nationalism.

In fact, there is, today, demonstrably more fascism than Marxism in the political beliefs of Ziuganov.[86] His statism and his nationalism are unmistakable markers. When Ziuganov speaks of governing, he talks of an "emergency gov-ernment of popular trust" that he will impose upon assuming power in Russia; and the rights that this government will provide will be those that were standard under the familiar "dictatorship of the proletariat."[87]

But there is also talk of progressive provisions: free public education and free medical care, for example. There is reference to a popular "Constitutional As-sembly" to craft a "new people's constitution." And there is an insistence that "basic human rights and freedoms will be enunciated and protected." But all this will take place in a political system that is not impaired by any "hollow separa-tion of powers" of the kind that deforms Western democracy. Such an infirm system would allow "traitors to the Fatherland" to carry out their obstructionist policies through a system of representation that would derail the national "col-lective will."[88] No less had ever been said by fascists of whatever stripe. All this recommends a careful consideration of the political system that Ziuganov is prepared to recommend. It is in this context that his reflections on Stalinism are instructive.

Ziuganov has consistently argued that Stalin, at the close of the Second World War, was prepared to abandon traditional Marxism–Leninism and undertake a "philosophical renewal" of the "official ideology of the Soviet Union." Stalin sought, according to Ziuganov, to "create an effective 'ideology of patriotism' . . . [as] a dependable philosophical basis for the . . . enormous Soviet State." Love of the Motherland would substitute itself for "class warfare," for all Russians would be fused in the fire of patriotism. Had Stalin succeeded in his enterprise, the Soviet Union, once again according to Ziuganov, would have "fully overcome the negative spiritual consequences of the revolutionary storms," the divisiveness, the anti-religiosity, and the stultifying materialism of the Bolshevik period.[89]

Under Stalin, Russia had become a major world power. It had "expanded to the utmost the zones of influence in the sea and oceanic directions, blocking henceforward any attempt at direct threats to the borders of the state." Had the "ideological restructuring" of Stalin been brought to its completion, Russia would have become the "most powerful alternative center of world influence," to continue, once again, its "geopolitical tradition."[90] Unhappily, Ziuganov maintains, Stalin succumbed before the "restoration of the Russian spiritual-state tradition" could be completed. Stalin was not yet cold before his successors turned back to the sterile anti-nationalist orthodoxies of the past.

What emerges from Ziuganov's account is an image of an ideal Stalinism—a Stalinism that is nationalist, statist, spiritual, and expansionist. Nothing is said to suggest that Ziuganov objects to the charismatic Stalin "cult of personality," the hegemonic party, or the rage for conformity, sacrifice, and obedience. Nothing serious is said of political democracy or pluralistic political arrangements.

For Ziuganov, as for many of the original Eurasianists, Stalinism shorn of its Marxist–Leninist trappings, infused with nationalist and statist sentiments, politically homogeneous, developmental in intent, and expansionist in practice, constitutes a political ideal. It is Stalinism stripped of all the "myths" and "fictions" carried over from its Marxist past. It is the "white communism" described by Sergei Kurginian. It is, for all intents and purposes, a transparently fascist ideal. Ziuganov has described a Stalinism transformed along the very lines anticipated, as we shall see, by the Fascist theoreticians of the 1930s.

Gennadi Ziuganov, the most important surviving representative of Soviet Marxism–Leninism has, in substance, identified a Russian fascism as his political ideal. He is the advocate of an expansionist, nationalist, interventionist, authoritarian state whose projected capabilities are supported by an exacting developmental program that allows the marginal existence of both private property and free market exchanges. He is dedicated to carving out a "Grand Space" for his nation in a struggle against "the destructive might of rootless democracy."[91]

The rise of a form of fascism in the former Soviet Union is an instructive irony. The Marxist theory of fascism that has dominated Western thought for more than half a century was largely the work of Soviet intellectuals. For decades it passed as the most comprehensive analysis of international fascism. Over the years it became increasingly devoid of specific cognitive content, and, finally, Marxists inside and outside the Soviet Union saw in whatever remained only a caricature of the century's first Fascism—and, as a consequence, failed to recognize its second coming.

At the close of the twentieth century, it is that caricature of fascism that is the bread and butter of many comparativists. Fascism is seen in the obscenities of skinheads and vandals. It is understood to be "necrophiliac," "pathological," "racist," and "reactionary," and as having nothing really instructive to say to our time.

How little understanding of fascism is purchased in these prevailing caricatures was evident years ago to anyone modestly apprized of the history of contemporary revolution. Even today most intellectuals on the Left fail to appreciate the irony of a leader of a Marxist–Leninist party finding his nation humiliated, reduced to servility, at the hands of an "international financial oligarchy," a "cosmopolian elite of international capital," turning to "national patriotic" forces to mobilize against the velleities, inefficiencies, and corruption of parliamentary democracy.[92] They fail to appreciate the painful similarities to another Marxist leader of the "revolutionary left," who seventy-five years ago abandoned all the dogmas about internationalism, class warfare, and the "withering away of the state," to give himself over to the mobilization of the "national patriotic" forces of another humbled nation, in order to resist what he took to be the impostures of foreign "plutocracy."

The fact is that what is now spoken of as "communofascism" and "Stalinofascism" serves as testimony to affinities long recognized by those who have refused to place the revolutions of the twentieth century on a continuum from Left to Right. There have always been deep and abiding similarities between Marxist–Leninist and fascist systems, albeit concealed by the fog of Marxist "theory."

All of which takes us back to the appearance of the first Fascism on the Italian peninsula, which grew out of the frustrations of an earlier cohort of revolutionary Marxists. At that time, it was one of the best-loved, most radical leaders of the Italian Socialist Party who created Fascism out of Marxism and the crisis of the First World War. An elliptical account of the story of that first Fascism may remind us of some important features of one of the most important political phenomena of the century. It may also reveal something important about Marxism as well.

Fascism and Bolshevism

That Marxist–Leninists and convinced socialists might find some variant of fascism attractive is not entirely incomprehensible. Between the two world wars, there were many who made the transition from one or another variant of Marxism to fascism—typified in the example of Henri De Man.

Henri De Man was a committed Belgian Marxist, judged to possess one of the finest intellects within the ranks of European "scientific" socialism. A socialist since 1902, De Man had become a fascist by the beginning of the Second World War. Like Marcel Déat and many other European socialists, De Man made the transition to fascism through an intrinsic critique of Marxism, as well as a response to the "realities" of his time.[1]

The record indicates that the transfer of allegiance from Left to Right among those in the ranks of revolutionaries throughout the interwar years was not unusual. In fact, that such transfers took place has never been thought unusual by those who have argued that the theoretical and practical relationship between Marxism–Leninism and Italian Fascism, for example, is curvilinear rather than rectilinear.[2]

That the affinities between Marxism–Leninism and Fascism are not regularly acknowledged probably arises from the fact that, from its advent, Mussolini's Fascism was characterized as intrinsically and inextricably "anti-communist." There have been those who have argued that, without the threat of communism, there could be no fascism. In general, among both conservatives and leftists, Fascism is conceived to have been the antithesis of communism and Marxism–Leninism. Winston Churchill considered Fascism primarily a reactive and defensive response to the "bestial appetites and the pathologies of Leninism."[3]

The early literature favoring Fascism tended to conceive of it as a movement mobilized to defend Europe from "all the horrors" of Bolshevism—the "brutalities and murders" that would have had all the Continent's "streets and cities . . . run red with blood."[4] Anti-Fascist literature, even when not Marxist in inspiration, deemed Fascism a paid tool of reaction, marshaled for the sole purpose of defeating communism and suppressing the political activity of workers.[5]

Actually, the relationship between Fascist and Marxist–Leninist revolutionaries was far more interesting than that. If *right-wing* and *left-wing* as political concepts have determinate meaning in local contexts, they seem to have relatively little significance in terms of the major revolutions of the twentieth century—a fact that has been grudgingly acknowledged by Marxist intellectuals in the Soviet Union and was fully anticipated in the abundant literature devoted to "totalitarianism."

Specialists in intellectual history, in a variety of places, have traced the complex threads that bind Mussolini's Fascism to Marxism and Marxism–Leninism.[6] That a form of fascism should resurface in post-Soviet Russia is not entirely unexpected. That some Marxists should find it doctrinally appealing is even less surprising.

Mussolini's own history as a socialist and a Marxist is now reasonably well known.[7] What is not as well known is the gradual transformation of a "subversive" Marxist commitment into the doctrine of revolutionary Fascism. That Fascism came to be identified as an unmollifiable "extreme right-wing" opponent of Marxism, socialism, and Marxism–Leninism is largely a function of the first "Marxist theory of Fascism," together with an early history of violent conflict. During the first years of the 1920s, Bolshevik theoreticians, still caught up in the euphoria of their successes in Russia, suddenly found themselves confronted by a powerful and popular "anti-socialist" mass movement that overwhelmed their confrères on the Italian peninsula.

The best among them recognized that the defeat of Leninism in Italy was both political and ideological. However much communist revolutionaries attempted to blame their defeat on the intervention of conspiratorial capitalist forces, the reality was that Marxism–Leninism in Italy had been outmaneuvered, marginalized, and overrun by an autonomous Fascist movement.

When the intellectuals of the Left attempted to explain the rise and success of Fascism, they had recourse to doctrines put together by Karl Marx and Friedrich Engels half a century before. There was recourse to the familiar account of class struggle and bourgeois perfidy. However enterprising the Marxist intellectuals, the story was never quite right. Stitched together out of the Marxism of the nineteenth century, what resulted was a fabric of thin plausibilities. Today, there are very few serious academics who invest much confidence in the original standard version of the Marxist–Leninist interpretation of Italian Fascism.

What we now know about the origins of Fascism as a political movement and an ideological persuasion suggests that Mussolini's enterprise resulted from the confluence of a number of evolving intellectual and political currents—including Italian Nationalism, Futurism, and revolutionary National Syndicalism—together exercising an impact on the millions of ferocious young men returning home from the worst military conflict in the history of humankind.[8] To fail to understand this is to misunderstand the first Fascism.

As has been argued, all the available historical evidence discounts the contention that the first Fascism was the simple creature of industrial capitalism or agrarian capitalism or of the "ruling class" in its entirety. This notion is entirely devoid of plausibility. Mussolini's Fascism was a complex product of an intricate sequence of events, shaped by complicated ideas and influenced by personalities and interests so numerous that no one can pretend to catalog them all.[9]

Among the elements that made Fascism attractive to many Italians, including war veterans, industrial workers, and the uncertain middle class, was its appeal to developmental nationalism—with its promise of class collaboration, economic growth, and political regeneration. Like Fascism's appeal to nationalism, the recourse to accelerated industrial development, "productivism," was intrinsically attractive to those faced with the difficulties that arise in a newly united nation facing an obscure future.[10]

Even before the turn of the century, Italian Nationalists had spoken of the necessity of rapid economic expansion and industrial development. They had spoken of a strong state, a renovated politics, and the future grandeur of the nation so long dismissed as a cipher by the "major powers" of Europe. Italian reactive nationalism, in general, born of the many humiliations that followed economic backwardness in an increasingly industrialized Europe, never had a sufficiently broad-based appeal to render it a truly revolutionary force before the multiple crises of 1918–22. Only then, in combination with other elements, was it to influence the history of the peninsula.

It is eminently clear that the thought of Mussolini, as a revolutionary, was influenced by that of the major theoreticians of Italian Nationalism: Enrico Corradini and Alfredo Rocco. But there was more to the ideology and political program of Mussolini than the substance provided by Italian Nationalism.[11] Italian Nationalism lent Fascism elements of its doctrine, as well as the collaboration of its principal leaders; but Fascism had already taken on most of its specific properties before its merger, after the march on Rome in 1922, with Corradini's Blue Shirts. Fascism's most direct ideological inspiration came from the collateral influence of Italy's most radical "subversives"—the Marxists of revolutionary syndicalism.

Mussolini, during the first years of his active political life, identified himself as a "syndicalist."[12] As such, he was a member of an intellectually aggressive socialist movement, led by Marxists well schooled in the traditions of their masters. Arturo Labriola, Sergio Panunzio, A. O. Olivetti, and Roberto Michels were among the many luminaries identified with the most radical expression of Italian Marxism.[13] Mussolini was not undistinguished among them. Italian Marxists, during the years before the First World War, considered Mussolini notable, and he was a welcome participant in socialist intellectual circles.[14] Ultimately, he was so well considered that he served as both political and intellectual leader of Italy's Socialist Party until the crisis of the First World War destroyed the unity of Italian socialism.

It was during the first years of the century, and as leader of Italy's socialists, that Mussolini developed the views on society and revolution that were to inform the doctrines of Fascism. Among the most important influences were those that originated with the syndicalists.

During the first years of the twentieth century, many Marxists in Italy were uncertain about how the doctrines inherited from the nineteenth century might be applied in the twentieth. This was particularly true among the most radical of them, the revolutionary syndicalists. As early as 1906, Olivetti—an early syndicalist, a confidant of Mussolini, and ultimately a major Fascist theoretician— reminded Marxists that the Italy of his time suffered from "a deficiency of capitalist development."[15] It was unclear just how revolutionary Marxism might apply in such circumstances. The argument was that without a mature economic base, the preconditions for socialist revolution could not be satisfied. Marxism, Olivetti argued, had always maintained that primitive economic conditions could produce only equally primitive politics and equally primitive classes. An "immature bourgeoisie" and an equally ineffectual urban "proletariat" were the necessary products of an essentially agrarian economic system.[16]

The logic of the argument was perfectly clear to Marxists: socialist liberation was predicated on the material abundance only made available by an advanced industrial system—and only advanced industrial systems produced politically mature proletarians, capable not only of overthrowing the old order of things, but equipped to manage the future socialist productive enterprise. Socialism could only liberate the proletariat at the end of the "bourgeois epoch" of industrial development.

Years later, as *Duce* of Italy, Mussolini reminded his followers of the argument. He told his audience,

> when I went to the school of socialism, my teachers and doctrinal sages told me that only determinate objective circumstances rendered socialism possible at all. I was told that socialism was only possible after capitalism had achieved its full maturity. . . . [I was told that socialism was possible only] at the conclusion of the bourgeois transformation of the medieval, into a

capitalist, economy. . . . Socialism would be impossible without a fully developed economic base and a class conscious, politically astute proletariat.[17]

Over the years, this very argument was to become central to the rationale of Fascism. Italy, before and after the First World War, was a marginally industrialized nation, totally ill suited to serve as the stage for Marxist revolution. Mussolini was rehearsing the arguments that had been made commonplace by Italy's syndicalists in the years before the Great War.

During those years, the young syndicalist Filippo Corridoni, who was to fall during the First World War, argued that in a community "still in its swaddling clothes . . . [with] three quarters of the nation . . . at precapitalist levels," one could hardly expect a Marxist revolution. In a largely agrarian nation one could only expect to find a small entrepreneurial bourgeoisie inadequate to its developmental tasks, and an equally small collection of politically immature urban wage workers uncertain in their loyalties and irresolute in struggle. In such a nation, the enjoinments of classical Marxism were all but totally irrelevant, and any talk of Marxist revolution was starkly unrealistic—and heavy with theoretical and historical anomalies.[18]

Marx and Engels had anticipated socialist revolution in the advanced industrial societies—in England, Holland, Germany, and the United States.[19] Only an advanced industrial system could produce the material abundance capable of supporting a classless society, in which "to each according to his needs and from each according to his abilities" might serve as an operative principle. Revolution in any other circumstances, Engels warned Marxists, would simply reproduce all the "old filthy business" of inequitable distribution of limited goods, endemic poverty, invidious class distinctions, and systematic oppression.[20] In an environment of anything less than full industrial development, there could be no talk of the "vast majority" of the work force being composed of "class-conscious proletarians."[21] Under such circumstances, revolution would have to be undertaken by declassed intellectuals leading petty bourgeois elements of the population—a prescription dismissed by both Marx and Engels.[22]

By the first decade of the twentieth century some of the major Italian syndicalists recognized that classical Marxism had very little to say to economically retrograde communities facing the revolutionary challenges of the times. There were those who argued that not only were the industrial preconditions for Marxist revolution absent in Italy, but their absence meant that Italians, without the general advantages of industrialization, were condemned to national inferiority, foreign cultural domination, and international humiliation.[23] Only rapid industrialization and economic growth could mitigate the magnitude of the threats.

All these notions gradually matured into what was later to be identified as the "revolutionary nationalism of the poor."[24] It was a variant of revolutionary Marxism designed to address the reality of less developed nations on the periphery of industrial capitalism. Its essentials included a mass-mobilizing strategy and a state-sponsored program of extensive and intensive economic development. It was a formula that was to appear and reappear among revolutionaries everywhere in the industrially backward parts of the globe where people perceived themselves as subject to the impostures of the "plutocracies."

All these convictions had made their appearance before the First World War. Before his death in that war, as a case in point, Filippo Corridoni argued that syndicalist revolutionaries should promote the peninsula's industrial development; they should assist the laggard bourgeoisie in their drive to industrialize; and to that end they should be the advocates of a market-governed system and liberal laws.[25] Blessed with abundant labor mobilized to good purpose, Italy would rapidly enter the machine age. Like the Italian Nationalists, Corridoni early identified revolution on the peninsula with reactive developmental nationalism—and dismissed orthodox Marxism, with its internationalism and class warfare, as an irrelevance.[26]

Thus, when Lenin pretended to bring Marxist revolution to economically primitive Russia in 1917, some of Italy's most aggressive Marxist theoreticians dismissed the claim. If Marxist revolution was impossible in Italy because of its primitive economic circumstances, it was equally impossible in industrially retrograde Russia.[27] Russia was no more industrially mature than the Italian peninsula. In the judgment of many of the revolutionary syndicalists, Lenin's revolution in backward Russia could not possibly pass as "Marxist." None of the minimum objective requirements for the advent of socialism existed there. Whatever had transpired with the succession of the Bolsheviks to power in the Russia of the tsars, it could not have been a "proletarian" revolution.

As early as 1919, Olivetti rejected the suggestion that the Bolshevik revolution had even the remotest connection with classical Marxism. Not only did the revolution violate every precondition established by classical Marxism as essential to proletarian revolution, but in the course of their coup, the Bolsheviks had not only destroyed fixed capital, but alienated those with technological and managerial skills as well. Lenin's revolutionaries had undermined the productive forces that were not only necessary for the ultimate attainment of socialism, but essential to the very foundation of collective life. Valuable plant, machinery, and essential infrastructure were consumed in the tide of violence precipitated by the Bolshevik coup, and there was no evidence that its leaders understood how all this might be rectified or how any of it made sense in the effort to establish socialism.[28]

For Olivetti all this was evidence not only of revolutionary ineptitude, but of a gross failure to understand the essentials of Marxism. He argued that Marxism identified the socialist revolution and the progress implicit in that revolution with the maximum development of productive forces. Not only had the Bolsheviks mounted a revolution before the forces of production had matured to the full measure required for the establishment of socialism; they had destroyed the forces of production in the process. For Olivetti, any organized violence that does not contribute to the extensive and intensive development of the forces of production, whatever its pretended doctrinal rationale, was irretrievably counterrevolutionary.[29]

By the early 1920s, these theses had become characteristic of the syndicalist critique of Bolshevism. Taking their cue from traditional Marxism, syndicalist thinkers identified revolution in the twentieth century with "superior productivity." Without the ability to sustain and enhance the productivity of the community, no meaningful social change would be possible. As a consequence of this conviction, syndicalists maintained that whatever had taken place in Imperial Russia in 1917 had very little to do with meaningful revolution—and still less with Marxist socialism. Bolshevism had brought almost complete devastation to the productive system of the community that it had captured. Having undertaken revolution in the wrong economic environment, the Bolsheviks had not only compromised Marxism, they had participated in what was the all but total destruction of the productive capacity of Imperial Russia.[30]

The logic of the assessment was clear. In countries lacking extensive industrialization, revolution could hardly be "proletarian." Revolution in less-developed economies required "bourgeois" enterprise. Classical Marxism had made it eminently clear that only the entrepreneurial bourgeoisie could industrialize retrograde economic systems. It was the bourgeoisie that would recreate the modern world in its own image and provide the material foundation for the liberating socialist revolution.[31]

Since the bourgeoisie had not completed their task in tsarist Russia, the Bolshevik revolution could not be "proletarian." The tasks before it were, in fact, "bourgeois." Like the Italian Nationalists, the syndicalists insisted that whatever the Bolsheviks had embarked upon in economically retrograde Russia, it could hardly have been "Marxian socialism."[32] The tasks the Bolsheviks faced in revolutionary Russia were those which Marx had assigned to the bourgeoisie—the economic development and industrialization of an agrarian anachronism. The Italian syndicalists insisted that, in the final analysis, "history" would require that the Bolsheviks discharge "bourgeois" responsibilities by industrializing their nation's economy. The syndicalists echoed the judgment of Enrico Corradini: that the "Bolsheviks in Russia were performing the same function as the revolutionary bourgeoisie in pre-industrial Europe during the French Revolution."[33]

Italian syndicalists, like the Nationalists of Enrico Corradini, simply repeated the admonitions of Engels. In 1850, when Engels addressed the issue of
revolution in economically primitive environments, he affirmed that any revolution that attempted to achieve social results that exceeded the productive capacity
of the economy was destined to fail. Under the circumstances, any revolutionary
effort to achieve the stated goals of Marxian socialism in economically backward
environments would inevitably find itself driven back to exceedingly "narrow
limits." When revolutionaries like the religious visionary Thomas Muenzer, for
example, sought to "emancipate the oppressed" in conditions of limited economic development, the effort could only be abortive. In a primitive economic
environment, the leaders of an "extreme party" could do little more than construct "castles in air." What could actually be accomplished was dependent not
upon the subjective will or intentions of revolutionaries, but "on the level of
development of the material means of existence."[34]

Since the Bolsheviks had captured a primitive economy, their task could not
be the easy production of equality and abundance promised by the nineteenth-
century socialism of Karl Marx. Their task could only be the arduous "right-
wing" rapid economic modernization and industrial development characteristic
of the "bourgeois epoch." If industrial development was not the inheritance of a
preceeding period of bourgeois enterprise, revolution in the twentieth century
required that the task be discharged by "classless" revolutionaries. Italian syndicalists, Nationalists, and Futurists were to argue that those revolutionaries
would be Fascists, not Marxists.[35] Fascism, they argued, was the socialism of
"proletarian nations."

By 1921, Fascist thinkers, who included in their number radical Marxists,
Nationalists, and philosophical Idealists, maintained that if the task that confronted retrograde Russia was the rapid development of its productive forces,
nothing less could be said of the tasks that confronted the revolutionaries of the
Italian peninsula. Several things followed, if the argument was accepted. If the
task of revolution in backward economic environments was the rapid industrialization and material development of society, then many of the policies imposed
on a prostrate Russia by the Bolsheviks were "ahistorical."[36] If growth and
modernization were the tasks of revolution, then class warfare and the abolition
of private property were clearly counterproductive. Disciplined collaboration of
all productive elements in a stable system would be a condition of rapid and
sustained economic growth.[37]

If a retarded economic and industrial system was to be extensively and
intensively developed, the continued existence of private property and the incentives that ownership afforded served a clear purpose in what remained essentially a "bourgeois epoch." The ownership of property provided performance

incentives, and the existence of a market provided a rational pricing system, essential to any program of economic development. If rapid industrialization and economic maturation were revolutionary responsibilities, private property recommended itself. The continued existence of private property contributed to conditions critical to the overall process of accelerated and technologically sophisticated growth.[38]

Fascist critics argued that once the purpose of revolution had been made transparent, hierarchical direction and control recommended themselves.[39] Development was understood to be a complex enterprise. It required political stability, collective commitment, and the provision of incentives in political arrangements that were structured and controlled. Developmental nationalism required the existence of a tutelary state—something the Bolshevik revolutionaries pretended not to understand.[40]

Beyond that, it was clear to Fascists, as developmental nationalists, that revolution in primitive socioeconomic systems would require not only an exemplary state presence, but individual and collective discipline and self-sacrifice as well. With only limited welfare benefits available, moral incentives would have to supplement them if collective effort were to be mobilized.[41] There would be material incentives, but the primitive state of the national economy precluded the possibility that material incentives alone would be sufficient to generate the energy required.[42] It would be necessary to elicit from the masses both self-sacrifice and an abiding commitment to the survival and enhancement of the community.[43] Nationalism would have to be an inextricable component of the revolutionary enterprise.[44]

Fascism inherited the bulk of those arguments from the radical Marxists who, by 1919, joined its ranks as organized National Syndicalists.[45] The National Syndicalists had argued that Italy, a "proletarian" nation, with a population that exceeded the support capacity of its soil, lacking raw materials, and capital-poor, would never escape the trap of collective poverty and powerlessness in the modern world unless political and social revolution united all its people in a disciplined national enterprise of systematic, expanding, increasingly sophisticated production. Such a program would necessitate a state-sponsored sacrificial program of frugality, intensive labor, and collective enterprise in the effort to create a "Greater Italy."[46] Material incentives were useful, but the ultimate energy had to be forthcoming from the enthusiasm of masses, mobilized to the national purpose in "heroic" commitment.[47]

Fascists were convinced that economic development constituted a reality that imposed itself on revolutionaries in backward economies. "Its iron laws" were considered "infrangible." Among the "infrangible laws" was that which required that "those who abolish property rights during the early phases of rapid industrial growth and economic modernization must necessarily restore them . . . and those who attempt to do without spiritual, intellectual and moral hierarchies during the unfolding process are constrained to reestablish them." Fascist intellectuals argued that the failures of the Bolsheviks in Russia were object lessons confirming the necessities of a market economy predicated on private property, the existence of a hierarchically structured state, and a program for mass mobilization in an enterprise of national regeneration.[48] Even before Fascism came to power, the National Syndicalists argued that Lenin's Bolsheviks had failed to understand the logic of their circumstances and, as a consequence, had brought ruin to tsarist Russia and its associated territories. The Bolsheviks had thrown Russia into turmoil in the pursuit of "proletarian internationalism," "class warfare," and egalitarian "socialism." The outcome was the destruction of much of the productive potential of Imperial Russia. By 1921, the Bolshevik revolution had brought the former Russian empire to the brink of total collapse, and its population to destitution.

By 1920 or 1921, most of the Marxist critics of Bolshevism in the ranks of Italian National Syndicalism had already marshaled themselves under the guidons of Fascism. As a consequence, orthodox Marxists dismissed their criticisms of Bolshevism as the flawed reasoning of Marxist apostates. Leninists chose to dismiss their arguments and gave themselves over to an interpretation of Italian Fascism devoid of substance and innocent of insight.

Not only did Marxist–Leninist theoreticians fail to understand Fascism, as a consequence of their dismissal of the substantive analysis of the Italian National Syndicalists, they were compelled, as a consequence, to attempt to put together their own interpretation of the curious revolution they had imposed on economically primitive Eastern Europe. To that end, between November 1919 and May 1920, Nikolai Bukharin, one of Bolshevism's major ideologues, produced a manuscript that attempted a Marxist explanation of the events that had overwhelmed Russia.[49]

Bukharin sought to deliver a persuasive interpretation of how Marxist revolution might take place in an environment not only devoid of an industrial base, but lacking the proletarian masses necessary for armed rebellion.[50] What resulted was a somewhat quaint manuscript that set the pattern for Marxist–Leninist responses for the next quarter-century.

In his Preface, Bukharin counselled the proletariat, the "Prometheus class" of world history, to prepare itself for the "inevitable pain of the period of transition" between capitalism and the liberation of communism.[51] That pain and privation were costs that would have to be borne by the Russian people was the consequence of the peculiar circumstances that surrounded the death throes of industrial capitalism. Nothing in the corpus of traditional Marxism suggested

that the revolution and the transition to a socialist society would involve privation of biblical proportions.[52] Lenin's *State and Revolution*, written almost immediately before the October Revolution, seemed to suggest that while the revolution itself would involve the violence of smashing the "bourgeois state" and all its
"repressive adjuncts," the transition from capitalist to socialist society would be
relatively painless.

In his account, Bukharin argued that revolution in Russia had been so difficult because it had been the first expression of what soon would be a universal
uprising against world capitalism. He maintained that the Great War signaled
the advent of the anticipated "General Crisis" of industrial capitalism. He maintained that the Great War had been the final tremor of a dying capitalism.
Compelled by the secular decline in the rate of profit, the rulers of capitalist
society had been driven by cupidity and intense competition into cataclysmic
armed conflict.[53] The war that followed had exacted its revenge. It had destroyed
the economic foundations of international capitalism. Driven to war in an effort
to restore their profits, capitalists had condemned their system to extinction.

The war had drawn off millions of laborers to serve as cannon fodder in the
trenches of Verdun and Flanders. The massacre of young men had cost the
system hundreds of millions of man-hours of labor, as well as a "massive anni-
hilation of productive forces."[54] The losses in manpower and capabilities fatally
impaired a system already grievously wounded by the extraordinary burden
placed upon it by the need to supply the appurtenances of war. In Bukharin's
judgment, once the war was over, capitalism would not be able to reconstruct the
international capitalist economy. Capitalism had lapsed into the final crisis predicted by Marxist theory. As a consequence of that eventuality, the proletarian
revolution had become inevitable and inescapable.

Marxism–Leninism had no choice but to lead a "proletarian" revolution in
circumstances largely devoid of proletarians. Revolutions are made where they
can be made. Like Lenin, Bukharin was convinced that revolution in Europe
and in the most advanced capitalist states would follow close on the heels of the
revolution in Imperial Russia. The postwar socialist revolution had become as
"historically inevitable" as the final crisis of capitalism.[55]

To fail to mount a revolution in such circumstances, whatever the seeming
proscriptions of classical Marxist theory, would be criminally irresponsible. It
would condemn humankind to unimaginable privations. It would postpone the
advent of socialism at a time when the catastropic contraction of economic
activity that would irresistibly follow capitalism's final crisis would threaten the
very survival of the species. Human beings would languish in preindustrial
destitution.

For Bukharin, the fact that Bolshevik Russia found itself in desperate economic circumstances was not the consequence of failing to understand the responsibilities of fomenting revolution in primitive economic conditions; it was the price paid by a vanguard for participation in what would inevitably be a victorious tide of "proletarian revolution." The worldwide victory of socialism would bring the missing industrial potential of capitalism with it, as a prize.[56] Socialism would have its material foundation, and the integrity of classical Marxist doctrine would be restored.

For Bukharin, the entire Bolshevik enterprise was perceived as an elaborate holding action, a preliminary for the final "ineluctable, and inevitable" universal proletarian revolution.[57] With the adherence of the world proletariat, the socialist revolution would finally deliver on the promises of Marxism.

Out of this argument, what was to become the orthodox standard interpretation of fascism was to be fabricated. Fascism was conceived of as an extension of the strategies employed by moribund capitalism to secure a future. Just as international capitalism had driven the world to war in a frantic effort to halt the declining overall rate of profit, so Italy's ruling bourgeoisie had created, subventionized, and directed Fascism to the same purpose. The defeat of the "proletarian revolution" in Italy meant that the peninsula was doomed to lapse into the most primitive forms of productive conditions. Wherever Marxists failed to foment the required revolution, the inability of capitalism to restore the productive levels of the prewar period meant a rapid decline in living standards and privations of a magnitude that would be intolerable. Only systematic recourse to violence and terror, inflicted amidst appeals to mystic irrationalities and ritual chauvinism, could sustain so retrograde and reactionary a system.

As we have seen, this was the interpretation of fascism produced by Marxist theory. It was to mesmerize not only Marxist–Leninists, but the majority of Western academics as well. It was the product of abstract reasoning from suspect premises.

Italian syndicalists had traversed much of the ground covered by Bukharin before the First World War. Those syndicalists who had joined the Fascist ranks after the war, probably without having read Bukharin's account, implicitly rejected all the principal theses of his *Economy of the Period of Transition*. First and foremost, Fascists rejected the notion that the revolutionaries of the twentieth century could anywhere expect a "saving international revolution" to solve urgent national problems.[58] Italian Syndicalists, Nationalists, and neo-Idealists all argued that the internationalism in which the Bolsheviks had invested so much confidence was a fiction. It was a fiction because the reality of the world was that limited associations of persons, identifying themselves through conceived or real affinities, sacrificed and struggled to enhance their survival potential in contests with similarly disposed groups in similar circumstances.[59] At various times and in various climes there would be different in-groups and different out-groups—but there would always be groups animated by dispositions that were group-sustaining.[60] In the world of the twentieth century, a seamless internationalism that failed to recognize the intense nationalism that arose in response to real and fancied humiliations was an implausible fiction that flew in the face of overwhelming evidence.

Given the economic and strategic demands of the modern world, the nation had become, for Fascist theorists, the most effective vehicle for group competition and survival. Fascist theoreticians always argued that Marx and the Marxists never understood the contemporary force of nationalism, because they failed to recognize its sources in the evolutionary history of humankind and its function in the modern world. As a result, Marxists always underestimated the psychological roots of national sentiment and so failed to appreciate the effectiveness of in-group identification and the utility of national symbols in the mobilization of the masses in the service of a collective enterprise.

If nationalism was an expression of an affirmative identification with a community sharing similar interests in an environment of intense competition, Fascists argued, then internationalism was a doctrinal fiction that served only the policy concerns of "sated" nations, those "plutocratic" commodity- and capital-exporting communities, that sought to insure their unrestricted access to market supplements and investment outlets in the less developed regions of the world.[61] Internationalism was the "moral" pretext for economic imperialism. Either that, or it served as the last refuge of timid souls.

Fascists argued that there was very little substance in the internationalism of Marxism—Leninism. There was absolutely no evidence that "proletarian masses" identified themselves with any expression of internationalism. The Great War had demonstrated that human beings identified with communities of limited compass, and that internationalism was an empty dream. Fascists argued that internationalism served conservative, rather than revolutionary, purposes in the world of the twentieth century. The advanced industrial nations, exploiting the less developed economies on their periphery, were the conservative advocates of international stability and peace.

"Proletarian nations," those beset by economic limitations and general poverty, could only be ill served by internationalism. Internationalism was a product of late capitalism, serving the "free trade" interests of imperialism and designed to disarm the resistance of the poor. The notion that nations suffering economic retardation in the modern world might be salvaged by some kind of international proletarian revolution was, at best, delusional.[62] It was far more likely that any commitment to internationalism would leave economically backward nations the victims of exploitation—in a state of perpetual dependency and inescapable underdevelopment. Long before the "New Left" of the 1970s discovered "dependency theory," the first Fascists had given it critical space in their interpretation of the modern world.

Fascist arguments were more critical of Bolshevik theoretical justifications than was suggested by their dismissal of internationalism and their invocation of a version of dependency theory. Very early in the period, for example, Mussolini argued against the claim that industrial capitalism had exhausted its potential and that the Marxist apocalyptic "final crisis" was at hand. Mussolini held that not only had industrial capitalism survived the Great War, but that it gave every evidence of embarking on an expanded cycle of growth. He went on to maintain that "capitalism has just commenced its trajectory of growth. . . . There are immense continents such as Asia, Africa, Australia, and a large part of the Western Hemisphere, that await development. Capitalism remains almost exclusively European, while it is clear that it is destined to become global."[63]

Given the rejection of some of the major premises of the Marxist interpretation of the economic, political, and social circumstances of the early twentieth century, Fascist intellectuals dismissed the entire argument extended by the early Bolsheviks. The Bolshevik revolution was not "inevitable." It was an adventure conducted by those who imagined themselves Marxists, but who had no clear conception of what they were about.

By 1924, the theoreticians of Fascism had rejected all Bukharin's arguments. Capitalism had not exhausted its potential, and the international proletarian revolution would not save the Russian Revolution. The Bolsheviks would have to make do with what they had. In doing with what they had, the Fascists argued, the Bolsheviks would find that they would be driven to fall back on nationalism, restore the preeminent and directive state hierarchy that sustains it, and embark on a developmental program for the devastated national economy.[64]

For at least those reasons, Mussolini insisted not only that Marxism was irrelevant to Russian circumstances, but that it was irrelevant to the history of our time. Mussolini conceived of the world as divided into advanced, "plutocratic" nations and those nations that were less developed. The industrially advanced nations would continue to profit through the expansion of capitalism— Marxism had very little relevance for them. Those nations that were "late developers," on the other hand, required not Marxist revolution, "proletarian internationalism," or "class conflict," but a state-directed strategy of rapid, massive, sustained economic growth and technological development.[65]

Mussolini argued that reality had thrust that truth on a reluctant Lenin. By 1920, Lenin had attempted to restart the Soviet economy with the improvisations of his New Economic Policy. He had allowed the reemergence of some private ownership and the restoration of free markets for the sale of some agricultural produce. He had allowed private enterprise on the margins of the system he had created. And he was prepared to make generous concessions to foreign capitalists if they would invest capital in, and help manage, the newborn "socialist" community. At some stage in that involutionary process, Lenin, the anti-capitalist Marxist revolutionary and irrepressible anti-nationalist internationalist, lapsed into extending concessions to capitalists and capitalism, as well as enjoining the revolutionary "proletarians" to serve their "socialist fatherland."[66]

By 1924 or 1925 it had become obvious that there would be no "saving revolution" in the West that would rescue the failing "proletarian" revolution in what had been the empire of the tsars.[67] Among the Bolsheviks, there was a scramble to provide a Marxist rationale for the unanticipated sequence of events and the implications it brought in its train. It was evident that Lenin had no clear idea of what was transpiring, nor did he offer a clear program of resolution. Even before his death in 1924, it seemed obvious that Lenin had lost control of his revolution.

In 1917, two months before the Bolsheviks seized state power, Lenin had written that, following the victory of the proletarian revolution, the abolition of the state bureaucracy would be the most distinguishing feature of the "dictatorship of the proletariat." At that time, Lenin was convinced that the revolution would inherit the institutional maturity of an advanced industrial economy. According to the notions of traditional Marxist theory, Lenin believed that by the time of the revolution, monopoly capital would have so simplified production and circulation that immediately after the "proletarian" seizure of power, the postrevolutionary economy could be governed by exceedingly simple operations—registration, filing, and regulation—nonmarket clerical activities that could be performed by any literate person.[68] Lenin imagined that there would be no need for a professional state bureaucracy in a "proletarian dictatorship."

In retrospect, it seems evident that either Lenin knew nothing about the primitive state of the Russian economy, or he imagined that the Bolshevik revolution would be immediately followed by world revolution. If the latter was the case, it soon became apparent that there would be no "saving revolution" from the industrialized West that might deliver the vast resources, technology, plant, and institutional and managerial sophistication required to render socialism viable.[69] As a consequence, once it became clear that the revolution would be confined to the political boundaries of the former Russian empire, Lenin was compelled to create a complex bureaucratic state apparatus to ensure the most elementary productive efficiency of the retrograde, primitive economy under his control.

In the years between the Bolshevik coup and his death, Lenin lamented the "primitive conditions" of postrevolutionary Russia. He complained of the "semi-

Asiatic incompetence" and "barbarism" of the Russian working class. He recognized that what the Bolshevik economy required was "Prussian railroad efficiency plus American technology and organization of trusts plus American public school education," and so forth.[70] In effect, what the emerging Soviet Union required was economic and industrial maturity. That economic maturity would have to be purchased by the revolutionaries by desperately hard labor. Italy's National Syndicalists had been right. The tasks faced by the revolution were not those Marx had identified as "liberating"; they were tasks that could only be discharged under the direction of an authoritarian state.

Before his death, Lenin recognized that his government would have to feed, clothe, and house an entire population. At the very least, the new government was required to "keep going until the socialist revolution [was] victorious in the more developed countries." The new regime could not endure unless "large-scale machine industry" and all its adjuncts could be put together in marginally industrialized Russia.[71] In order to satisfy its responsibilities, the Bolshevik leadership undertook a "strategic retreat" to "re-create" a form of capitalism that would be "subordinate to the state and serve the state."[72] The unabashed appeal to the tutelary, managerial, and hierarchical state confirmed all the anticipatory judgments advanced years before by the Italian National Syndicalists and the heretical Marxists among the Fascists.

Once Lenin passed into history, those who followed were compelled to pursue some variant of the course he had initiated. Before his death, Lenin made Josef Stalin General Secretary of the Party, and it was Stalin who decided to embark upon an intense program to "build socialism in one country." Bolshevism had taken on all the major features of a developmental dictatorship. By the time Stalin made that decision, anyone with independent judgment could recognize what had happened. By then, even Bukharin recognized that the circumstances in which the "proletarian revolution" found itself required a developmental strategy vastly different from anything to be found in the works of traditional Marxism.

Bukharin advocated a developmental strategy involving the collaboration of the proletariat, the peasantry, and the bourgeoisie under the auspices of the "proletarian state." Over and above the conditional collaboration of classes, the state would ensure the civil peace and order essential to rapid industrialization and development.[73] The nonregime Marxists in Europe, including those who had passed into Fascist ranks, had been correct. "Socialism" in the Stalinist Soviet Union had devolved into a state- and party-dominant system that would have been totally unrecognizable to Marx or Engels.

"Marxist Russia" had been transformed into a developmental nationalism. The state, with all its "bourgeois" attributes, was restored. It would ensure social tranquility, control labor, extract surplus, and mobilize resources to serve the ends of the "socialist fatherland," all under the auspices of a hegemonic party dominated by a "charismatic leader."[74] Already at that stage in the process of involution, there were many Marxists and non-Marxists who recognized the emerging features. Bukharin, originally a major architect of the new political system, began to be troubled.

Evgeni Preobrazhenski, certainly less troubled, provided a new "Marxist" rationale for the emerging system. Because the post-Leninist system required not only restarting a stalled economy, but its extensive and intensive growth, Preobrazhenski recommended a program of "primitive socialist accumulation" of capital that, by the late 1920s, would grow into massive "tribute" to be extracted from the peasant and urban working classes. Incalculable sums were to be invested by the state in a capital-intensive developmental program.

Once the decision had been made to industrialize a peasant economy, the new Soviet state assumed more and more onerous extractive functions in order to supply the capital necessary to fuel and sustain economic growth and development. It also assumed more and more directive functions as those parts of the economy allowed to operate through market exchanges contracted. More and more of public life was governed by a complex hierarchy of bureaucratic state institutions responsible only to a small, self-selected committee of party stalwarts. "Soviet patriotism" provided the focus for collective sacrifice and obedience— and Josef Stalin loomed ever larger over the entire system as the *Vozhd*, the "Leader" and "Father of Peoples."

In the course of all this, the entire system took on the further properties of an epistemocracy. Rule in the Soviet Union was reserved exclusively to those who knew and accepted the "Truth." In 1924, Trotsky had unselfconsciously insisted that all Marxists commit themselves to the proposition that the Communist Party (Bolshevik) was "always right."[75] By the time Stalin assumed dictatorial control, "Marxism–Leninism"—the "only true social science"—legitimated single-party rule and was accorded the role of inerrant guide to the conduct of all Marxist revolutionaries. Just like Fascism, Stalinism had discovered that charismatic rule implied that leadership must be understood to be "always right." Leadership, party, and state dominance of an entire complex system could rationally be justified only by a claim to inerrancy.

By the time of these developments, Bukharin's misgivings were irrepressible. He began to allude to the "fascist" features of the emerging system.[76] By the early 1930s, the "convergence" of Fascism and Stalinism struck Marxists and non-Marxists alike. In 1934, Drieu La Rochelle was "profoundly convinced that Stalinism was a semi-fascism."[77] By the mid-1930s, even Trotsky could insist that

"Stalinism and fascism, in spite of deep difference in social foundations, are symmetrical phenomena."[78]

During those years, a number of Fascist authors alluded to the doctrinal and institutional features shared by Italian Fascism and Stalin's socialism. They did so in part to affirm the "universality of the Fascist idea" and in part to confirm the predictive competence of the earliest Fascist theorists, whose schooling in traditional Marxism had led them to anticipate the kinds of social and political instrumentalities that the accelerated economic development of a primitive economy would require in the modern world.

As early as 1934, Fascists had argued that "in the course of its development, the Russian revolution has gradually given evidence of fully abandoning Marxist postulates and of a gradual, if surreptitious, acceptance of certain fundamental political principles identified with Fascism."[79] Just as the National Syndicalists had suggested, Bolshevism could be viable only if it abandoned the substance of the Marxism it pretended was its inspiration.

More than that, toward the end of the 1930s, serious Fascist theorists sought to emphasize the fact that Bolshevism, as a form of Marxism, had entirely misconstrued the challenges of the contemporary world. Soviet doctrinal literature continued to feature internationalist, democratic, anti-statist, and socialist themes—at a time when Stalinism was becoming increasingly more nationalist, authoritarian, and statist, and manifestly less socialist.[80]

By the 1930s, Stalinism had transformed itself in its efforts to respond effectively to challenges it had not anticipated and with which it was not prepared to cope. In attempting to address the problems generated by the effort to industrialize the Soviet Union, the Stalinist regime reinterpreted the central theses of classical Marxism and "dialectically" transformed the anarcho-syndicalist and anti-statist ideas of Lenin into "political formulae calculated to galvanize the Russian people to the service of industrial development and nationalist purpose."[81]

With the redefinition of the goals of the revolution came a series of programmatic revisions. There was no longer any pretense of "proletarian" or working-class control of the means of production. Production, its organization, and its management were all state-governed. Labor unions became agencies of the state, "transmission belts" for directives from the Kremlin. By the mid-1930s, Stalinism had created the most complex, hierarchical, authoritarian state structure in history.[82] Together with the state, Stalin created one of the most impressive coercive machines ever. For national security, vast quantities of scarce capital and technology were invested in the Soviet armed forces. Never again was Russia to be defeated in battle because of its "backwardness." The military was to become a dominant Soviet institution, and its heroes were to serve as models for Soviet citizens.

For domestic security, resources were lavished on agencies designed to control an unarmed population through state-sponsored demonstrative and prophylactic terror. Together with state control of information and education, all these population management mechanisms produced the requisite compliant behavior. Gone was the "left-wing" frenetic anti-nationalism, anti-statism, and anti-militarism of the early days of the revolution that had made socialism the mortal enemy of "right-wing" Fascism.[83] There was a pervasive recognition that Stalinism, as a system, had "dialectically thrown overboard the principles in whose name" the Bolshevisk revolution had been undertaken, and that "Marxist–Leninist principles" had been transformed into their " 'contraries,' that is to say, the ideas that provide body and substance to the Fascism of Mussolini."[84]

Fascist theoreticians pointed out that the organization of Soviet society, with its inculcation of an ethic of military obedience, self-sacrifice and heroism, totalitarian regulation of public life, party-dominant hierarchical stratification, all under the dominance of the inerrant state, corresponded, in form, to the requirements of Fascist doctrine.[85]

The people of the Soviet Union were urged to work and sacrifice in the collective effort to assure their nation's greatness, to secure its historic boundaries, and ensure its sovereignty in a hostile world.[86] Soviet citizens had a mission, determined not by class consciousness or simple economic imperatives. It was a mission informed by Soviet patriotism, by a compelling sentiment of community, and an irresistible sense of obligation—all imparted by systematic inculcation through central control of general education. All this, Fascists argued, constituted a clear recognition that Marxism, in whatever guise, had failed, and that "the Kremlin was ready to tread the path already undertaken by Fascism."[87]

Towards the end of the 1930s, few Fascist intellectuals denied that the social and political system put together in the Soviet Union substantially overlapped that fashioned by Fascism.[88] Whatever distinctions were drawn, and however emphatically those distinctions were insisted upon, no Fascist intellectual failed to note the significant institutional and behavioral similarities of Fascism and Stalinism.

In 1933, after the Fascist regime had passed through periods of relative liberalism and economic *laissez-faire*, Mussolini announced that "corporativism," the preferred productive system of the Fascist state, involved the "complete organic and totalitarian regulation of production with a view to the expansion of the wealth, political power and well-being of the Italian people."[89] As early as the end of the 1920s, Fascists had spoken of the corporate state as "controlling, coordinating and harmonizing all the forms of productive energy" that contribute to the progressive increments in material wealth of the nation.[90]

With that characterization of the Fascist state, Fascist theorists were prepared to acknowledge that not only had Soviet "communism gravitated increasingly to the right, . . . Fascism had moved increasingly toward the left. The
conviction that there was an absolute antithesis between Moscow and Rome on
matters dealing with the national economy, was false." Fascist intellectuals anticipated that both systems would ultimately fuse, to produce the general outline of
an economy that satisfied the needs of the twentieth century.[91]

Fascism's major intellectual spokesmen did not hesitate to identify the similarities of Fascism and Stalinism. Ugo Spirito, one of Fascism's foremost theoreticians, maintained that Fascism and Bolshevism, as the two revolutionary systems of the modern world, shared fundamental affinities. He argued that those
affinities would ultimately lead to a "synthesis": Fascism, a "superior revolutionary form," would absorb "everything alive and fruitful" to be found in that
Bolshevism that had already abandoned the critical postulates of Marxism.[92]

Mussolini himself argued that because of the singular conditions of the
twentieth century, the "corporate solution" would "force itself to the fore everywhere." He was convinced that the Soviet Union had already traversed much of
the distance between the "Sovietism" of the Bolshevik revolution of 1917 and a
future Fascism, through the "crypto-fascism" of Josef Stalin.[93]

Within the similarities, Mussolini identified some of the major distinctions
separating Fascism from Stalinism. Among them were Fascism's qualified defense of private property and a disposition to proceed "circumspectly in the field
of economy."[94] Fascism, he maintained, was prepared to experiment with various forms of control and guidance of the nation's economy but was ill disposed to
exclusively bureaucratic institutionalization.[95] In Fascist Italy, the basic features
of an essentially market economy were to be preserved.

The fascism that Mussolini anticipated would become dominant in the twentieth century would be a fascism having all the major attributes of the Stalinism
of the Soviet Union, but allowing private property and the market, to provide
both a rational price structure for the entire system and some measure of overall
productive efficiency.[96] The suppression of private property and the market in
the Soviet Union of Josef Stalin was sufficient, in the eyes of Fascist theoreticians,
to distinguish it from the paradigm.

Stalinism was only one of the modern systems gradually adapting itself to the
model. Fascist theorists fully expected to see such systems ultimately transform
themselves into perfect analogs of the model they had provided on the Italian
peninsula. They fully expected the twentieth century to be a century of Fascism.

By the end of the 1930s, Italian Fascism had entered its final phase. War had
been successfully fought in Spain, and Fascism had embarked upon the acquisition of colonies that it imagined would provide the raw materials fundamental to

the self-sustained and self-sustaining industrialization of the Italian peninsula.[97] By the middle of 1937, Fascism was being drawn further and further into the maelstrom of what would be the Second World War.

For Mussolini, Fascist Italy faced the "plutocratic nations" in what he conceived to be a decisive contest for sovereign independence, cultural autonomy, space, resources, and international prestige.[98] The inequities of the modern world were to be finally resolved.[99] The "proletarian peoples" would finally secure their place in the sun.

Fascism was consumed in the world war that followed. What it left behind was an interrelated set of concepts that afforded an interpretation of Stalinism, an accounting of the revolutionary movements of our time, and an interpretation of how Fascism itself was to be understood. Through the two decades that followed the advent of Fascism on the Italian peninsula until its disappearance in the Second World War, Marxist–Leninist thinkers persisted in the interpretation of fascism they had jerry-built out of the conjectures of Nikolai Bukharin. During the interwar years they had used this interpretation to very little theoretical effect. Captives of that interpretation, Marxist–Leninist theoreticians failed to understand not only their own system, but almost everything of importance that was occurring around them. In the decades that followed, they and the regime that Marxism–Leninism had built were swept away. Out of the collapse, the anticipated Russian fascism made its fulsome appearance.

Fascism, Marxism, and Race

That Soviet Marxists, with the collapse of the regime they had legitimated for seven decades, found themselves drawn to some variant of fascism is explicable, it can be argued, once one understands something of Mussolini's Fascism. Without the thicket of confusions that impaired Marxist thought after the failure of anticipated revolution in the advanced capitalist countries, the reactive nationalism that had always inspired Russian radical thought took on the logic of Fascism. Fascism spoke to the revolutionary leadership of those nations that conceived themselves as treated as inferiors by the "advanced powers." The informal logic of reactive nationalism reveals itself in the postures assumed by less developed countries in the twentieth century.

With the collapse of the Soviet Union from "superpower" to a nuclear armed "third world nation," the entire psychology of a humbled nation is engaged. In the ruins of the former Soviet Union, humiliation and despair fuel a reactive nationalism that should be familiar to those who know something of revolution in the twentieth century. The mythic appeals to a glorious past, the anti-liberal and anti-democratic posturing, the irredentist reconstruction of empire, the appeal to a "magnificent state," and the anticipated role of "heroic" elites—are all reminiscent of the Fascist revolution.

Beyond that, however, is something more ominous. If Marxism in less developed environments is condemned to devolve into some form of fascism, how much of fascism will be accommodated in the process? One of the features of fascism that Western academics have tended to identify as peculiarly "right-wing" is "racism." Racism has been made the defining property of "right-wing extremism" and singularly characteristic of fascism.

That racism has surfaced in the political notions of Russia's new nationalists and old communists has created a puzzle for those who divide the political universe into left and right wings. Because of the presence of "racist thought" among former communists and current nationalists in Russia, many commentators have begun to refer to the "die-hard communists" of Eastern Europe as "right-wing extremists." Entirely unselfconscious about the paradox involved in such creative naming, these commentators have stumbled on a feature of senescent Marxism they would rather leave unexplored.

There is an interesting historic connection between Marxism and racism that is rarely considered. That contemporary Marxists have found refuge in one or another form of racism has perplexed analysts, simply because no thought is given to that connection. Most recently, the convoluted ethnobiological work of Lev Nikolaevich Gumilev has become a doctrinal favorite among those Marxist–Leninists in post-Soviet Russia who have made the easy transition from "left" to "right." Gumilev's major work, *Ethnogenesis and the Biosphere*, was written as a supplement to, and an application of, the historical materialism of Karl Marx, and was published as such by the Marxist–Leninist state publishing house before the definitive collapse of the Soviet Union.[1]

Concerned with the rise and fall of civilizations and the formation and decline of *ethnoi*, Gumilev's work has been assessed as "racist" by critics.[2] Whether credible or not, it is clear that Gumilev's discussions turn on the evolution of ethnic communities that, in time, stabilize themselves as nations and civilizations—not simply as socioeconomic and political communities, but as "biophysical realities . . . surrounded by a social envelope of some sort."

Gumilev insists that his concepts have nothing to do with traditional racial theories, but he does speak of ethnogenesis as a complex biological process that, over time, sees ethnoi organized as tribes, clans, city-states, and more complex configurations, ultimately to find expression in the history of nations. He speaks of ethnoi as "stable collectives of individuals each of which opposes itself to all other similar collectives."[3]

In opposing themselves to out-groups, the survival needs of ethnoi compel the cultivation of behaviors "by which the interests of the collective will become higher than personal ones." Gumilev holds that "group sentiment," out-group enmity and in-group amity, is a common element in the evolution of ethnoi and the history of nations, and that collectivities must inculcate norms of behavior that enhance the survival, perpetuity, and prevalence of the community.[4]

The entire life of ethnoi is sustained by emotions of attraction and repugnance, of self-sacrifice, commitment, discipline, and "drive." Ethnoi arise, expand, stabilize, contract, and decay in response to "an irrational . . . passionate . . . craving for power" that invests not only individuals, but entire ethnoi, in the perpetual struggle for survival and triumph that is at the center of ethnogenesis.[5]

The ethnoi that survive and prevail in that struggle, create "superethnoi"—civilizations that shape the history of the world.

Ethnoi are "natural," complex products of geography, genetic mixture, biology, group affinities, economic, cultural, and political influences all finding expression in a mode of production, language, faith, and a sense of historic destiny.[6] Each ethnos results from the "creation of a new stereotype of behavior" that defines it, with each new "stereotype" arising from "peoples' instinctive activity."[7] The new "stereotype" is cultivated in each political community by sanctioned social norms communicated through education and often through symbol and ritual.

However one wishes to interpet all this, Gumilev's ideas share considerable similarities with Fascist doctrine as formulated by some of Fascism's most notable thinkers. There is the suggestion that nationalism and some form of "racism" share some relationship in the ideologies of reactive nationalism. In Fascism, explicit biological racism played only a marginal role.[8] It bore very little, if any, similarities to the biological determinism that was at the heart of Hitler's National Socialism. Fascism's "racism" was a form of racism that grew out of the intense nationalism that animated the system. As such, it was an integral part of Fascist doctrine before the appearance of National Socialism. It was a predictable product of reactive nationalism.

A case for the contention that some form of racism is a product of reactive nationalism can be made by considering Fascist thought as a paradigmatic instance of reactive nationalism. Fascism gave rise to a form of racism that the more competent Fascist thinkers articulated, Fascist intellectuals celebrated, and which, in our own time, Marxist–Leninists have begun to mimic.

Fascists identified their revolution with a "new era of [national] development."[9] This notion implied that the international community had entered into a protracted period of revolution in which poor and less developed nations would be compelled to put together a strategy designed to allow them to effectively compete against those nations that enjoyed the advantage of early industrialization.[10] Such a strategy almost invariably involved "proletarian nations" in a program of rapid economic development in order to produce a domestic industrial base for industrially retarded nations capable of providing credible defensive potential as well as substantial power projection.

Given these sorts of convictions, Sergio Panunzio, one of the regime's most prominent ideologues, identified the "breaking out of the vicious circle of underdevelopment" as one of Fascism's principal responsibilities. Italy, capital-poor, oppressed by the burden of overpopulation, and without natural resources, would have to undertake an arduous program of rapid industrial development and economic growth if it were to survive and prevail in the frenetic competition of the twentieth century. Sustained, intense collaboration between all population elements, under the superintendence of an authoritarian "national discipline," would be required if that were to be accomplished.[11]

To assure the requisite discipline, a "unitary and monolithic" state would have to assume pedagogical, administrative, security, and executive responsibilities that would provide in such a way that "everything was within the state, nothing outside the state, and nothing against the state."[12] For Fascism, the state must, of necessity, be "totalitarian."[13]

For Fascists, the nation, given structure by the state, was understood to afford the promise of collective and individual realization, without which life was without meaning or purpose. The nation was conceived of as the gift of antecedent generations, the moral foundation of self-realization, the hope for oneself and one's children, and the inspirational "myth" of the present.[14] Given explicit form by the state, the "nation" was the central empirical and normative concept in Fascist theory. It was the nation that must arm itself in order to pursue its renovative mission. A nation united, inspired by its antiquity and its accomplishments, led by a charismatic elite, and informed by a strong state, would create the material means necessary to prevail against "plutocratic" enemies.

In theory, Marxists refused to consider the possibility that nationalism could serve any such ends. For Marxists, nationalism had to be a subterfuge, a contrivance employed by the "class enemies" of the proletariat to serve capitalist interests and corrupt revolutionary "class consciousness."

For Fascists, nationalism was their primary "myth," and around that "central and dominant" concept, all the "thought, doctrine and literature of Fascism" collected itself.[15] It was a mythic "exaltation of the Fatherland" that was to serve as the emotional foundation intended to assure system maintenance and the realization of developmental goals.[16] The nation, its history, its past glories, its antiquity and its attainments all occupied space in the political imagery of Fascist mobilization.

In Italy, in the decade before and the two decades of the regime, proto-fascist and Fascist theoreticians generated an enormous body of doctrinal literature devoted to an analysis and explication of the concepts *nation* and *nationalism*.[17] Some of the most interesting and important material in this body of literature was the work of some of the century's most gifted political theorists—Roberto Michels among them.[18] Michels was not only a classic political theorist, he was a major Fascist ideologue as well.[19]

Michels, unlike the Marxists of his time and since, treated the concepts *nation* and *nationalism* seriously. He treated both as historical products, the consequence of popular response to a shared culture, a common history, and psychological suggestion, in a specific historic environment.[20] Michels, like many proto-fascist and Fascist theoreticians, was prepared to argue that human beings were intrinsically disposed to identify themselves with one or other collectivity—which one being determined, in large part, by time-conditioned circumstances.[21] Within the loose constraints of those circumstances, suggestible masses could be led by resolute elites.[22]

For proto-fascist and Fascist thinkers alike, human beings were understood to be, by nature, social, associative, political creatures. They seek out, and live out their lives in association with, their similars. Language, culture, territorial affinity, social visibility, religious conviction, together with the memories of ancient glories, a shared history, or an anticipated future, provide the grounds for a durable sense of in-group identification.[23] Nationalism was one dramatic form assumed by that identification and could be expected to recur in the course of revolutionary crisis throughout the twentieth century.

In the course of history, identification of the individual with a group, a tribe, a city-state, or a nation would be the product of a number of complex influences. The community with which individuals identify could be the result, among other things, of demanding collective enterprise, external threat, or economic necessity. It could be the consequence of enduring humiliation, the result of a sense of inadequacy in the face of challenge by out-groups, or the reactive product of real or perceived predations suffered at the hands of others.[24] In the modern era, it was argued, national sentiment is very often the reactive product of group affirmation in the face of challenge, provocation, threat, oppression, and hopelessness.[25] Michels framed all these notions as though they were lawlike regularities.

Michels, like those who preceded him and those who followed him, argued that in the modern world it is the nation with which the individual characteristically identifies. Lesser communities—tribes and city-states—no longer offer the prospect of protection, opportunity, and survival they once did.[26] Michels argued that although humankind had harbored the disposition to organize itself in self-regarding communities since time immemorial, only in the modern period had the nation served that purpose.[27] In the modern world only the nation can provide the resources and capabilities sufficient to ensure the survival and prosperity of the individual in the face of challenge.[28]

Given this kind of assessment, proto-fascists and Fascists alike rejected the entire theoretical schema offered by classical Marxism as an interpretation of nationalism in the nineteenth and twentieth centuries.[29] For Michels, nationalism was a time- and circumstance-specific response to the generic human disposition to identify with some determinate group of similars. It was natural to the human condition.

The sense of nationhood—nationalist sentiment—was the group response to prevailing objective conditions as well as psychological suggestion. In some special circumstances—as the result of trauma associated with international or domestic confict or catastrophic economic failure, for example—human beings become particularly susceptible to group-building influences.[30]

Nation building is a concrete instance of the human disposition to identify with one or another or a collection of organized aggregates. This disposition is the product of a psychology shaped in evolutionary time by the protracted human struggle for survival in hazardous environments.[31] In almost any conceivable "natural" environment, survival threats overwhelm the solitary individual and recommend his identification with a larger community. Those ill disposed to identify with a larger group perish. Individuals who do so identify tend to have a greater survival potential and correspondingly higher reproductive rates. Over time, those given to identification with a community of similars predominate among populations everywhere. Given such convictions, all major Fascist thinkers could argue that *Homo sapiens* was, by nature, a social animal.[32]

Nationalism is the reaction of human beings as group animals to the challenges and risks of the twentieth century—and a function of the incitements and suasion of elites.[33] Nationalism is the abiding sense of belonging that fosters the individual's identification with an articulated community wherein he not only survives, and perhaps prospers, but in which he defines himself as well.[34] Nationalism, Fascists argued, would be a recurrent and inevitable feature of the revolutionary twentieth century.

In effect, all Fascist ideologues, whether social scientists, jurists, philosophical idealists, or apologists, explicitly rejected the classical Marxist notion that nationality and the sentiment of nationality were simple reflections of elite economic interests.[35] They also implicitly or expressly rejected the liberal notion that individuals, in the "state of nature," survive in solitary "freedom" and only come together as a consequence of a social contract predicated on self-regarding interest.

Fascist theoreticians of the caliber of Michels, Giovanni Gentile, Sergio Panunzio, and Carlo Costamagna put together an understanding of nationalism that conceived of it as a historic product influenced, but not determined, by affinities of ethnicity, language, history, and culture.[36] The sense of nationality is established, cultivated, and enhanced by intellectual elites who use all the instruments of suggestion, moral suasion, and pedagogy in its furtherance.[37]

In one of the more important pieces of legislation of the Fascist regime, the nation was spoken of as "an organism having ends, life, and instrumentalities superior in power and in duration to those of the individuals or aggregates of individuals of which it is composed. It is a moral, political and economic unity that achieves integral realization in the Fascist state."[38] For Fascist theoreticians, the state is the concrete embodiment of the nation. While the state is "trans-historical" in essence, since every organized aggregate of human beings requires governance, at any given time it is the product of that time's psychology and that time's circumstances.[39] At any of those junctures, the state provides concrete form to the material provided by history.[40]

Fascists argued that in the modern world, the state, particularly the state that has charged itself with a revolutionary mission, discharges enormous respon-sibilities. In its revolutionary commitment to the creation of a "Greater Nation," it must restore lost territories, defend its boundaries, protect its culture, assure the continued prosperity of the community by securing its productive base, provide for its freedom from the dominance of foreign influence, mediate be-tween the assertive corporate interests of business and labor, inculcate the princi-ples that enhance collective life, as well as train successive generations of those who will implement national policy.[41]

By the end of the Great War, the first Fascists were consistently arguing that the primary task of a truly revolutionary state would be the "salvaging, protect-ing and assisting [the nation's] magnificent industrial development," the founda-tion of a new and greater Italy.[42] As early as 1914, Michels had counseled Italians that only industrialization could assure them a place in the modern world.[43] All this would require enormous discipline, self-sacrifice, and commitment to the larger community.

Fascists always considered the world a hostile place—a place in which com-petition was intense and weakness a fatal flaw. It was a place in which the "hegemonic nations" had seized not only most of the earth's surface, but its resources as well, and in which the advanced industrial powers systematically sought to thwart the industrialization of those less developed, in what was seen as a veritable "class struggle" between nations.[44]

The sense of disadvantage—the conception that the nation, both poor and less developed, might forever remain the servile inferior of the more advanced industrialized powers—became a constant incitement among Fascists. The ap-peal to the glories of the past and hope in the future were calculated to mobilize effort, discipline performance, provide noneconomic benefits, and ensure un-coerced commitment.

Fascists maintained that for those nations undergoing late development, it was necessary to tap the deep sense of humiliation, the prevailing feeling of collective privation that typified their populations, if revolutionary leaders were to mobilize them to developmental enterprise. In order to sustain the tempo of development once undertaken, Fascist theorists were convinced that it would be necessary to engage whole populations at the most profound level of collective sensibilities.

In order to mobilize the forces for revolution and to engage and sustain an entire population in a renovative and transformative enterprise, "nonlogical" appeals through sign, symbol, and ritual helped to assure commitment, obedience, and endurance. Fascists anticipated that all developmental regimes would have to assume some of these strategies if they were to be successful in the twentieth century. There was little that was "irrational" in any of this. Fascist social theorists argued that the vast majority of human beings characteristically respond to emotive appeal, to symbols and ceremonial ritual. Fascists rejected the notion that human beings in general could be moved to intense labor and selfless sacrifice through exclusively rational appeal. In their judgment, most human beings were largely creatures of passion, ideals, will, and impulse—a conviction that is not uncommon among contemporary social psychologists.

Fascists were convinced by the arguments found in works like those of Gaetano Mosca, Vilfredo Pareto, and Gustav Le Bon, that individual and collective human action, more likely than not, was motivated by suggestibility, passion, and "nonlogical" influences.[45] The judgment that such was the case was not consequence of mystical intuition; it was based on the then available sociological evidence. Fascist judgments in this regard were the result of rational calculation. In order to undertake mass mobilization, to succeed in eliciting compliance behavior, it would be necessary to engage the passions, the ideals, and the sentiments of subject populations.[46]

Fascists argued that the intensity with which the entire collection of group-building sentiments were cultivated, celebrated, and rewarded created the conditions for the appearance of "charismatic" leaders among "suggestible" masses.[47] More than that, those same group-building sentiments produced a propensity to conceive the community as organically bound together not only in moral union, historical continuity, and cultural homogeneity, but through biological affinity as well.[48]

Even before the march on Rome, Mussolini indicated that Fascism had dedicated itself to creating out of the forty million citizens of the peninsula a "great family," united by blood in "one single pride of race" and steeled by an abiding "racial solidarity."[49] The biological continuity of a people that had given the world the "grandeur of Rome" and the "Universal Church," as well as the art, science, architecture, and literature of the Renaissance, was identified as "racial." Fascists regularly spoke of Italians as a "race" of "sublime heroes" who had made their prodigal contributions to civilization against all odds.[50] The race was traced back to the earliest antiquities of the Italic peninsula.

More often than not, the term *race* was used as though it were synonymous with *people* or *nation*.[51] As the regime matured, however, an entire body of literature was produced that provided the term with relatively specific biological reference.[52] In its most sophisticated use, the term *race* was used among scholars and social scientists in Fascist Italy to refer to a breeding population that had been subject to relatively long reproductive isolation. Such a population, isolated by geography, in-group sentiment, out-group enmity, culture, or politics, reproducing within the confines of a restricted breeding-circle, would gradually take on properties, "stereotypical behavior," that could be represented in terms of statistical modalities—sometimes spoken of as "national character" or "racial traits."

The best of the theoreticians in Fascist Italy entertained a conception of *race* as a dynamic constant, the product of geographic and social isolation, attendant inbreeding, natural and artificial selection, and genetic variability.[53] According to the thesis, any "breeding-circle," isolated by whatever circumstances, was a potential race.[54]

Fascists thus spoke of nations as "races in formation," infilling the nation with still more significance. "Long established nations," it was affirmed, can, over time, "solidify themselves into races, become new races."[55] Thus, there was talk of a "mesodiacritic" Italian race, formed in relatively "pure" breeding isolation for almost a thousand years.[56]

These notions concerning race developed, in substantial part, before the advent of National Socialism in Germany. Fascist racism was not mimetic. Independent of National Socialist influence, Fascist racism, together with statism, developed effortlessly and coherently out of reactive nationalist enthusiasm. In fact, major Fascist theoreticians, more often than not, rejected the "materialistic" implications of biological determinism that typified the racism of Hitler's Germany.[57] Race, for Fascists, whatever the mixed ethnic elements out of which it arose, was a historic product, forged over an extended period of time in the crucible of rule-governed institutions.[58] It was shaped by political will and sustained by a sense of cultural integrity.[59]

For our present purposes, what is most interesting in these theoretical developments is the fact that some of those most responsible for the argument were originally radical Marxists. However unorthodox their Marxism may have been as revolutionary syndicalists, Marxists in Italy recognized them as "comrades in socialism." Some scholars have found it difficult to understand how some of the most radical Marxists of pre–First World War Italy could, by the commencement of the Second World War, lend their intelligence to any doctrine of racism whatsoever. Yet, there are precedents and significant instances which suggest the real possibility that Marxism and Marxists in the revolutionary crises of the twentieth century have followed a similar process of transformation that has concluded not only in emphatic nationalism, but in one or another form of racism as well.

Among the revolutionary syndicalists who ultimately contributed to the articulation of the Fascist doctrine of "natioracism," Roberto Michels, Sergio Panunzio, and Paolo Orano were perhaps the most important.[60] They made a transition, common to an entire class of Marxist radicals, from being the advocates of a proletarian, anti-capitalist, universal social revolution to being adepts of nationalism, statism, and a form of racism.

In our own time, we have witnessed a similar process in the last days of the Soviet Union. By that time, Lev Gumiliev's "ethnogenesis" had captured the imagination of some of the foremost intellectuals in the ranks of Marxism–Leninism. Gumiliev's "ethnogenetic Eurasianism," alive with the notion of the evolution of ethnoi from tribal communities to nation-states to civilizations, traces an intellectual course all but identical to that of the "racism" of paradigmatic Fascism. By the time of the disappearance of the Soviet Union, Gumiliev's "racism" had captured the imagination of Gennadi Ziuganov and his "national patriotic" Marxist–Leninists.

Among the leaders of the Communist Party of the Russian Federation, the "racist" conjectures of Gumiliev have found a place. Reactive nationalism is so emotionally intense that it is not difficult to understand the urgency with which the nation is given more than a philosophical rationale, but one that is enduring—not only historical, economical, cultural, and philosophical, but biological as well.

The "racism" of the anti-democratic opposition in post-Soviet Russia is the predictable product of an intense reactive nationalism. It is a "natural" product of the intense emotion associated with the nationalism of deprived and humiliated peoples. That reactive nationalists have a tendency to invoke an enduring biological basis for their nationalism is evidenced by the history of contemporary revolutionary thought. A singular example of the relationship, in fact, is provided by the life history of Moses Hess, the "communist rabbi" credited with having made a communist of Karl Marx.

More than half a century before the Fascist march on Rome, Moses Hess wrote a singular tract entitled *Rome and Jerusalem*. He followed an intellectual itinerary remarkably like that of the Marxist syndicalists of pre-Fascist Italy. Deeply involved in the Marxist movement of his time, Hess wrote a treatise in which his ideological cohorts were surprised to discover that he argued for "nationality" as a "force" independent of the "economic and class" determinants that governed "bourgeois society."[61] Between the years when his intimacy with Marx and Engels led to his collaboration in the preparation of some of their most important theoretical works and the publication of *Rome and Jerusalem* in 1862, Hess made the progression from ineluctable, universal "class revolution" to emphatic Jewish nationalism and an unmistakable form of racism.[62]

Hess was candid in accounting for the changes in his ideological position. With the publication of *Rome and Jerusalem*, he spoke of reaffirming a sentiment he had denied for two decades—a sentiment he believed that he had literally suppressed beyond recall. Hess credited the rebirth of his Jewish nationalism to his recognition that history had entered a "new age of nationalism," in which the future of humankind would be shaped by nationality. Whereas, as a young man, he had allowed "the suffering of the proletariat in Europe" to anesthetize him to the suffering of his own "unfortunate, maligned, despised, and dispersed people," the reality of nationality had reoriented his consciousness. "After twenty years of estrangement," he rediscovered the cause of his people and finally allowed his "Jewish patriotism" to find expression. Hess had become a reactive nationalist. The humiliation suffered by his "unfortunate, persecuted, and maligned people" compelled Hess to mobilize his energies in their service.[63] In and through them he sought fulfillment.

Typical of reactive nationalism, Hess made a point of the unique gifts of his humiliated people. More than an effort to simply shield his people from opprobrium, Hess reminded his contemporaries that it was historic "Jewish genius" that provided the "seed of a higher and a more harmonious development" for all mankind.[64] He was convinced that "Judaism alone has divine revelations" that reveal "the unity and holiness of divine law in nature and history."[65] Not only had the Jews provided the world with the substance of Christian thought, Hess insisted, but it was a Jew, Spinoza, who laid the foundation for all modern philosophical, social, and political reflection.[66] In fact, Hess reminded both Jews and Gentiles alike that it had been the destiny of the Jewish people, "since the beginning of time, to conquer the world—not like heathen Rome with its force of *arms*, but through the inner virtue of its *spirit*."[67]

For Hess, the Jews constituted a nation that, however humiliated and despised by those more powerful, was of primary historical significance. Hess enjoined Jews to unite and mobilize themselves around a program of national development in the Holy Land, the land of their ancestors. If the New Israel was not to succumb to a "parasitic way of existence," Hess went on, if it were to maintain its own population and sustain itself with equity and security in the modern world, it would have to develop its own "science and industry" on "its own soil," secure in its own "national independence."[68] Jewish nationalism would have to be largely autarkic and developmental.

The reaffirmation of Jewish nationalism would have to be redemptive, and that program of redemptive development would be sustained by a "cult of nationality," "the primal power of nationalism." It would be carefully cultivated by "the patriotic spirit of [Jewish] prophets and sages [that would serve] as an antidote to destructive rationalism." There would be the promotion of symbolism and ritual to reinforce the reawakened national spirit and inform the "restoration of the Jewish state," because Hess argued that the "masses are never moved through intellectual abstractions towards progressive ideas, whose mainsprings everywhere lie far deeper than the socialist revolutionaries themselves knew."[69] Hess was convinced that nationalism was a "natural and simple sentiment," sustained and enhanced by traditional ritual observance, symbol, and song. Emotion reinforced the patriotic determination to prevail in the inevitable strife that accompanies development.[70]

For Hess, one of the principal functions of nationalism would be the dissipation of class tensions during the desperate struggle for the creation of the Jewish state. "On the common basis of Jewish patriotism the . . . poor and rich will again recognize themselves as the descendants of the same heroes" who suffered the "two thousand year martyrdom and . . . carried aloft and held sacred the banner of nationality."[71]

Hess's plan for the patriotic revival of the Holy Land recognized that the nation, in order to realize its purposes, would have to be organized as a state and establish and maintain the social institutions that would effect its purposes.[72] The state would appeal to Jewish and non-Jewish capital to establish and foster the growth of "Jewish organizations for agriculture, industry and commerce in accordance with Mosaic, i.e. socialistic principles." Whatever the transfer of capital and talent, the new Jewish state would not allow foreign dominance of the process.[73]

All this displays the major features of reactive, developmental nationalism. More than that, it also exemplifies a further property of the intensive nationalism that inspires the entire process. Hess's nationalism took on manifest racist features, affording a firm biological basis for the sense of identity, community, and collective destiny on which his nationalism depended. Hess spoke of the Jews as a "primary race," apparently one of the races rooted in the origins of humankind. It was a race that "remained indelibly the same throughout the centuries."[74]

There is no doubt that, for Hess, race provided the biological foundation for Jewish nationalism. For him, "all of past history was concerned with the struggle of races and classes. Race struggle is primary; class struggle is secondary." In fact, he argued that "life is a direct product of race, which patterns its social institutions after its own innate inclinations and talents."[75]

Hess's racism seems to have arisen spontaneously out of the intensity of reactive nationalism. In and of itself, that need not necessarily be ominous. Hess conceived of racial differences as contributing to a diversity in development that would ultimately culminate in a world in which racial and social inequities would resolve themselves in universal harmony.[76]

The history of the twentieth century does not allow one to be sanguine with respect to all this, however. Some notable Fascists voiced humane sentiments very much like those of Moses Hess. Balbino Giuliano, a minister in the Fascist government, for instance, insisted that the regime held that "all human beings deserve respect because they are human beings bearing the imprint of divine creation; like us they love and have responsibilities; like us they labor, directly or indirectly, in the enhancement of civilization." He went on to insist that "the Fatherland, at its foundation, is humanity itself seen and loved in the distinct and concrete form provided by life."[77]

None of this precluded the promulgation of anti-Semitic and anti-miscegenation legislation during the tenure of the regime. However benign the sentiments expressed by representatives of the regime, an exacerbated nationalism generated a form of racism that shaped domestic policy at the cost of civil liberties and public freedoms.[78] The signal tragedies that have attended racial conflict in the twentieth century make it extremely difficult to review racial doctrines with equanimity. None of this can be gainsaid, but the purpose of the present review is not to credit the protestations of benignity on the part of doctrinal racists, but rather to trace the transformation of Marxism from a universalistic, class-determinate creed to a nationalism that takes on racist overtones.

Marxists, from the very inception of Marxism, have, with some regularity, transferred their loyalty from class warfare to nationalism—and, just as frequently, to some form of racism. There have been historic instances when that transfer has been catastrophic in its consequences.

Evidence that it has not been difficult for Marxists to make such a transition from proletarian international revolution to nationalism, and from there to some form of racism, is found throughout the history of modern revolution. Italian revolutionary syndicalists provided by no means either the first or the only instance. Moses Hess provided a dramatic, illustrative instance of the same phenomenon before the turn of the century.

Some Marxists have traversed the distance from orthodox Marxism to nationalism and thence to racism at exorbitant cost to humanity in general. There has been at least one instance of a major Marxist theoretician transforming his Marxism into an expression of racism and thereby bringing tragedy to an entire generation. More than a century before Marxists in the former Soviet Union began to attempt to buttress nationalism with allusions to racial origins and racial continuities, Ludwig Woltmann made the same transition.

Born in Solingen, Germany, in 1871, Woltmann joined the German Social Democratic Party before he was twenty-eight and became one of his nation's most competent Marxist theoreticians. In 1890, he published his *Der historische Materialismus*, which was so faithful and competent a treatment of classical Marxism that Lenin recommended it to all his followers.[79] By the first years of the twentieth century, Woltmann was overwhelmed by a growing preoccupation with the future of Germany. He had been transfixed by what he took to be Germany's inestimable contributions to civilization. He had convinced himself that German influence was to be found wherever human beings had made scientific, literary, architectural, and graphic arts progress, though this was nowhere acknowledged. Germans were treated as inferiors. Woltmann's reactive response was to discover trace evidence of German creativity in the military, political, and literary achievements of France and the artistic, scientific, and literary accomplishments of the Italian Renaissance.[80] Employing physiological blondism as a marker, Woltmann traced German creative influence throughout Europe.

In the course of his studies, Woltmann noted that not all German nationals shared the same overt somatic traits. He observed variability in the population. He began to draw a sharp distinction between Germans in general and members of what he called the "German race."[81] This race was pandiacritic, its members sharing overt, measurable, heritable properties that identified them.

By 1902, Woltmann had begun to raise so many objections to the orthodox Marxism that had originally inspired him, that even Marxist revisionists were no longer prepared to consider him a "Party comrade." Woltmann dismissed technological dynamics, relations of production, and class struggle as determinate factors in world history and settled instead on group sentiment, nationality, ethnicity, and racial biology.[82] In his reactive quest to assure Germany a place in the modern world, Woltmann abandoned the proletarian revolution for national and, ultimately and exclusively, racial regeneration. Marx, Woltmann maintained, had neglected the organic basis of human development. Quoting from Das Kapital, Woltmann pointed out that Marx had indicated that the productiveness of labor and, by implication, all subsequent social history was "fettered by physical conditions . . . all referable to the constitution of man himself (race, etc.)."[83] Apparently, Woltmann argued, Marx was prepared to recognize that the inherent, biological properties of human groups might influence the course of history, but he had failed to pursue this insight. By the time of his death in 1907, Woltmann had not only entirely abandoned Marxism, he had also dismissed nationalism as secondary to the spiritual rebirth of Germany. He had surrended himself entirely to the biological racism that, in time, would inspire the ideology of Adolf Hitler's National Socialism.[84]

Woltmann was not the last Marxist to allow his nationalism to transform itself into homicidal racism. The experience in former Yugoslavia is recent enough. There, Marxists, often from the highest ranks of the Communist Party, have employed nationalism as a warrant for the "ethnic cleansing" that has horrified the contemporary world.[85]

That Marxists, throughout the twentieth century, have abandoned the ortho-doxies of their ideology and transferred allegiance from class to nationalism and, to some measure, to racism is reasonably well attested. The massive defection of Japanese Marxists to the national cause in the years between the two world wars is yet another arresting instance of the same phenomenon. In the interwar years, between 1929 and 1933, successive groups of Japanese Marxists, members of the Communist Party of Japan—some members of the Central Committee of the Comintern—underwent "conversion (*tenko*)" and made the transition from pro-letarian internationalism to reactive, developmental nationalism.[86]

Sano Manabu, perhaps the most prominent among them, in the course of time formulated a program of national socialism that abandoned international-ism and sought to embrace the nation (*kokutai*) and protect the race (*minzoku*).[87] His conversion to the cause of the nation, like that of his party comrades, was genuine. Marxism had failed to address the problems that afflicted a moderniz-ing Japan facing the multiple threats that international tensions brought in their wake. Neither class warfare nor international revolution could redress the short-ages of raw materials, enhance the amount of arable land, or augment the limited fossil fuels available to Japanese industry. Only national socialism could redress Japan's national disabilities in its contest with the advanced industrial nations.

By the end of the 1920s, and particularly after it became apparent that Japan might face a war on the Asian mainland and increasing opposition from the advanced industrial democracies, many Japanese Marxists were forced to make a choice between the defense of the nation and adherence to Comintern policies that gave every appearance of being in the service of the Soviet Union. It became more and more evident that Marxism, either in the form left as an inheritance by Marx or in the version provided by Lenin or Stalin, offered little that might resolve the policy dilemmas of the Japanese.

By the end of 1933, the majority of the leadership of the Communist Party of Japan had defected, seeking reconciliation with the *kokutai*, to once again pursue their destiny as members of the Japanese people (*kokomin*). Class warfare and proletarian revolution had dissolved in the solvent of nationalism.

Between the mid-1930s and the Second World War, Japanese Marxists sought to transform Marxism and Marxism–Leninism into a political ideology that would allow the Japanese people to resist what were perceived to be the economic and military predations of the advanced industrial powers.[88] There was a frantic effort to conceive of a state structure and a national policy that could remove the Western preserve in China and shepherd the Japanese nation through its survival crisis to mature industrialization, national independence, assured sovereignty, economic self-sufficiency, and international respect.

Independent Marxists like Ryu Shintaro had by that time conceded that

Japan required not "proletarian revolution," but an intense collaboration of all classes in the interests of expanding the nation's "productive power."[89] Japan's dense population, its lack of domestic capital, its dearth of immediately available entrepreneurial skills, as well as the absence of those resources necessary for industrial growth, together with the perceived indisposition of the Western powers to allow its economic expansion into East and Southeast Asia, were all cited as compelling reasons for the abandonment of orthodox Marxism or any of its extant anti-national variants. What Japan required was not Marxist revolution, but sufficient "living space" to assure its immediate survival and the perpetuity of its "singular racial gifts."[90]

Japan's problem was seen as that of any less developed nation in the years between the two world wars. There was the perceived need to create a powerful national state, capable of mounting an adequate response to the economic, military, and cultural threats that attended Western imperialism and assuring the protection and survival of the "superior Japanese *minzoku*."[91] Japan's Marxists followed the same trajectory of ideological transformation as Moses Hess and the Italian revolutionary syndicalists decades before.

The declining Soviet Union witnessed very much the same phenomenon. As the system went into irreversible decline, years before the final collapse, Marxist theoreticians abandoned the orthodoxies of the past to support various forms of nationalism, and some of them, as has been suggested, abandoned themselves to the rankest expressions of biological racism.[92]

We have become increasingly familiar with the attempts of Marxists to deal with the critical problems of the twentieth century. Fascists had early anticipated something like this process taking place in all Marxist–Leninist systems. What is suggested by all this is that Fascist theoreticians anticipated some of the principal features of revolution in our time—and gave expression to their insights in "theory." It also appears that the failure of Marxism to address the issue of national sentiment contributed both to its general irrelevance to our own time and its decay. Nationalism frequently grows out of such decay, fertilized by the frustration experienced by Marxist theoreticians disillusioned by the failure of their inherited doctrine to even address, much less solve, the most vexing problems of our time.

Since statism and elitism frequently accompany the emergent developmental nationalism that results from Marxism's compounded failures, revolutionaries often have awesome coercive power at their disposal. Since such nationalism is frequently, if not always, nurtured by an abiding sense of individual and collective humiliation, it is not uncommon to find it accompanied not only by belligerence, but by homicidal rage as well. Possessed of power and animated by rage, what results may well be the kinds of horror that history has documented in the mass murders of the twentieth century.[93]

A racism that arises out of a nationalism born of failure, real or perceived status deprivation, and protracted exposure to threat may be capable of unimagined bestialities. This is the fear that haunts many commentators who see only future horrors in the rise of nationalism in the former Soviet Union.[94]

Even those Fascist theoreticians who foresaw so correctly the changes that would ultimately transform Marxist–Leninist systems and who so well appreciated the failures of Marxist theory never anticipated all that would emerge out of the revolutions the twentieth century. To a significant extent, Fascist ideologues never really understood what it meant to say that not Marxism, but "Fascism [was] the idea of the twentieth century."[95]

"Fascisms"

It seems unlikely that we will ever have an adequate explanation of why academicians, Marxist and non-Marxist alike, have generally failed to understand Fascism, Fascist theory, or fascisms in general. Still less likely is the prospect of ever fully understanding the peculiar relationship between Marxism, Mussolini's Fascism, and modern revolution.

Nonetheless, the disintegration of Marxism into developmental nationalism and its accommodation of one or another form of racism in its effort to prove itself relevant to our time are instructive. The Fascism of Italy's heretical Marxism has demonstrated its durability and its appeal to a wide variety of revolutionaries in the twentieth century.

It is hard to account for why so much of this has remained obscure. Part of the answer may lie in the fact that Italian Fascism was identified at its very inception as implacably "anti-Marxist." In reality Italian Fascism was more anti-Leninist, in its insistent anti-nationalism, than it was specifically anti-Marxist. Many of the principal theoreticians of Fascism, as we have seen, had been schooled in Marxism and, like Giovanni Gentile, demonstrated a competence in the material that won the admiration of Lenin himself.[1]

The fact was that the philosophical neo-idealism that served Fascism as its normative foundation shared its origins with orthodox Marxism through their common connection to Hegelianism. Both had a conception of human beings as intrinsically social animals. Like Marx, Gentile rejected the "liberal" conviction that human beings are best understood as independent, self-sufficient monads, possessed of inherent freedoms, interacting only at their convenience.[2]

Fascism and Marxism were both collectivist in orientation, and fundamentally anti-liberal. They shared a conception of society as an organism in which individuals survived and matured into persons only as constituents in complex, interdependent relationships. Implicit in such notions was the tenet that society somehow had priority over the individual. It was a philosophical belief that perceived individuals as essentially and "naturally" social in character. In consequence, the liberal view—that persons entered into social relationships only as a consequence of calculation—was dismissed as an immoral fiction. It was a view that remained constant among both Fascists and Marxist–Leninists throughout the lives of their respective regimes.[3]

None of this was at issue when the leadership of Italian socialism identified those Marxists who had come out of its ranks to fight in the Great War as "renegades." As has been suggested, the breach in the ranks of socialism was the consequence of a difference regarding Italy's participation in the First World War. The Marxists who had rejected the official party position with respect to Italy's neutrality in that war were deemed traitors to socialist universalism. Rejecting neutrality and universalism, they had become nationalists.

By the end of the First World War, those same Marxist heretics sought the fulfillment of the nation's promise. Having dismissed the possibility of proletarian revolution, they sought development, enhancement of the nation's prestige, restoration of lost lands, and acknowledgement of Italy's place among the major powers. They opposed themselves to the anti-nationalism of official socialism. They were to become the first Fascists. As anti-nationalists, the more orthodox Italian Socialists and revolutionary Leninists totally rejected the Fascist position. As Leninists, the pro-Soviet revolutionary Marxists found Fascism a direct competitor on the peninsula. Given the circumstances, it was politically expedient to define Fascism as "anti-Marxist" and "right-wing" in principle. The relationship was deemed adversarial, and the armed conflict that followed fixed this characterization indelibly in history.

The consequence since then has been that Fascist and Marxist–Leninist systems have been dealt with as antipodal. Both Marxist and non-Marxist analysts have tended to accept the thesis at considerable cognitive cost. The issues that divided the first Fascists from their adversaries turned less on Marxism *per se* than on an assessment of the options opened to a marginally industrialized Italy in a world of Darwinian conflict.[4]

The differences between Fascism and Marxism that arose out of the First World War were inflamed by the enmities bred of the long, venomous, violent conflict in the postwar period. The conflict reached such an intensity that Marxists of whatever variety refused to acknowledge the heretical Marxist origins of the first Fascism.[5] Marxists attributed the "defection" of some of their foremost intellectuals simply to venality and opportunism. The next step in the logic of denial was to conceive of Fascism itself as venal and opportunistic. The final step was to see Fascism as the "tool of capitalist reaction," since only monied "reaction" could offer enough in benefits to those motivated by nothing more than personal material advantage.

The very intensity of recrimination led Marxists and leftist enthusiasts of all sorts to insist that Fascism could be nothing more than the defense of capitalism. This was deemed the "reality" of Fascism. The result was a densely written interpretative "theory" of Fascism that had little to recommend it but that succeeded, above all, in misleading both Marxists and non-Marxists. The intellectual costs were only slightly less than the price paid by Marxists in revolutionary failures. Few ever succeeded in understanding the real threat posed by fascism for the twentieth century.

However flawed, this entire treatment of Fascism influenced all subsequent assessments attempted by Marxists and non-Marxists alike. A more profitable analysis of Italian Fascism in particular and generic fascism in general might do better to begin with the recognition that Marxism–Leninism and Fascism share a common origin in response to some common problems. In fact, some of the more astute non-Marxist analysts of our time have acknowledged that Marxism and Fascism were animated by a "related ideology" and employed "almost identical and yet typically modified methods."[6]

As has been indicated, many Fascist theoreticians, throughout their active political lives, acknowledged the affinities between Fascism and Marxism–Leninism.[7] There were even Italian Marxist–Leninists—including Nicola Bombacci, one of the founders of his nation's Communist Party—who conceived of Fascism as the only viable form of Marxism for economically retrograde communities.[8] In the years that followed, many other Marxist–Leninists acknowledged as much, and many more offered confirmation not only by adopting Fascist policies, but by articulating a Fascist rationale in their support.

Among academics in general, Fascism and Marxism have been dealt with so long as diametrical opposites that there has been a general failure to treat their intrinsic affinities with the skill and attention they deserve. After more than half a century of puzzlement, it would seem that the time has come to attempt an assessment of Fascism, fascisms, and contemporary Marxism that might illuminate, rather than obscure, some of the major features of the revolutionary twentieth century.

As has been argued, many of the earliest Fascists, as well as some of Italy's first Nationalists, were originally Marxists. They subsequently shared many affinities with the Marxist–Leninists of the interwar years, and the surviving Marxist–Leninists of the present continue to display properties that have always been part of the criterial definition of fascism.[9]

Of criterial definitions of fascism, there is an abundance. In general, they share overlapping properties that have been rehearsed throughout the present discussion.[10] What has been absent has been an accompanying "explanatory" text that would supply the grounds for the observed similarities. Marxists, as we have seen, have sought to radically distinguish fascism from Marxist–Leninist regimes by identifying the former with a defense of "moribund capitalism." However impaired their effort, it has influenced intellectuals everywhere in the world. In the absence of a persuasive alternative text, there has been a manifest failure on the part of most academics and political analysts to recognize the similarities of "leftist" Marxist–Leninist systems and paradigmatic "right-wing" Fascism. Marxist–Leninists themselves either failed to see, or attempted to explain away, the common traits.

More and more frequently, in the recent past, it has been observed that some of the most obvious traits of Marxist–Leninist movements and regimes tend to approximate those of fascism. It has been more and more regularly acknowledged that there is "a tendency . . . for the extremes on the right and left, to meet."[11] The criterial traits of the one overlap, in significant measure, those of the other. The resemblances between Fascism and Marxist–Leninist regimes are substantial. If those resemblances are to be treated as anything more than curiosities, they must be associated with some common factors that, taken together, provide some understanding of complex past events and allow some anticipation of future events. Such treatment generally appears as a discursive "text" in which "causal" factors are associated with shared similarities. Observed similarities are related to socioeconomic and political factors in an explanatory narrative.

Each of the features that constitute the grounds of a family resemblance is characteristically selected because that trait is somehow deemed important to the explanatory text. Traits are related to each other in a nexus that adds an increased measure of plausibility to the narrative. The traits themselves are directly or indirectly observable, contribute to easy storage and retrieval, result in the provision of reasonably discrete but related categories, assist in the formulation of complex hypotheses, and in general further empirical theory generation.

The fact that Marxist theoreticians insisted on a fundamental distinction between fascism and Marxism–Leninism, because they chose to identify Italian Fascism with the defense of capitalism, confounded any analysis that might have arisen from the evident fact that fascism and Marxism–Leninism shared not only observable institutional properties, but some elemental socio-philosophical affinities. Even Leon Trotsky, who recognized the "fateful similarities" between fascism and Stalinism, failed to pursue the analysis to any cognitive purpose, because he could not disabuse himself of the notion that the Soviet Union was a "workers' state" and Fascist Italy was not. Inextricably caught up in the notion that revolution must be either "proletarian" or "bourgeois," Marxists never really understood reactive nationalism, developmentalism, or the political dynamics of the twentieth century. As a consequence, they failed to understand very much about the twentieth century.

The more Marxist theoreticians spoke of "internationalism" and "proletarian democracy," the more nationalist and authoritarian their systems became. The more they spoke of "proletarian democracy," the more clearly did rule pass to the national political, technical, and bureaucratic "state bourgeoisie."

Whatever the acknowledged similarities, however, to this day many have continued to distinguish fascism from Marxist–Leninist systems presumably because there is an insistence that one cannot understand what "fascism means" unless one can appreciate what "lies behind the hatred and destructiveness [it] unleashes"—as though "hatred" and "destructiveness" are unique and exclusive to fascism—and any attempt to deal with the subject independent of that recognition is dismissed as evidence of cognitive impairment.[12]

Any account of generic fascism must deal with the issue of the high emotional salience and attendant violence that accompanied almost all its manifestations. At the same time, it must also be acknowledged that such features were associated with almost every manifestation of revolution in general and Marxism–Leninism in particular.

Every serious commentator has cited the highly charged environment in which Italian Fascism developed. Fascists themselves acknowledged that Fascism could only "live in an atmosphere of strong ideal tension."[13] Marxist–Leninists were rarely as candid, but it is hard to overlook the excess of emotion that accompanied almost all their revolutionary activities. At some point in their history, almost all revolutionary movements display very much the same intensity. They are almost invariably attended by violence. For some reason, however, fascist intensity and fascist violence have been seen as unique. Fascists were peculiarly "xenophobic" and "pathologically ethnocentric." They were given to "ultranationalism," and their violence and genocidal fury were its natural by-products.[14]

Such accounts enjoy a certain measure of plausibility. The first Fascists were fervent nationalists. Italian Fascism was a form of reactive, anti-democratic, irredentist, developmental nationalism.[15] It conceived of itself as a reaction to the treatment of Italians as a backward, supine, servile, dependent people in an international universe dominated by advanced industrial nations.[16] At its inception, Fascism's self-assertiveness evoked a deeply felt affirmative response among large sectors of the population of post–First World War Italy. After their sacrifices in the Great War, Italians demanded that Italy be treated as an equal by the "Great Powers," and no longer as a mendicant among the powerful.

The reactive passions of the first Fascism extended across boundaries of gender, class, category, and age. Although at first composed disproportionately of young veterans of the Great War, membership in the ranks of Fascism soon included substantial numbers of the urban and rural middle classes, as well as the proletariat of the manufacturing centers. For its intellectuals, and those population elements caught up in its political theater, Fascism was, in substantial part, the vital, aggressive, intense, regenerative response of a long-suffering and proud people to the arrogance of the "Great Powers."

That the First World War provided the occasion for the rise of Fascism can hardly be gainsaid. The charged environment of domestic internal conflict and the economic, political, diplomatic, and military challenges from without all contributed to its eventuality as well as its aggressiveness. The availability of millions of mobilizable young men, schooled in war, gave Italian Fascism an inimitable and forbidding aggressive individuality.

But other revolutionary movements were to arise in the interwar years and in the years after the Second World War that did not share those same immediate circumstances or demographic resources, and yet, in the course of time, took on many, if not all, of the major features of fascism. Fascism seems to respond to far deeper collective needs than a simple reaction to the dislocations of international war or some specific economic crisis.

Fascism, as some contemporary Russian analysts have suggested, seems to be, at least in substantial part, an expression of collective outrage. It arises from a sense of profound and protracted, real or fancied, group humiliation. In the nineteenth and twentieth centuries such humiliation was often a direct or indirect result of economic retardation. The inability to meet the military challenges of the advanced industrial nations often left less developed nations with an enduring sense of inefficacy and inferiority, which revolutionary minorities often succeeded in stoking into a reactive frenzy.

Under the aegis of such minorities, a mobilizing rationale may flow very easily from reactive nationalism, to a rage for domestic homogeneity, to ethnocentrism, to xenophobia, and, in the most extreme instances, to justification of murderous violence against indigenous "indigestible" minorities or foreign opponents—and "fascist traits" make their commonplace appearance. What is significant is that Marxist–Leninist regimes have gradually assumed an increasing number of just such traits. State-sponsored violence against citizens, mass murders, and, at the extreme, genocidal carnage, have come to typify Marxist–Leninist systems with no less frequency than they have their fascist counterparts. In fact, Marxist–Leninist systems have destroyed more of their own nationals through systematic political violence than any fascist regime ever did.[17]

In the effort to come to grips with all this, the suggestion has been made that an explanation of such collective dispositions is to be found in the emotional intensity of the critical identification of individuals with a community of similars.

Very recently, comparativists have put forward the argument that throughout history human beings, in the course of their individuation, have identified with groups of limited compass.[18] In those communities, individuals find recognition, a sense of self, and self-esteem. But when the host community is humiliated, the individual is humiliated as well. The individual's search for personal worth through "self-transcendence" in the community is frustrated—with reactive hostility as its natural consequence.[19]

The social science literature devoted to collective life is rich with allusions to the individual's identification with his or her community.[20] Individuals achieve a level of recognition and a sense of personal worth as part of a group. In the past, individuals identified themselves with their tribes or clans or city-states in order to achieve the desired sense of self-esteem. Many contemporary social scientists speak of the disposition to identify with a collectivity as a generic human trait.[21]

By the nineteenth and twentieth centuries, as part of this universal process, individuals tended to identify themselves with the nation-state, the ultimate repository of sanction, the final arbiter between alternatives open to the community, and the supreme defender of life lived in common.[22] The contemporary argument is that nationalism is the modern form of tribalism, and thus that thwarted nationalism can give rise to anachronistic, barbaric violence.

In the very recent past, others have spoken of the "struggle for recognition" that is at the center of the individual's life lived in common, making allusion to the critical role that group life has played in the psychosocial process of self-articulation throughout the twentieth century.[23] The clear intimation of these kinds of social science speculations is that if a human being fails to find requisite recognition through normal group life, he or she seeks it in "unnatural" group life—in an extreme sensitivity to real or fancied slights directed at their community, an aggressiveness in defense of that community, a tendency to exaggerate the accomplishments of their group, and a readiness to sacrifice themselves or others in its service.

These dispositions have been observed in exaggerated form among the populations of communities undergoing late economic development during the latter part of the nineteenth and the beginning of the twentieth century. In the nineteenth and twentieth centuries economic growth and technological development have largely determined rank in the order of nations. The place occupied by a person's nation in that order significantly influences each individual's sense of worth.

In the nineteenth and twentieth centuries, retarded economic development carried so many disabilities in its train that it soon became evident that the national community, whatever its past, would suffer grievously at the hands of others unless it could effectively protect itself economically, politically, and militarily. The drive to industrialize became a project at the conclusion of which nations expected to achieve the necessary military capabilities to ensure survival, security, and stature. In the process, their populations, individually and collectively, would find satisfaction in the "powerful experience of self-transcendence" in a community enjoying international recognition.[24]

Frustration in the course of such a complex resolution precipitates "irrational" and "pathological" responses. Influenced by an indeterminate number of time-specific, local intervening factors, forms of exacerbated reactive nationalisms make their appearance. Thus we are told that although human beings, throughout history, have identified with groups of restricted membership, finding in them a sense of personal identity and accomplishment, in our own time, nations serve as the vehicle of individuation and self-affirmation. "When a people, having gone through the first phases of economic modernization, is denied both national identity and political freedom," one can expect frustration to intensify all features of group life. "Thus," the account proceeds, "it is not surprising that the two Western European countries to invent fascist ultranationalism, Italy and Germany, were also the last to industrialize and to unify politically, or that the most powerful nationalisms in the immediate aftermath of World War II were those of Europe's former colonies in the Third World. Given past precedent, it should also not surprise us that the strongest nationalisms of today are found in the Soviet Union or Eastern Europe where industrialization was relatively late in coming"—and, one might add, where populations have long suffered from a sense of inadequacy and conceive their treatment at the hands of the more industrialized nations as humiliating and demeaning.[25]

However synoptically expressed, what all this suggests is that under certain conditions, human beings, as group animals, become particularly mobilizable and eminently aggressive. In the twentieth century those conditions engage a disposition shared by human beings "since time immemorial" to intensively seek personal fulfillment in a *national* "community of destiny."[26] Should all this be persuasive, the fact that Fascist recruitment in Italy, Bolshevik recruitment in Russia, and Chinese Communist recruitment in revolutionary China were never really governed by class or status considerations becomes easily comprehensible. Revolutionaries in industrially retrograde environments, whatever their political persuasion, have always recruited wherever they could; and nationalism, overtly or covertly and in the last analysis, supplied the ideological solvent of class, category, or status differences. Anyone, or any group, that did not or could not merge without remainder into state-engineered homogeneity became an "outsider," an enemy, and the potential object of violence.

The initial attractiveness of specifically fascist appeal in such circumstances is to a sense of national, not class, outrage. Fascism appeals to the abiding conviction that an entire people has been systematically, over a long period of time, humiliated by its more "advanced" counterparts. Ultimately, Marxist–Leninists were to exploit essentially the same sentiments, and, in time, class appeals were transformed into "patriotism."

What distinguished Fascists in all this was that Fascist intellectuals provided an unambiguous ideological rationale. Fascists invariably perceived the world as a place in which privileged nations sought to maintain and perpetuate their hegemony against the demands of the "proletarian poor."[27] It was a view of the world in which the dignity, security, and life of the poor are purchased and assured only through *national* struggle. In the judgment of Fascists, struggle and competition are at the heart of every human activity; and in the modern world, the struggle between poor and rich nations shapes events and determines futures.[28] Contemporary Marxist–Leninists, with their allusions to the struggle of "socialist" nations against "imperialist" nations, say, increasingly and emphatically, very much the same thing.

In the contemporary world, there is a general recognition among less developed communities that an effective defense of group life can only be undertaken and sustained by the development and maintenance of an adequate economic base.[29] The adequacy of that base is largely determined by technological innovation and industrial growth. Within such a conception of the world, national economic development becomes critical to the self-esteem, security, and prestige of peoples who have remained essentially agrarian in a world environment increasingly dominated by industry. In the modern world, the struggle for survival makes rapid industrialization an inescapable necessity for late developers. What is eminently clear is that rapid industrialization and modernization are undertaken not to reduce poverty or restore equity or achieve universal harmony. Industrialization is the necessary condition for securing the nation, for fulfilling the nation's mission, for restoring "lost" territories, and for uplifting the self-esteem of entire peoples.

It became abundantly clear to the first Fascists that the exigencies of defensive, and ultimately offensive, military power required the heavy equipment and technological sophistication made available only through fairly substantial industrialization. The revolutionary demand for "national economic development" was thus driven not by a search for wealth or to sustain a program of "proletarian redistribution," but by a recognition of its necessity for the establishment and expansion of domestic and international power.[30]

For Fascist intellectuals formulating their thought at the beginning of the twentieth century, the world was composed of competing national units, each animated by a tradition as old as the life of the community. For Italy that tradition was Roman, and for Fascists, it deserved to survive and prosper even against the overwhelming material power of the "demoplutocracies."[31] In the judgment of the leaders of Fascism, only a strong, centralized state, animated by an ideology of obedience, class collaboration, and an ethic of heroic self-sacrifice, could manage extensive and intensive industrial development and economic growth—the necessary preconditions for national salvage, reconstruction, and transformation in a world of intense competition.

These were the central convictions of Fascism, and they can serve, for the purposes of classification, as the criterial properties of generic fascism. The collectivist persuasion, the nationalist sense of mission, the anti-democratic stat-ism, the militarism, and the posturing that tend to accompany such regimes are familiar to comparativists. In a political environment animated by a rage for unanimity, the invidious out-group, ethnic, racial, or class discrimination that often follows is equally well known, whether that system identifies itself as Fascist or not. All the traits of such political and economic regimes are the functional by-products of an intense, reactive nationalism. They are all found, in varying strengths, in the failed experiments in Castro's Cuba and Kim Il Sung's Democratic People's Republic of Korea. Their violence against "unassimilable" groups can vent itself in incarceration or deportation—or, in the last analysis, in mass murder.

In the recent past such systems have been observed, often in caricature, among the less developed nations of sub-Saharan Africa. They were found in uncertain variants compatible with their national traditions during the interwar years in Getulio Vargas's Brazil, and after the Second World War some of the same features surfaced in Juan Peron's Argentina.[32] They are found in truncated forms in the Arab and Islamic dictatorships in the Middle East at the end of the twentieth century.[33]

The ideology of late industrial development expresses itself in a set of fea-tures that has now become increasingly familiar. Whatever their postures at the beginning, movements of anti-democratic reactive nationalism take on, over time, common traits. Compelled by functional requirements, in an environment of threat, contemporary reactive nationalisms tend to display common ideologi-cal and institutional features. Thus, at its inception, Bolshevism spoke a language and sought ends totally alien from those that typify reactive and developmental nationalism. Only with the passage of time and under the pressure of circum-stances did Bolshevism transform itself into one of fascism's variants.

Similarly, among those movements and regimes identified as "fascist" during the interwar years were some initially lacking some of the essential proper-ties identified here as central to the concept. Among the successor states that emerged from the dissolution of the Austro-Hungarian Empire at the end of the First World War, for example, were anti-communist movements of reactive nationalism, which academics have traditionally identified as "fascist," that were initially devoid of the developmental features typical of the species or sub-species.[34] Anti-communist nationalists in Hungary and Romania, as cases in point, initially sought the defense of their traditions in a program that was essentially anti-, or at least, nondevelopmental. Such reactive nationalists sought Hungarian or Romanian palingenesis in defense of the virtues of the peasant smallholder and the traditional economic system—against the seductive "corruption" of foreign "stock-jobbers" and "shopkeepers." Nationalist revolutionaries in the successor states of the Austro-Hungarian Empire sought national salvation in a return to the cultural roots of their nations' preindustrial past.

While such ideas were predominant, for example, in the early years of Hungarian "fascism," by the mid-1930s, the "vast majority of radicals [had] succumbed to the inexorable logic of their militant nationalism once they realized that the exigencies of military power . . . made the industrialization of the country inevitable."[35] Thus, initially anti-developmental Hungarian revolutionaries, like the Bolsheviks before them, were driven by the irresistible logic of their circumstances to promote the industrialization of their domestic economy. The effort to secure the nation in a world of intense competition compelled Hungary's fascists to attempt to industrialize under authoritarian auspices.

Of course, each such fascism has its own history. Reactive nationalists in Romania, for example, understood their several movements to be a response to circumstances that found the people of Romania threatened by the real probability of permanent international "inferiority."[36] They feared that the nation would forever be subject to the yoke of foreigners.[37]

In 1938, the *Romanian Encyclopedia*, in formulations that have long since become familiar, complained that imported manufactured commodities were sold in Romania at high prices, while domestic primary goods were purchased abroad at "very low prices"—affording the wealthy industrialized nations every advantage in economic exchange. It was argued that, as a consequence, Romania was in danger of "being permanently a colony, open or disguised, of the foreigners."[38]

The initial response to this common sense of national vulnerability on the part of what is now generally referred to as Romanian fascism was, in many respects, unique. In making what they considered an appropriate response, the anti-communist intellectuals of the Romanian Legion of the Archangel Michael appealed to the virtues of peasant life and religious mysticism to supply the nation's renovative strength.[39] According to the ideologues of the legion, traditional virtues and an absolute commitment to God and the Savior, Jesus Christ, would make Romania "honored and powerful."[40] In fact, there was something reminiscent more of primitive cargo cults than of paradigmatic Fascism in the original ideology of Corneliu Zelia Codreanu, the leader of the legion.[41]

In the organizational manual of the legion, members were admonished to pray to "the mysterious forces of the invisible world. . . . Those forces . . . will provide for your defense. . . . They will sow panic and terror among your enemies, paralyzing them. In the final analysis, victories do not depend on material preparations . . . but on the collaboration of spiritual forces."[42]

Codreanu, the charismatic "Captain" of the movement, seems to have been a genuine mystic who distinguished his movement from Fascism by insisting on its religious inspiration.[43] While he clearly sought a "great and powerful Romania," he conceived of his salvific mission as essentially religious in character. The "new men" who were to be created by the legionary regime would be heroic, loyal, obedient, diligent, and self-sacrificing—as they are expected to be in all movements of reactive nationalism—but, more than that, they would be "pure of heart," because God could dwell only in a pure heart. Where purity was absent, there Satan dwelt.[44]

Codreanu's entire strategy was "spiritual." At the very foundation of his program for Romanian renewal was a grueling process of spiritual regeneration. Codreanu intended to transform the best of Romanians into transcendent "new men" who would create a "new Romania." None of this involved industrial development and economic growth. Codreanu's "new men" would be ascetics, not modernizers. They would deny themselves the most elementary indulgences, not to supply capital for the growth of heavy industry, but to sanctify themselves. Codreanu's "new men" would commit themselves to chastity and poverty, the better to overcome the temptations of the flesh. Fasting was undertaken as a purification prior to prayer in the effort to render themselves worthy of the intercession of the invisible spiritual forces they invoked.[45]

Other than the regenerative liturgy that informed legionary practice, there was really no explicit social, economic, or political policy that uniquely characterized the revolutionary program of the legion of the Archangel Michael or its Iron Guard. Codreanu took pride in the fact that the legion had no specific program.[46] What there was, was a collection of ideas common to reactive nationalists. The thinkers of the legion spoke of the creation of the Romanian nation as a product of millennia of struggle, ethnic conflict, and religious persecution. They spoke of the nation as a product of reproductive relationships and traditional culture, of a continuity in place, biology, and history.[47] General favor was accorded corporativist ideas, the organization of functional economic categories under the superintendence of the state.[48] Governance was understood to be, in principle, hierarchical and authoritarian. The ideal was totalitarian—the total integration of all individuals, classes, sects, and functional components into the resurgent nation.[49] But there was no enthusiasm for technological development or the creation of domestic industry. It was only after the murder of

Codreanu in 1938 that the ideology of the movement, for whatever reason, took on more of the developmental features of paradigmatic Fascism. The work of Mihail Manoilescu, attracted to leadership after Codreanu's death, brought new dimension to the doctrines of the movement.

In a manner almost entirely absent in the works of Codreanu, Ion Motza, or Horia Sima,[50] the ideologues of the legion, Manoilescu spoke of the necessities of industrial development in the twentieth century. He addressed the issue of the exploitation of the less developed agrarian economies of the world at the hands of the advantaged "plutocracies." He spoke of national rebirth through the agency of rapid economic development and industrialization and of maintaining political control, through the institution of a single party, over an economy undergoing major systemic changes.[51]

Thus, by the beginning of the 1940s, ignoring the chaos that surrounded Romania, the legion of the Archangel Michael and the Iron Guard took on some of the more elemental attributes of paradigmatic Fascism. By the early 1940s, one major feature distinguished the legion of the Archangel Michael and the Iron Guard from the Fascism of Mussolini—its implacable anti-Semitism.

Unlike the sometimes anti-Semitism of Fascism, the anti-Semitism of the legion was central to its every political conviction. Legionaries saw the Jews as the unregenerate enemies of Christ. Those who could not have Jesus in their hearts made a place for Satan. Like all fascisms, the fascism of the Iron Guard had its distinguishing characteristics. At the center of the regenerative ideology of the legion and its guard was their concept of "ethnic purity." In substance, what this meant was a dogged purge of all Jewish influence from Romanian life. The putative Satanic influence of the Jews and its expression in the "Jewish question" served as the linchpin of the ideology of Codreanu and his legion in ways that were totally absent from the thought of Fascism's major intellectuals. In the judgment of the intellectual and political leadership of the legionary movement, development and corporativism were entirely secondary to the resolution of Romania's Jewish question.[52] Anti-Semitism was an irrepressible constant in the nationalist writings of the intellectuals of the legion.

Unlike the anti-Semitism of National Socialism, Romanian anti-Semitism was religious, not racist, in derivation. Legionaries insisted that the Jews, prominent in the economic and intellectual life of Romania, constituted a threat to its "true" Christian culture. Romanian fascism, reactive in origin, elitist by disposition, irredentist in intention, and, during its final years, resolutely developmental in character, was, in a clear sense, *sui generis*. Like Fascism, it was prepared to protect property and social distinctions if they contributed to the nation's program of survival and prevalence. Like Fascism, it was multi-class in origin and recruitment, with a preference for peasant members and peasant values.[53]

It was doctrinal anti-Semitism and doctrinaire religion that distinguished the legion from Italian Fascism. While Mussolini, like Stalin, entertained a form of vulgar anti-Semitism and after 1938 imposed anti-Semitic legislation on Italy, the Jewish question was never an essential component of Fascist ideology any more than it was of Stalinism.[54] While Fascism, and (ultimately) Stalinism, accommodated religion, religion did not constitute the core of their respective belief systems.[55]

In retrospect, it has become evident that revolutionary and anti-democratic, reactive, and developmental nationalisms had emphatic similarities. Marxism–Leninism, almost from the moment of its accession to power in 1917, was compelled to embark on a course of intensive economic growth and industrial development even though such a program had no place in its original revolutionary agenda. Economic, civil, and political rights were sacrificed in the service of extensive and intensive growth. By the time Josef Stalin assumed control of the process, it had become clear that if the Soviet Union were to survive, more than anything else, it would be required "to overtake and outstrip the advanced technology of the developed capitalist countries."[56] Like Fascist Italy, either the Soviet Union would "outstrip" the advanced industrial democracies, or it would be "forced to the wall."[57] By the time Stalin held sway over the system, the entire program of Lenin's "proletarian revolution" had been transformed into the forced-draft industrialization of the Soviet Union in order to "emancipate" the "whole of Russia from the yoke of world imperialism" and transform it "from a colony into an independent and free country."[58] The Soviet Union of Josef Stalin, like the Italy of Mussolini's Fascism, had assumed the major features of a reactive developmental nationalism.

Like Fascism, Marxism–Leninism in the Soviet Union, under authoritarian auspices and single-party rule, undertook the rapid industrial and agricultural development of a nation facing international threats of a magnitude that jeopardized its survival. In its pursuit of security, the leadership of the Soviet Union exploited its industrial and agricultural labor force in order to fuel its programs of development. The Soviet Union was a "poor and retrograde" community in a world of aggressive, advanced industrial powers. In its defense, everyone was expected to make sacrifices; but it is evident that the sacrifices fell more heavily on the workers than on the bureaucracy or the political elite.

As has been argued, the first Fascist theoreticians anticipated most of those developments. In a world in which the more advanced industrial powers "colonized" those that were less developed, one did not need much sophistication to anticipate the reactive rise of developmental nationalisms on the periphery. However uncertain the goals of the Bolshevik revolution may have been for Marxist–Leninists at its inception, for Fascist theoreticians, the revolution in economically retrograde Russia was actually the first of many "revolutions of poor nations . . . against the . . . tyranny of [established international] capitalism."[59]

Stalin recognized that in less developed countries "the struggle against impe- rialist oppressors" would produce a nationalism that would act as a "powerful predominating factor," drawing "the revolutionary forces of the country to- gether into one camp."[60] In effect, whatever one might have expected from Marxist "theory," Stalin was prepared to recognize the multi-class nature of "revolutionary forces" in those industrially and economically less developed countries that found themselves confronting "imperialism."

Whatever the political dynamics of the Maoist revolution in China, in retro- spect it is evident that Chinese Communists sought the rapid industrial and economic development of their nation in the effort to establish its sovereign place in the modern world. However confused and incompetent Maoist strat- egies of national development proved to be, there is little doubt that their pur- pose was the establishment of China as a major power in the modern world. At its most coherent, Marxism under Mao Zedong meant reactive nationalist eco- nomic and political policies.[61] However much Maoism was larded over with Marxist jargon, its purposes ultimately became manifestly clear in its behavior. Against the threats and power of foreign imperialism, Maoists sought to restore China to its rightful place at the "center of the world." Once this is understood, all Mao's invocations concerning "class struggle" and "proletarian internation- alism" are seen as obstructions to what were, in fact, the primary tasks of the revolution.

On the Chinese mainland, only the death of Mao freed the leadership of the People's Republic of China from the anti-market prejudices of orthodox Marx- ism. Only then were China's "capitalist roaders" free to embark on a program of rapid economic and industrial growth—the real purpose of the long Chinese revolution. Only then could they allow the effective existence of private property, the exercise of individual initiative, and the pursuit of personal profit to influence the allocation of resources as well as the investment of capital. Only after the death of Mao could the Marxists of Communist China allow property, profit, and personal initiative to fuel the impressive industrial growth that has distinguished post-Maoist China from its Maoist past.[62] With the attendant transformation, the distinctions between generic fascism and Chinese Marxism–Leninism have be- come increasingly threadbare.

By the mid-1990s, the inspiration for the Herculean efforts of the mainland Chinese to develop their nation economically turned on "love of country" and continued resentment of "the humiliations" suffered by China at the hands of "foreign aggression."[63] By that time, all notions of domestic "class struggle" had been abandoned. In their place, a conception of an international struggle between "poor" and "rich" nations was embraced without equivocation.[64]

Not only are "class distinctions" to be tolerated in post-Maoist China, but the leader of the Communist Party of China, Jiang Zemin, instructed the party to foster the union of all Chinese, whatever their "class," in the effort to further national development. The party was counseled to reconstruct itself "under the new banner of nationalism."[65] For the most modern spokesmen of contemporary China, patriotism, the commitment to the national state, has become a cardinal virtue to be invoked and/or inculcated in the masses of the mainland. Patriotism has become a form of national affect ignited by a communal celebration of the millennial culture of China. Where the memory of past glories is absent or weak, it must be stoked by ritual incantation.[66] Nothing less was advocated by Fascist pedagogues in the 1930s.[67]

The ideology that today legitimizes the rule of the Communist Party of China is identified as "socialism with Chinese characteristics." It is a "socialism" that has long been familiar to fascists. It is a socialism in which economically defined classes collaborate, under the aegis of a single-party state, in the furtherance of national developmental purpose. As a reactive nationalist, elitist, etatist, authoritarian, irredentist, anti-democratic, developmental, single-party-dominant, and increasingly militaristic regime, post-Maoist China shares an unmistakable family resemblance to paradigmatic Fascism.[68]

What was used in the past to distinguish the class of fascisms from Marxist–Leninist regimes was the latter's doctrinal objections to private property and the existence of a market through which the bulk of resource allocations were made and commodities were exchanged for money. With the passage of time and changed circumstances, Marxist–Leninists in the former Soviet Union, in post-Maoist China, and in Vietnam have shown themselves prepared to tolerate private property and market influences in accelerated economic development. As a consequence, the distinctions between "left" and "right" single-party, elitist, nondemocratic growth regimes has become increasingly less substantial.

In Fascist Italy, private property and the market were treated as instrumental to government purposes. Irrespective of the massive intervention of the Fascist state, the exchange of goods and services in the market supplied the price structure by virtue of which allocations could be rationally undertaken, profits fixed, wages established, and collective goals pursued.[69]

However different Marxist–Leninist systems were, and are, from paradigmatic Fascism, given their different histories and national circumstances, the family traits are evident. Both systems conform to the informal, but demanding, logic of anti-democratic reactive developmental nationalism. A syndrome of properties emerge out of all this—too familiar by now to warrant rehearsal. It features the traits of a class of reactive, developmental nationalisms that includes many of the late developing countries of the twentieth century, of which Italian Fascism was the illustrative instance.

Acknowledging all this, there is a sense in which specialists like Renzo De Felice are correct. There was only one Fascism, that of Benito Mussolini.[70] It was a product of the First World War, without which it would not have existed.[71] No other movement had its history, and no other movement, by definition, could have had its history. That granted, everything in the world is unique in the same way and the same sense. Everything in the universe has had a unique history; but there is very little cognitive profit in acknowledging that. With an insistence on the uniqueness of every single thing, speech itself, not to speak of empirical generalization, becomes impossible. We would be condemned to experience the world, but never to have any cognitive purchase on it.

The fact is that we do generalize, typologize, classify, and taxonomize. We tease out similarities and observe family resemblances. We stipulate meanings and offer operational definitions—all in the effort to bring order to our domains of inquiry. We do this for "pretheoretical" purposes, in order to provide, on occasion, for the easy storage and retrieval of otherwise complicated information. We sometimes do it for heuristic purposes, to suggest what to look for among instances of the same putative category of objects or events. And sometimes we do it to establish functional relationships between categories of objects and/or events. All this we do in the hope that viable theory will be forthcoming.

Social science has not been particularly successful in generating predicative theory.[72] Historians and social scientists have provided us with relatively informal typologies and taxonomies intended to provide us some pretheoretical leverage on understanding. Thus Richard Pipes recently reminded us that "Bolshevism and Fascism were heresies of socialism" and shared important species traits, a fact that was early acknowledged by Mussolini himself.[73]

That differences nonetheless distinguished the two can hardly be gainsaid. But differences distinguish any two things—and we still categorize, typologize, and generalize.

Mussolini's Fascism was very different from Hitler's National Socialism, as from Codreanu's legion. More interesting than the confession of differences is the question of how the remaining similarities are to be classified. Given the history of all these revolutionary movements in the twentieth century, perhaps the most reasonable way to classify them would be to identify a genus, "reactive, developmental nationalism," of which "democratic" and "nondemocratic" would be distinguished as species. Developing India, for example, might fall under the rubric of a "democratic" reactive, developmental nationalism.[74] Under the species "nondemocratic" one might find reactive nationalist authoritarianisms and autocracies as subspecies as long as they gave evidence of developmental intent. "Fascisms" would be a subspecies of nondemocratic, reactive, developmental nationalisms. The criterial properties of the subspecies would include possession of a formal ideology inspired by a collectivist socio-philosophy, a clear commitment to accelerated economic growth and development, an institutionalization of elitism and hierarchical arrangements, "charismatic government," mass mobilization, and the inculcation of an ethic of essentially militaristic service and sacrifice, as well as extensive state control of the economy and the flow of information.

As reactive nationalisms, elements of "masculine protest" would be evident. Uniforms would be prevalent. The military would serve as a model for citizens. There would be an emphasis on unanimity in opinion, faith, and sacrifice. Political discourse would feature the language of "manhood," war, struggle, and sacrifice. Irredentism would be a common, if not universal, feature of the subspecies. There would be an aggressive agenda to restore the nation's "true" boundaries. Equally common would be the appearance of a singular "charismatic leader" who would be identified with the "never-setting red sun" or the "millennial genius" of his nation. Should the system survive, charisma would be routinized or bureaucratized. An effort at autarkic self-sufficiency would episodically recommend itself. There would be constant appeal to past glories and a call to a transcendent mission.

Among the subspecies, religious fundamentalisms, various forms of nonspecific authoritarianisms, some racisms and nativisms, as well as incoherent fascisms, would be found—all members of a subspecies sharing some family resemblance. While such a resemblance urges itself upon comparativists, it is not clear what measure of similarity is required to define categories. Even less clear is how similarities are to be quantified. As a consequence, there are questions of degree. How much mobilization must take place if a movement or regime is to qualify as "mass mobilizing"? Should that mobilization find expression in political party mobilization? What might qualify as a "formal ideology"? And how much intervention in the economy qualifies as "extensive"? How many of the traits must a regime display in order to qualify for entry? And what of movements that have not established themselves as regimes? How is one to treat the ideology of a movement that is at demonstrable variance with regime behaviors?

There is, in effect, no end of questions. And there are no easy answers. As in all the informal sciences, what is required is judgment. Taxonomic efforts are pretheoretical. They are undertaken to bring order into an otherwise disorderly universe of inquiry. In the search for order, it is logically possible to generate an "infinite number of schemes."[75] In the human sciences, those that are, in fact, attempted are, more often than not, intended to bring not only order with them, but understanding as well.

"Understanding" can be taken to mean the reduction of puzzlement concerning some complex sequence. Evidence for its success is an avowal on the part of an audience. "Understanding" can also be taken to mean that some recommended ordering of things make possible "generalizations about how the presence, absence, or clustering of certain combinations of variables affect politics."[76] "Theoretical understanding" can be taken to mean that the generalizations forthcoming are testable and afford a measure of predictive competence.

With respect to this final understanding, social scientists have not been notably successful. They have perhaps been least successful in their treatment of Fascism, fascism, Marxist theory, and Marxist–Leninist systems. As a consequence and for the foreseeable future, we will probably not have much that might pass as theoretical understanding of some of the most important political phenomena of our time.

In such parlous circumstances, we can offer very little insight into the future of a "Russian fascism," or the more likely "Chinese fascism" that will occupy space in—and threaten the peace of—the twenty-first century. For all that, in some indeterminate future, perhaps a century from now, social scientists will wonder why we failed to predict the political eventualities of their time, given what they would then perceive to have been the clear anticipations provided by our own.

Appendix:
The Devolution of Marxist "Theories" of Fascism,
A Narrative Chronology, 1919–1995

First Period: 1919–1924   The Fascist movement was formally founded in March 1919. It was an uncertain collection of groups and individuals, whose ideological orientations ranged from those of the left-wing revolutionary national syndicalists to those of the iconoclastic Futurists of F. T. Marinetti. Veterans of the First World War comprised, numerically, the largest single component.

The characteristic Fascist political posture was resistance to the threat of socialist revolution on the Italian peninsula. Fascists specificaly opposed the anti-nationalism and the class warfare commitments of organized socialism. The socialist response was to identify Fascism with "reaction."

At its first appearance, and with its rise to prominence, efforts to provide an interpretative account of Fascism were made by relatively unknown socialist authors like Julius Braunthal (an Austrian Social Democrat) and Julius Deutsch (a German Social Democrat). Fascism was immediately identified as a "creature" and/or a "tool" of simple "class" reaction against the inevitability of the "progressive" world revolution of the "working class."

Fascism's class sponsor was taken to be the "bourgeoisie." Neither the term *bourgeoisie* nor how any such class might create this kind of movement or render it obedient was explored with any rigor. This disability continued throughout the entire period of Marxist speculations concerning *Fascism* as a specific and *fascism* as a generic term.

Such interpretations were by-products of a long Marxist methodological and empirical tradition that defined politics in terms of omnibus bourgeois interests as opposed to those of a "Promethean proletariat." Neither definition of critical terms nor empirical evidence to support the claims of Marxist commentators was forthcoming. It was clear that the earliest interpreters were uncertain which elements of the collective bourgeoisie had ordered, subventionized, directed, or utilized the Fascists in their war of resistance to progress.

Second Period: 1924–1926   The first serious intellectual efforts at interpretation appeared. Gyula Sas (Aquila) (1893–1943), a Hungarian Marxist, produced for the

Comintern Information Department one of the first reasonably coherent accounts of what Marxists understood Fascism to be. He identified *the leaders of Italian industry* as the occult masters of Fascism. Klara Zetkin (1857–1933), the German head of the women's section of the Comintern and member of its Central Committee, followed the lead of Sas and conceived Fascism as the simple instrument of major industrial interests in Italy. The evidence in support of that account was supplied by the unilateral interpretation of the first legislation passed under Fascist control of the Italian political system.

Third Period: 1927–1930   By now it had become evident that it was far from satisfactory to interpret Fascist political behavior exclusively in terms of the interests of the Italian industrial bourgeoisie. Many more interests appeared to be involved. Palmiro Togliatti (1893–1964), Italian Communist Party member and a member of the Presidium of the Comintern, argued that Fascism represented *an entire consortium of propertied classes* on the Italian peninsula. This meant that it would be difficult, if not impossible, to identify any political consequences of such control. Fascism could conceivably formulate, pursue, and implement contradictory policy practices without confirming or disconfirming any or all claims that such activities were class-based. *Whatever* Fascism did could be interpreted as serving one or another bourgeois interest.

Fourth Period: 1931–1935   During this period, Fascism revealed itself to be more than a function of the peculiarities of Latin circumstances and Latin temperament. Adolf Hitler's National Socialism made its appearance in one of the most advanced nations of Europe. What Marxists sought was a comprehensive account that was applicable to both Italy and Germany, as well as to those fascist-like movements that had emerged in various other European and non-European environments during the same period. A "standard version" of what would pass as the "Marxist theory of generic fascism" appeared with the publication in 1934 of the work of Rajani Palme Dutt (1896–1974), an Indian–English Marxist–Leninist, who argued that fascism was the *specific reactionary response of finance capital* to the apparent "general crisis" that had overwhelmed industrial capitalism in 1929.

Karl Marx had left his followers with a theoretical expectation that the average profit rate of capitalism must at some point inevitably sink to "absolute zero," bringing the entire Western industrial enterprise to a halt. Palme Dutt interpreted the Great Depression of 1929 as that anticipated final crisis. Since there could be no rational resolution of such a crisis, the masters of Western capitalist industry, the finance capitalists, acted as sponsors, organizers, financiers, and directors of fascism in their effort to artificially sustain their revenues. Hitler and Mussolini were the "supine agents" of their creators. They were assigned the task of monopolizing their respective industrial systems in order to produce goods at planned low levels, so as to maintain sustainable profit levels.

Fascists were to destroy education in order to suppress technological innovation in a system that, according to traditional Marxist theory, derived profits exclusively from human labor. Fascism was designed to obstruct any industrial improvements, because capitalism, in its final crisis, was compelled to reduce productivity. Moribund capitalism was committed to a "new dark age"—and fascism was its instrument.

As a consequence, the standard of living throughout the capitalist countries must gradually, but systematically, decline. The means of production must be destroyed, because improvement in those means would generate increases in supply that could not be distributed by capitalism at a profit. According to the thesis, the declining rate of profit was the nemesis of industrial capitalism. Fascism was the spawn of that "internal contradiction," finance capitalism's pathological response to its final crisis.

In 1935, the substance of this account appeared in a report authored by Georgi Dimitroff (1882–1949) that served as the main report of the Seventh Congress of the Communist International, thereby receiving the official imprimatur of Soviet Marxism–Leninism. Generic fascism was "the open terrorist dictatorship of the most reactionary, most chauvinistic, and most imperialistic elements of finance capital."

Trotskyists like Daniel Guerin (1904–1988) attempted to make the same case at approximately the same time. Other Marxists, not affiliated with either wing of Marxism–Leninism, argued that the official standard version was impaired in a number of critical ways.

Even before the close of the fourth period, a major work by the German Marxist Franz Borkenau (1900–57), "The Sociology of Fascism," which appeared in the *Archiv fuer Sozialwissenschaft und Sozialpolitik* in February 1933, argued that the standard version was predicated on the notion that the "historic tasks" of fascism were to *retard* economic growth and industrial modernization, when in fact *Italian Fascism sponsored developmental programs* for the Italian peninsula. At about the same time, the Austrian Marxist Otto Bauer (1881–1938) argued that generic fascism had *demonstrated political independence from any specific bourgeois faction* and operated as an "independent force" sustained by a *multi-class base*. It was the product of a political environment in which no single class could dominate.

Fifth Period: 1936–1940 This period was characterized by important intellectual developments. While the official Marxist–Leninist interpretation remained that of Georgi Dimitroff, it was evident to many that Fascism could not be dismissed as opportunistic.

While the vagueness and ambiguity of the term *bourgeois* allowed fascism to be identified, in some sense, with the class required by traditional Marxist theory, the clear evidence of its developmental properties and political independence could not be accounted for so easily. Fascism could be identified with the bourgeoisie, because *it provided protection for private property and for the role of private enterprise in economic activities*, but *it could not be identified as a creature or tool of capitalism*. More than that, Leon Trotsky (1879–1940), an anti-Stalinist Marxist–Leninist, recognized the "substantial similarities" between fascism and Stalinism.

Sixth Period: 1941–1949 The effort to provide a convincing interpretation of generic fascism largely ceased during the period of the Second World War and its immediate aftermath. Soviet intellectuals simply repeated the standard version of 1935, and the employment of what were taken to be the defining properties of generic fascism became increasingly commonplace. Fascism was seen to be a bourgeois political system, designed to defend private property and industrial capitalism. Its overt political features included (1) the leadership principle (rule by a charismatic figure); (2) a hegemonic party (single-party rule); (3) large-scale state intervention in the economy (state monopoly capitalism); (4) extensive control over education, communication, and social life; (5) nationalism, chauvinism, and aggressiveness; (6) militarization of the economy; (7) invocation of an obedience and sacrifice ethic; in (8) the service of a national mission; with (9) the restoration of lost lands as part of a comprehensive policy of return to national grandeur.

The "fascist powers" were defeated in the course of the Second World War, but Mao Zedong (1893–1976) identified the forces of Republican China as a "fascism" that had survived, and he proceeded to pursue the resolution of a civil war that had beset mainland China since the 1920s. The definition of Chinese fascism was understood to conform to the standard Marxist–Leninist account of the interwar years. The leadership of Republican China was *the tool of the generic Chinese bourgeoisie or the "foreign imperialists" or both together*.

Seventh Period: 1950–1962   Little in the way of responsible interpretation of generic fascism was attempted during this period. The lines of struggle had been drawn, and the Korean War (1950–53) had pitted the United States and its allies against the Soviet Union, Mao's China, and North Korea: the "imperialists" against the "worldwide proletarian revolution."

The death of J. V. Stalin (1878–1953) precipitated events that gave impetus to changes in the official Marxist–Leninist interpretation of fascism. N. S. Khrushchev's denunciation of Stalin in 1956 created intellectual space in which Soviet and non-Soviet Marxist–Leninists and Marxists could attempt a more cognitively persuasive interpretation of fascism.

At the end of this period in Italy, the Communist Party theoretician Paolo Alatri argued that Italian Fascism was *multi-class in origin and, while bourgeois "in essence," developmental in character*. In some sense, it was a variant of "bourgeois dictatorship" that shepherded the economy of the peninsula from one to another, more progressive level. The relationship between the owners of property and industry and Fascist rule was not direct. Fascism was no longer seen as simply a "class phenomenon," but as a complicated political system that arose in a complex political environment.

Eighth Period: 1963–1969   At the end of the seventh period, because of growing bilateral tension, the Marxists of Mao Zedong began to identify the Soviet Union as a "robber imperialist state." Krushchev was declared a "number one capitalist-roader" attempting to restore capitalism to the Soviet Union, creating thereby a "*social-fascist dictatorship*." The increasing intellectual independence that appeared with the Khrushchev "thaw" saw scholars such as Alexander Galkin arguing that fascism, hitherto arbitrarily interpreted in accordance with the contrived artificialities of the Comintern, might best be characterized not as a product of the "final crisis" of capitalism, but as *a response to the demands of a "new stage" in the development of "state monopoly capitalism."* The leadership of fascism was *neither the creature nor the tool of* *any specific class, if class is defined in terms of the ownership of the material means of production.*

According to this evolving thesis, fascism was a sort of "Bonapartist" political system, which, while serving the "general interests of the bourgeoisie," was not created, sustained, controlled, or directed by the bourgeoisie. Under crisis conditions, fascism ushered the capitalist industrial system from one level of development to another. It was simply one form of modern state monopoly capitalism, with the traditional prerogatives of capitalists surrendered to a politically independent dictatorship capable of dragging industrial capitalism into wars of mass destruction.

At about the same time, Mihaly Vadja, a member of the Hungarian Academy of Sciences, argued that Italian Fascism, in particular, was a *"progressive" response to the crisis of industrial capitalism* on the peninsula. The "proletarian forces" that threatened Italy with socialist revolution after the First World War were "reactionary," because, had their demands been met, Italy would not have been able to accumulate the capital, retain the entrepreneurial talent, or provide the incentives for economic growth and industrial development. Had the socialist revolution prevailed in post–First World War Italy, that country would have languished at the level of marginal industrial growth.

It is in this context that the major work of Nicos Poulantzas (1936–79) appeared in Europe. His was clearly an effort to provide some Marxist–Leninist understanding of the worsening Sino–Soviet split.

If fascism could no longer be identified as a direct consequence of bourgeoisie ownership of the means of production, it might better be seen as *a result of political class struggle between elements of the bourgeoisie*—agrarian, petty, commercial, industrial, and financial. Further, since such "class struggle" was political, it need not be directly associated with the ownership of property; so *"fascism" could exist in environments innocent of private property and capitalist industry*. All that was required was a collection of persons who entertained bourgeois intentions—a "class" of "capitalist-roaders." Thus, it could be argued that the Soviet Union, where private property had been abolished with the revolution, had been transformed into a "fascist state."

The Soviet Union had established a new class system in which those who *controlled* collective property could employ it to their advantage. To protect their "social-fascist state," the Soviet Union's "capitalist-roaders" took on all the subsidiary properties of traditional fascism. They become oppressive with respect to their domestic population and aggressive and exploitative in dealing with their neighbors. Poulantzas had supplied a Maoist interpretation of fascism that allowed the Soviet Union to be identified as an exemplar of the class.

Ninth Period: 1970–1980   What Poulantzas had done was to provide, for Westerners, a fairly coherent account of generic fascism as that account became standard in the writings of the intellectual and political leaders of China's chaotic "Great Proletarian Revolution." Yao Wenyuan, Zhang Chunqiao, and Wang Hongwen had made their case in essays that had been widely distributed throughout China and the West as a vindication of Beijing's denunciation of Soviet fascism.

At about the same time, commencing before the end of the preceding period, various Soviet authors came to perceive *Maoism as a form of "petty bourgeois revolutionism" and an identifiable form of fascism*. Not only had the Chinese leadership declared Soviet Marxism a "class enemy," but by the first years of the 1970s they had begun a *rapprochement* with the "imperialist" United States.

Since Marxist–Leninists in general no longer identified fascism as the instrument of a particular class of property owners, it might be associated with any collection of persons in authority, controlling but not owning property, who used their power for their own benefit. Such persons could be found in any "socialist" environment.

Soviet authors cited the "bourgeois character" of the leadership of Maoism, its anti-intellectualism, its aggressiveness, its invocation of force in the service of political ends, its express nationalism, its reliance on mass mobilization through ritual and liturgy, its appeals to charismatic leadership, its fostering and sustaining of single-party dominance of the system, its militarization of the economy, as well as its flirtation with "imperialism," as evidence of a Chinese fascism. Chinese Marxist–Leninists, in turn, identified the reintroduction of market elements into the command economy of the Soviet Union, Moscow's increasing appeals to the state and national interests, its use of military force against "fraternal socialist states" such as Czechoslovakia, Hungary, and Poland, together with its domestic "restoration of capitalism" and its abandonment of proletarian values, as compelling evidence of its fascist character.

By the end of the period, Marxist–Leninist commentators in both the Soviet Union and the People's Republic of China were characterizing the political, economic, and social system of the other as fascist. Fascism was perceived in terms of *political intentions* rather than any empirical class properties. A fascist political and economic system was one that supported material class, sectoral, and regional differences and was geared to the industrial and technological maintenance and expansive support of an institutionalized military. It was a system that had abandoned class warfare as a "key element" and was nationalistic, essentially chauvinistic, and territorially aggressive. Its leadership was animated by a conviction of its own inerrancy. It was essentially anti-liberal, anti-democratic in practice, elitist in disposition, and episodically mass-mobilizing.

On 9 September 1976, Mao Zedong died. China was immediately plunged into political crisis. Mao's hand-picked successor, Hua Guofeng, was dismissed, and Deng Xiaoping acceded to power. The leaders of Mao's Gang of Four, architects of the devastating Great Proletarian Cultural Revolution, were arrested.

At the same time, the protracted economic crisis of the Soviet Union steadily worsened. Various desultory attempts were made to reform the dysfunctional command economy. A series of ineffectual leaders succeeded Leonid Brezhnev.

Final Period: 1981–1995   In 1985 Konstantin Chernenko died and was succeeded, on 10 March 1985, by Mikhail Gorbachev. The Soviet Union subsequently lapsed into a systemic crisis from which it was not to emerge.

By then, Western Marxists like Charles Bettelheim had identified the reformist system introduced into China by Deng as fascist. Chinese domestic critics like Wang

Xizhe rendered similar judgments. The Marxist–Leninist theory of fascism, transformed by six decades of revision, served as grounds for such judgments.

In the Soviet Union, Marxist–Leninist theoreticians who were opposed to Gorbachev's "new thinking" finally articulated those theoretical, institutional, and practical differences between "Marxism–Leninism" as it had dogmatically been presented throughout the Soviet period and the truly revolutionary ideology that promised salvation to the threatened Russian state and the people it served. Sergei Kurginian and Alexander Prokhanov prepared a "spiritual" and "patriotic" program for the "national-patriotic forces" organized behind Gennadi Ziuganov, leader of the Communist Party of the Russian Federation. The proposed program, designed to salvage the nation in its mortal struggle with foreign powers, was predicated on extensive class collaboration, qualified defense of private property, and employment of market adjuncts to direct the economy. Russia was to continue its "historic responsibilities" as the Eurasian "gatherer of lands" and recover its dominance throughout what had been the Soviet empire.

The national-patriotic forces committed themselves to the restoration of Russia's status as a major military power. They anticipated a political system that would not suffer from the disabilities of liberalism. The entire ideological system was supported by an appeal to the ethnobiological convictions of Lev Gumilev (1912–92), who understood nations to be bioethnic units structured over time, sustained by an in-group amity and an out-group enmity that found expression in patriotism, and which, under special leadership, in times of "passion," entered into a process of major territorial and cultural expansion. Gumilev argued that all these notions were fully compatible with the Marxism–Leninism that inspired them.

What almost everyone else has maintained is that Gumilev's ideas share major theoretical affinities with the "natioracism" of Fascism. Further, both Kurginian and Prokhanov have acknowledged the general similarities of their ideological convictions with those of classical Fascism. In substance, the ideology that inspires the national-patriotic forces of Ziuganov's Communist Party shares demonstrable resemblances to the Fascism of Mussolini. The nationalism, the domestic class collaboration and the international "class conflict," the commitment to a vanguard party and rapid domestic economic and technological development, the irredentism and the potential appeal to autarky, the inculcation of a work, obedience, and sacrifice ethic, are all classical Fascist postures. Marxism–Leninism, as a consequence of its own internal "dialectic," has transformed itself into what is manifestly a form of paradigmatic Fascism.

Notes

Preface

1. Robert Soucy, *French Fascism: The First Wave, 1924–1933* (New Haven: Yale University Press, 1986), p. xi.

2. Mark Neocleous, *Fascism* (Minneapolis: University of Minnesota Press, 1997), p. x.

3. See Peter H. Merkl and Leonard Weinberg (eds.), *The Revival of Right-Wing Extremism in the Nineties* (London: Frank Cass, 1997).

4. See the entire discussion in works like Roger Griffin, *The Nature of Fascism* (London: Routledge, 1991), and Roger Eatwell, *Fascism: A History* (New York: Penguin, 1995).

5. See A. James Gregor, *The Fascist Persuasion in Radical Politics* (Princeton: Princeton University Press, 1974).

Chapter 1: On Theory and Revolution in Our Time

1. The term *revolution* will be used throughout to mean "any systemic change in the sociopolitical order that is the consequence of the use, or the threat of the use, of violence."

2. The term *Fascism*, capitalized, will refer throughout to the Fascism of Benito Mussolini. The term *fascism*, lowercase, will refer to the class of generic fascisms.

3. See, e.g., the views of Peter H. Merkl, "Introduction" to Peter H. Merkl and Leonard Weinberg (eds.), *The Revival of Right-Wing Extremism in the Nineties* (London: Frank Cass, 1997), pp. 1–16.

4. Glyn Ford (ed.), *Fascist Europe: The Rise of Racism and Xenophobia* (London: Pluto, 1992), pp. x–xiii.

5. To be told that "common to all movements of fascism" was "brutality . . . a contempt for the individual and a love of violence," tells us very little. With such a descriptive characterization, one could anticipate an almost infinite number of candidates for membership of the class "fascist." See the discussion in H. R. Kedward, *Fascism in Western Europe 1900–45* (New York: New York University Press, 1971), pp. 4, 26.

6. As with *Fascism/fascism*, the term *communism* refers to the class of systems so identified. It will be capitalized when preceded by a specifying term, so "Soviet Communism" or "Chinese Communism."

7. Roger Griffin, *The Nature of Fascism* (London: Routledge, 1991), pp. 183, 229.

8. As cited in Paul Hollander, *Decline and Discontent: Communism and the West Today* (New Brunswick, N.J.: Transaction, 1992), p. 127.

9. See Norman Mailer, "A Country Not a Scenario," *Parade Magazine*, 19 August 1984, as quoted in Paul Hollander, *The Survival of the Adversary Culture* (New Brunswick, N.J.: Transaction, 1988), p. 54; the discussion in J. Arch Getty, *Origins of the Great Purges: The Soviet Communist Party Reconsidered* (New York: Cambridge University Press, 1985); and R. J. Barnet, *The Giants—Russia and America* (New York: Simon and Schuster, 1977), pp. 93, 106, 111, 119, 168–169, 171–175.

10. See the discussion in Paul Hollander, *Political Pilgrims* (New York: Oxford University Press, 1981).

11. See, e.g., A. James Gregor, *The Fascist Persuasion in Radical Politics* (Princeton: Princeton University Press, 1974), chaps. 2–4, and *idem, A Survey of Marxism: Problems in Philosophy and the Theory of History* (New York: Random House, 1965), chaps. 5, 6. More recently, the Bolshevik revolution has been described as "a daring move by a handful of zealots leading a motley crowd of soldiers, workers, and sailors . . . to seize power" (Adam B. Ulam, *The Communists: The Story of Power and Lost Illusions 1948–1991* [New York: Scribners, 1992], p. 487).

12. Paul Hollander, "Durable Significance of Political Pilgrimage," *Society*, 34, no. 5 (July/Aug. 1997): 45–55.

13. Roger Eatwell, *Fascism: A History* (New York: Penguin, 1995), chaps. 11–14.

14. As late as 1990, Sheldon Wolin could still argue that the communist regimes, being of the left, were the "only ones that professed, and to some degree achieved, a commitment to equality" (Sheldon Wolin, "Beyond Marxism and Monetarism," *Nation*, 19 Mar. 1990, p. 373).

15. Piero Ignazi, "The Extreme Right in Europe: A Survey," in Merkl and Weinberg (eds.), *Revival*, p. 48.

16. Walter Laqueur, *Fascism: Past, Present, Future* (New York: Oxford University Press, 1996), p. 90.

17. See the discussion in Ignazi, "Extreme Right," pp. 48, 49.

18. Peter Merkl, "Introduction" to Merkl and Weinberg (eds.), *Revival*, p. 2.

19. More than a generation ago, the similarities between the Right and the Left were argued in Gregor, *Fascist Persuasion in Radical Politics*.

20. Mikhail Agursky, "The Soviet Legitimacy Crisis and Its International Implications," in Morton Kaplan (ed.), *The Many Faces of Communism* (New York: Free Press, 1978), p. 150.

21. Peter Viereck, "The Mob within the Heart," in P. Juviler and H. Morton (eds.), *Soviet Policy Making* (New York: Praeger, 1967), p. 27. See Agursky's comments, "Soviet Legitimacy," p. 167.

22. Henry E. Carey, "Post-Communist Right Radicalism in Romania," in Merkl and Weinberg (eds.), *Revival*, p. 149.

23. Merkl, "Introduction," in ibid., p. 8.

24. See Gennadi Kostyrchenko, *Out of the Red Shadows: Anti-Semitism in Stalin's Russia* (Amherst, N.Y.: Prometheus, 1995), and Arkady Vaksberg, *Stalin against the Jews* (New York: Knopf, 1994). See the account in Mikhail Agursky, *The Third Rome: National Bolshevism in the USSR* (Boulder, Colo.: Westview, 1987).

25. While it is to the "extreme right" that the author addresses his comments, it is clear that communist systems, no less than fascist ones, demonstrate these same properties (Ignazi, "Extreme Right," pp. 48–49).

26. Ibid.

27. As quoted by Walter Laqueur, *The Dream that Failed: Reflections on the Soviet Union* (New York: Oxford University Press, 1994), p. 78.

28. That was the central thesis of my *Fascist Persuasion in Radical Politics*.

29. See, e.g., Richard Pipes, *Russia under the Bolshevik Regime* (New York: Vintage, 1995), chap. 5.

30. See the discussion in A. James Gregor, " 'Totalitarianism' Revisited," in Ernest A. Menze (ed.), *Totalitarianism Reconsidered* (London: Kennikat, 1981), pp. 130–145.

31. Pipes, *Russia*, p. 245.

32. Stephen F. Cohen, "Bolshevism and Stalinism," in Menze (ed.), *Totalitarianism*, p. 67.

33. See the discussion in Michael Mann, "The Contradictions of Continuous Revolution," in Ian Kershaw and Moshe Lewin (eds.), *Stalinism and Nazism: Dictatorships in Comparison* (New York: Cambridge University Press, 1997), esp. pp. 135f.

34. See the discussion in Pipes, *Russia*, pp. 275–278.

35. See the entire discussion in ibid., chap. 5.

36. See the discussion in Kenneth Murphy, *Retreat from the Finland Station: Moral Odysseys in the Breakdown of Communism* (New York: Free Press, 1992).

37. Martin Malia, "From under the Rubble—What?," *Problems of Communism*, Jan.–Apr. 1992, p. 105.

38. See Hollander, *Political Pilgrims*.

39. See the discussion in Bill Brugger and David Kelly (eds.), *Chinese Marxism in the Post-Mao Era* (Stanford, Calif.: Stanford University Press, 1990), pp. 171–175.

40. See the discussion in Carl Linden and Jan S. Prybyla, *Russia and China on the Eve of a New Millenium* (New Brunswick, N.J.: Transaction, 1997), chap. 2.

41. Pipes, *Russia*, p. 242.

42. Ibid., p. 253.

43. Ibid., p. 264.

44. Ibid., pp. 245 and 253.

45. A selection of the variety of Marxist notions of fascism advanced during the interwar years is available in David Beetham (ed.), *Marxists in Face of Fascism: Writings by Marxists on Fascism from the Inter-War Period* (Manchester: Manchester University Press, 1983).

46. See the discussion in A. James Gregor, *An Introduction to Metapolitics: A Brief Inquiry into the Conceptual Language of Political Science* (New York: Free Press, 1971).

47. See the discussion in Gregor, *Survey of Marxism*, chaps. 1, 2, 5, 7.

48. See the insightful discussion in Fred M. Gottheil, *Marx's Economic Predictions* (Evanston, Ill.: Northwestern University Press, 1966).

49. See the discussion in Arif Dirlik, "Postsocialism? Reflections on 'Socialism with Chinese Characteristics,' " in Arik Dirlik and Maurice Meisner (eds.), *Marxism and the Chinese Experience* (Armonk, N.Y.: M. E. Sharpe, 1989), pp. 363–376.

50. See *London Times*, 2 Nov. 1929; and George Sabine, "State," in *Encyclopaedia of the Social Sciences* (New York: Macmillan, 1934), vol. 14, p. 330.

51. Pipes, *Russia*, p. 242.

52. Ibid., p. 245.

53. See the suggestions in Laqueur, *Fascism*, chap. 3; Alexander Yanov, *Weimar Russia and What We Can Do About It* (New York: Slovo-World, 1995); Vladimir Kartsev, *Zhirinovsky!* (New York: Columbia University Press, 1995); Vladimir Solovyov and Elena Klepikova, *Zhirinovsky: Russian Fascism and the Making of a Dictator* (New York: Addison-Wesley, 1995).

54. See the discussion in Alexander Yanov, *The Russian New Right: Right-Wing Ideologies in the Contemporary USSR* (Berkeley: Institute of International Studies, 1978).

55. James P. Scanlan, "From Samizdat to Perestroika: The Soviet Marxist Critique of Soviet Society," in Raymond Taras (ed.), *The Road to Disillusion: From Critical Marxism to Postcommunism in Eastern Europe* (Armonk, N.Y.: M. E. Sharpe, 1992), p. 37.

56. A. Volkov and V. Mironov (eds.), *The Phenomenon of Socialism: Essence, Regularities, Perspectives* (Moscow: Global Research Institute, 1990), pp. 43–44, 90, 159, 183.

57. See Kershaw and Lewin, "Afterthoughts," in *idem* (eds.), *Stalinism and Nazism*, pp. 343–358.

58. Anthony Daniels, *Utopias Elsewhere. Journeys in a Vanishing World: North Korea, Cuba, Albania, Romania, Vietnam* (New York: Crown, 1991), p. 9.

59. See the comments in Pipes, *Russia*, p. 280.

60. See Zeev Sternhell's discussion of fascism in France: *Neither Right nor Left: Fascist Ideology in France* (Los Angeles: University of California Press, 1986).

61. Ibid., p. 270.

62. See A. James Gregor, *Phoenix: Fascism in Our Time* (New Brunswick, N.J.: Transaction, 1999).

Chapter 2: The First Marxist Theories of Fascism

1. See the account in A. James Gregor, *Young Mussolini and the Intellectual Origins of Fascism* (Los Angeles: University of California Press, 1979). The most substantial account of the early history of Fascism is to be found in the definitive biography of Mussolini written by Renzo De Felice; see his *Mussolini il rivoluzionario* (Turin: Einaudi, 1965) and *Mussolini il fascista: La conquista del potere 1921–1925* (Turin: Einaudi, 1966).

2. Mussolini regularly maintained that while Fascists opposed the politics of communists, it shared with them "intellectual affinities" (Mussolini, "Per la vera pacificazione," in *Opera omnia* [Florence: La Fenice, 1953–64], vol. 17, p. 295).

3. Only in the English edition of the *Manifesto* of 1888, years after Marx's death, did Engels attempt to define the concepts *bourgeoisie* and *proletariat*, and then the definition was *lexical*—i.e., without quantification or measure. Much the same can be said about almost all the central concepts of classical Marxism. None are defined with measurable or testable precision. That includes essential concepts such as *material forces of production*, *productive relations*, and *subsistence wage*. Some of these issues are dealt with more extensively in A. James Gregor, *A Survey of Marxism: Problems in Philosophy and the Theory of History* (New York: Random House, 1965), chaps. 1, 2, and 5, esp. pp. 273–281.

4. For a more elaborate account, see A. James Gregor, *The Fascist Persuasion in Radical Politics* (Princeton: Princeton University Press, 1974), chaps. 2 and 3.

5. See Karl Marx, *Capital* (Moscow: Foreign Languages, 1954), vol. 3, pp. 227–230; Joseph M. Gillman, *The Falling Rate of Profit* (London: Unwin, 1957).

6. See the more ample discussion in Gregor, *Fascist Persuasion in Radical Politics*, pp. 62–75.

7. See E. Galli della Loggia, *La III Internazionale e il destino del capitalismso: l'analisi di Evghenij Varga* (Milan: Feltrinelli, 1973), pp. 980–1015.

8. Julius Braunthal, "Der Putsch der Faschisten," *Der Kampf*, 22, no. 11 (Nov. 1922): 323.

9. Julius Deutsch, *Die Faschistengefahr* (Vienna: Volksbuchhandlung, 1923), p. 5.

10. See John M. Cammett, "Communist Theories of Fascism, 1920–1935," *Science and Society*, 31, no. 2 (1967): 150–155.

11. The original text is very difficult to obtain. The available translation, G. Aquila, "Il fascismo italiano," in R. De Felice (ed.), *Il fascismo e i partiti politici Italiana* (Rocca San Casciano: Cappelli, 1966), is a translation of the German text. A revised, enlarged edition, *Fascistkoi Italia*, appeared in Moscow in 1929; see p. 421.

12. Karl Marx and Friedrich Engels, *The Communist Manifesto* (New York: International, 1987), p. 11.

13. In the third volume of *Das Kapital*, Marx spoke of an "infinite fragmentation of interests and rank created by the social division of labor among laborers, capitalists and landlords." The putative relationship between ownership of the means of production and "class interests" appears increasingly uncertain in a number of places in the Marx corpus. See Marx, *Capital*, vol. 3, p. 863.

14. Ibid., pp. 477–479, 482, 494.

15. Clara Zetkin, "Der Kampf gegen den Faschismus," in Ernst Nolte (ed.), *Theorien ueber den Faschismus* (Munich: Kiepenheuer & Witsch, 1967), pp. 88–111.

16. Aquila, "Il fascismo italiano," p. 469; Zetkin, "Der Kampf gegen den Faschismus," p. 99.

17. Cf. Aquila, "Il fascismo italiano," pp. 458–467, and Zetkin, "Der Kampf gegen den Fachismus," pp. 99–105.

18. "La lotta di classe e il fascismo," in C. Casucci (ed.), *Il fascismo* (Milan: Mulino, 1961), p. 271; emphasis added.

19. Ibid., pp. 275, 276.

20. As cited in R. Palme Dutt, *Fascism and Social Revolution* (New York: International, 1934), pp. 88–90, my emphasis.

21. Palmiro Togliatti, "A proposito del fascismo," in Casucci (ed.), *Fascismo*, p. 291.

22. Ibid., pp. 292, 298; cf. p. 294.

23. See the comments in Ernst Nolte, "Introduction," in Nolte (ed.), *Theorien*, p. 54.

24. Georgi Dimitroff, *The United Front against War and Fascism* (New York: Gamma, 1974), p. 7.

25. Daniel Guerin, *Fascism and Big Business* (New York: Pathfinder, 1973; 1st ed. in French in July 1936); and R. Palme Dutt, *Fascism and Social Revolution: A Study of the Economics and Politics of the Extreme Stages of Capitalism in Decay* (San Francisco: Proletarian Publishers, 1974; 1st ed. in June 1934).

26. See Leonardo Rapone, *Trotskij e il fascismo* (Rome: Laterza, 1978), pp. 12–16, 21.

27. I have attempted to unpack the logic of the claim that the rate of profit in industrial capitalism *must* decline over time in Gregor, *Fascist Persuasion in Radical Politics*, chaps. 2 and 3.

28. Guerin, *Fascism and Big Business*, p. 22.

29. Thus, one of Leon Trotsky's followers gave expression to a proposition that had become a commonplace among most Marxists: "The whole basis of Fascism arises out of the decomposition and decay of capitalism" (E. R. Frank, "Introduction," in Leon Trotsky, *Fascism: What It Is; How to Fight It* [New York: Pioneer Publishers, 1944], p. 8).

30. Ibid., p. 24.

31. See esp. Guerin, *Fascism and Big Business*, pp. 209, 239, and 284.

32. These notions were the *deductive* consequences of holding some antecedent premises to be true. There are few economists who accept the notion that the value of commodities is determined by the amount of "concretized living labor" they incorporate. Fewer still believe that increments in investment in research and development, technological improvement and machinery, must necessarily reduce the rate of profit. In this context, see the interesting analysis of Marx's deductive system in Fred Gottheil, *Marx's Economic Predictions* (Evanston, Ill.: Northwestern University Press, 1966).

33. See Jane Degras, *The Communist International 1919–1943: Documents* (London: Pluto, 1956), vol. 2, p. 418.

34. As quoted in T. Pirker (ed.), *Komintern und Faschismus, 1920–1940* (Munich: DTV, 1966), pp. 176, 180.

35. Guerin, "Preface to the 1945 French Edition," in *Fascism and Big Business*, p. 7.

36. Palme Dutt, *Fascism and Social Revolution*, pp. 13, 24.

37. Ibid., pp. 245ff.

38. Ibid., p. 16.

39. Ibid., pp. 73, 77, 308.

40. See the discussion of the rates of real growth in industrial production in Italy during the Fascist regime. Shepard B. Clough, e.g., indicated that by 1926 Fascist Italy had regained its pre–First World War levels of production and rates of consumption per capita (*The Economic History of Modern Italy* [New York: Columbia University Press, 1964], pp. 226–227). The period between 1922 and 1929 in Fascist Italy was characterized by rapid industrial and agricultural expansion. See Rosario Romeo, *Breve storia della grande industria in Italia* (Rocca San Casciano: Cappelli, 1967), pp. 134–135.

41. Ibid., p. 19.

42. See the discussion in ibid., chap. 12.

43. See the discussion in Gregor, *Young Mussolini*, chap. 10.

44. In this regard see Angelo Tasca, *Nascita e avento del fascismo* (Milan: La nuova Italia, 1950), pp. 513–525; De Felice, *Mussolini il rivoluzionario*, chap. 14; *idem, Mussolini il fascista*, chaps. 1–4; Mario Missiroli, *Il fascismo e il colpo di stato dell'Ottobre 1922* (Rome: Cappelli, 1966); Roberto Michels, "Elemente zur Entstehungsgeschichte des italienischen Faschismus (1922)," in *Sozialismus und Faschismus in Italien* (Munich: Meyer & Jensen, 1925), pp. 251–324.

45. In this regard, see Roland Sarti, *Fascism and the Industrial Leadership in Italy: 1919–1940* (Los Angeles: University of California Press, 1971).

46. In this context see some of the discussion in Renzo De Felice, *Mussolini il fascista: l'organizzazione dello stato fascista* (Turin: Einaudi, 1968), chap. 3.

47. See, e.g., Galeazzo Ciano, *Ciano's Hidden Diary: 1937–1938* (New York: Dutton, 1953) and *The Ciano Diaries: 1939–1943* (New York: Doubleday, 1946); cf. also G. Rumi, *Alle origini della politica estera fascista* (Bari: Laterza, 1968); Luigi Villari, *Italian Foreign Policy under Mussolini* (New York: Devin-Adair, 1956).

48. For years after the Second World War, Marxist theoreticians insisted that Fascism had imposed "stagnation" on the peninsula's economic system. That this contention could not be supported was argued by Italy's major postwar economists. See Gianni Toniolo, *L'economia dell'Italia fascista* (Rome: Laterza, 1980), chap. 1.

49. Nicos Poulantzas, *Fascism and Dictatorship* (London: NLB, 1974), p. 98; emphasis added.

50. "On the one hand, the massive introduction of capitalism into agriculture clearly produced some spectacular results in Italy: notably the yield of cereal production, which was chronically inadequate." By 1939, Poulantzas reported, Fascist Italy was producing enough grain to satisfy the needs of the nation (ibid., p. 119).

51. W. Welk, *Fascist Economic Policy* (Cambridge, Mass.: Harvard University Press, 1938), p. 200; see also pp. 191–205.

52. See, e.g., E. Ragionieri, "La storia politica e sociale," in *Storia d'Italia* (Turin: Einaudi, 1975), vol. 4, pt. 3, p. 218.

53. See the discussion in Bruno Caizzi, *Storia dell'industria Italiana* (Turin: UTET, 1965), chap. 15, and the comments of Stanley Payne, *A History of Fascism 1919–1945* (Madison: University of Wisconsin Press, 1995), chap. 14.

54. Angus Maddison, *Economic Growth in the West* (New York: Twentieth Century Fund, 1964), appendices A, E, H, and I.

55. See August Thalheimer, "Ueber den Faschismus," in W. Abendroth (ed.), *Faschismus und Kapitalismus* (Hamburg: Europaeische Verlangsanstalt, 1967), pp. 19–38.

56. Arthur Rosenberg, "Der Faschismus als Massenbewegung," in Abendroth (ed.), *Faschismus und Kapitalismus*, p. 114.

57. Otto Bauer, "Der Faschismus," in Abendroth (ed.), *Faschismus und Kapitalismus*, pp. 143–167, esp. pp. 151, 153, 156, 162.

58. Franz Borkenau, "Zur Soziologie des Faschismus," in Nolte (ed.), *Theorien*, pp. 156–181.

59. Ibid., esp. pp. 164, 165, 178.

60. The germ of these notions appeared in Otto Bauer, *Die oesterreichische Revolution* (Vienna: n.p., 1923), pp. 242–248, 275–291.

61. As quoted in Gerhard Botz, "Austro-Marxist Interpretation of Fascism," *Journal of Contemporary History*, 11 (1976): 133.

62. According to Guerin, the bourgeoisie, faced with the crises of "decaying capitalism," "handed over the state to completely subservient politicians"—the fascists (*Fascism and Big Business*, p. 32; see also pp. 39, 113, 115, 117, 137). Guerin claimed that Hitler frequently and simply "obeyed his financial backers" (p. 142) or went "in person to Krupp, in Essen, to get his orders" (p. 145). Both Mussolini and Hitler were compelled to "obey" their financial masters (p. 204) and "capitalist magnates" (p. 239). For Guerin, fascism was simply the obedient tool of "monopolistic heavy industry" (p. 287). For Palme Dutt it was the "decision of the bourgeoisie" to put "fascism in power" (*Fascism and Social Revolution*, pp. 144, 145), and it was to the bourgeoisie that fascists owed allegience and obedience.

63. Palme Dutt, *Fascism and Social Revolution*, p. 213.

64. "Resolution of the VII Congress of the Communist International," in T. Pirker (ed.), *Utopie and Mythos der Weltrevolution* (Munich: DTV, 1964), p. 226, and Palme Dutt, *Fascism and Social Revolution*, p. 8.

65. Borkenau, "Zur Soziologie," p. 178. See the discussion in Salvatore La Francesca, *La politica economica del fascismo* (Rome: Laterza, 1973), *passim*.

66. As quoted in Botz, "Austro-Marxist Interpretation of Fascism," p. 133.

67. Leon Trotsky, *The Revolution Betrayed* (New York: Doubleday, 1937), p. 278.

68. Bruno Rizzi, *La lezione dello Stalinismo* (Rome: Opere nuove, 1962), p. 38.

69. G. Prezzolini, "Ideologia e sentimento," and R. Mondolfo, "Il fascismo in Italia," both in De Felice (ed.), *Il fascismo e i partiti politici Italiani*, pp. 522f., 549.

70. Karl Renner, like many Marxists of the period, recognized that fascism was a "new state system," not simply a variation of the traditional "rule of the bourgeoisie" (*Wandlungen der modernen Gesellschaft: Nachgelassene Werke* [Vienna: Buchhandlung, 1953], vol. 3, pp. 68–70, 77–80).

71. See Borkenau, "Zur Soziologie," pp. 171–181.

Chapter 3: The Marxist Theory of Fascism after the Second World War

1. M. Rosenthal and P. Yudin (eds.), *A Dictionary of Philosophy* (Moscow: Progress, 1967), p. 158; cf. also G. Klaus and M. Buhr (eds.), *Philosophisches Woerterbuch* (Berlin: VEB, 1966), p. 191. For treatments by Soviet theoreticians immediately after the Second World War, cf. S. M. Slododskoi, *Storia del fascismo* (Rome: Riunti, 1962), originally published in Moscow in 1945. A German edition appeared as *Der italienische Faschismus und sein Zusammenbruch* in 1948; see also Iring Fetscher, "Faschismus und Nationalsozialismus," *Politische Vierteljahresschrift*, 3/1, no. 43 (1962): n. 2.

2. Boris Lopukhov, "Il problema del fascismo italiano negli scritti di autori sovietici," *Studi storici*, 6, no. 2 (1965): 255.

3. Alexander Galkin, "Capitalist Society and Fascism," *Social Sciences: USSR Academy of Sciences*, 2 (1970): 80–85.

4. This assessment corresponds quite well with that offered by Mussolini himself. See

Benito Mussolini, *Storia di un anno: il tempo del bastone e della carota*, in *Opera omnia* (Milan: La Fenice, 1953–64), vol. 34, pp. 301–474.

5. Paolo Alatri, *Le origini del fascismo* (Rome: Riuniti, 1963), pp. xv, xxi, 264.

6. Ibid., pp. 24, 108.

7. R. Kuehnl, *Formen buergerlicher Herrschaft: Liberalismus-Faschismus* (Munich: Rowohlt, 1971), pp. 123ff.

8. Mihaly Vajda, "On Fascism," *Telos*, 8 (Summer 1971): 43–63; *idem*, "The Rise of Fascism in Italy and Germany," *Telos*, 12 (Summer 1972): 3–26; *idem*, *Fascisme et mouvement de masse* (Paris: Le sycomore, 1979).

9. Vajda, *Fascisme et mouvement de masse*, p. 15.

10. Ibid., p. 63.

11. Ibid., pp. 29–30.

12. See Vajda, "On Fascism," pp. 47f.

13. Ibid., p. 51.

14. Vajda, "Rise of Fascism in Italy and Germany," pp. 5ff., 11ff., 13.

15. Vajda, "On Fascism," p. 44.

16. The one "conservative" feature of fascist politics on which Vajda remarked was fascism's general failure to "attack the principle of private property." In a qualified sense, fascists continued to guarantee the "right of property"—extending to all classes a "perspective whereby they could accumulate property" and enjoy the social and economic mobility so essential to the "myths" of contemporary capitalism. Thus, Italian Fascism was a revolutionary and progressive arrangement, "conservative" and "bourgeois" only insofar as it tolerated the institution of private property and the market exchange of goods. At the same time, it was acknowledged that Fascist political power was exerted with independence—whatever the existing legal arrangements for the protection of private property as an institution. See ibid., pp. 47–48.

17. See Vajda, "Rise of Fascism in Italy and Germany," pp. 10, 12; *idem*, *Fascisme et mouvement de masse*, pp. 74, 78.

18. Vajda, *Fascisme et mouvement de masse*, p. 74.

19. Galkin, "Capitalist Society and Fascism," p. 130.

20. See the book jacket of Nicos Poulantzas, *Fascism and Dictatorship* (London: NLB, 1974).

21. Ibid., p. 11; see pp. 310–312.

22. Ibid., pp. 16, 17.

23. Ibid., pp. 38, 39, 40; see pp. 42, 44.

24. Ibid., pp. 98, 120. Poulantzas was particularly emphatic in his rejection of the views of Palme Dutt; see p. 58, n. 5.

25. See esp. ibid., pp. 54–64.

26. Such categorical judgments are found throughout Poulantzas's text, but the more outrageous examples are on pp. 354 and 355. See p. 351.

27. Ibid., pp. 134, 308.

28. See ibid., p. 42, n. 8; pp. 78, 140, 225, 228, 230f.; see also pp. 43, 48, 60.

29. Ibid., p. 228.

30. See ibid., pp. 43f.

31. See the discussion in A. James Gregor, *A Survey of Marxism: Problems in Philosophy and the Theory of History* (New York: Random House, 1965), pp. 158–185.

32. Karl Marx, *Contribution to the Critique of Political Economy*, in Karl Marx and Friedrich Engels, *Selected Works* (Moscow: Foreign Languages, 1965), vol. 1, pp. 362f.

33. Marx, in a letter to Annenkov, 28 Dec. 1846, in Marx and Engels, *Selected Works*, vol. 2, p. 442.

34. Karl Marx, *The Poverty of Philosophy* (Moscow: Foreign Languages, n.d.), p. 122.

35. See the discussion in A. James Gregor, *Marxism, China and Development* (New Brunswick, N.J.: Transaction, 1995), pp. 33–41.

36. See the discussion in Maria Hsia Chang, "What is Left of Mao Tse-tung Thought," *Issues and Studies*, 28, no. 1 (Jan. 1992): 18–38.

37. See Mao's extensive criticisms of the Soviet Union, which, by the mid-1960s, had been codified in Party documents: Mao Zedong, *A Critique of Soviet Economics* (New York: Monthly Review, 1977).

38. "Soviet Revisionists' Fascist Dictatorship," *Beijing Review*, no. 4 (1974), trans. in *Social Imperialism: Reprints from Peking Review* (Berkeley: Yenan Books, n.d.), pp. 16–18.

39. See *Long Live Leninism!* (Beijing: Foreign Languages, 1964); see the materials in Edward Crankshaw, *The New Cold War* (Baltimore: Penguin, 1963).

40. G. Apalin and U. Mitayayev, *Militarism in Peking's Policies* (Moscow: Progress, 1980), p. 13.

41. " 'Thought of Mao Tse-tung' versus Marxism," in *Maoism through the Eyes of Communists* (Moscow: Progress, 1970), p. 47.

42. *A Destructive Policy* (Moscow: Novosti, 1972), p. 44. See the entire discussion in V. A. Krivtsov and V. Y. Sidikhmenov (eds.), *A Critique of Mao Tse-tung's Theoretical Conceptions* (Moscow: Progress, 1972).

43. See the "Moscow Declaration of 1957," in David Floyd (ed.), *Mao Against Khrushchev: A Short History of the Sino–Soviet Conflict* (New York: Praeger, 1963), p. 249; cf. the specific reference to "the existence of bourgeois influence" and the "internal source of revisionism," in *Long Live Leninism!*, p. 10.

44. See the collection *The Great Socialist Cultural Revolution in China* (Beijing: Foreign Languages, 1966), vols. 1–10.

45. *Circular of the Central Committee of the Chinese Communist Party (May 16, 1966)* (Beijing: Foreign Languages, 1967), p. 3.

46. Yao Wenyuan, *On the Social Basis of the Lin Piao Anti-Party Clique* (Beijing: Foreign Languages, 1975), p. 3.

47. "Mao Tse-tung's Thought is the Telescope and Microscope of our Revolutionary Cause," in *Great Socialist Cultural Revolution in China*, vol. 3, pp. 11–17.

48. Ibid., pp. 14, 15.

49. "Sweep Away All Monsters," in *Great Socialist Cultural Revolution in China*, vol. 3, p. 5.

50. "Never Forget the Class Struggle," *Liberation Army Daily*, 4 May 1966, in *Great Socialist Cultural Revolution in China*, vol. 1, pp. 20, 26; and Yao Wenyuan, "On 'Three Family Village,' " in ibid., p. 58.

51. In this context see the Maoist works of Bob Avakian, *For a Harvest of Dragons: On the "Crisis of Marxism" and the Power of Marxism Now More than Ever* (Chicago: RCP, 1983), and *Phony Communism is Dead . . . Long Live Real Communism!* (Chicago: RCP, 1992).

52. "Soviet Revisionists' Fascist Dictatorship," *Beijing Review*, no. 4 (1974); repr. in *Social Imperialism: Reprints from Peking Review* (Berkeley: Yenan Books, 1974), pp. 16–18.

53. See *Betrayal of Proletarian Dictatorship is the Heart of the Book on "Self-Cultivation"* (Beijing: Foreign Languages, 1967), pp. 8–9.

54. See the argument in Zhang Chunqiao, *On Exercising All-Round Dictatorship over the Bourgeoisie* (Moscow: Foreign Languages, 1975), pp. 3–4.

55. Poulantzas, *Fascism and Dictatorship*, pp. 223–233; see esp. pp. 230 and 231.

56. Ibid., pp. 16, 44, 50, 63, *passim*.

57. See ibid., p. 22, n. 6.

58. James D. Cockcroft, André Gunder Frank, and Dale L. Johnson, *Dependence and Underdevelopment: Latin America's Political Economy* (Garden City, N.Y.: Doubleday, 1972), is a classic statement of this thesis.

59. See the discussion in ibid., pp. xxvi, 138, 178, 400.

60. One of the more popular expressions of these theses can be found in Noam Chomsky and Edward S. Herman, *The Washington Connection and Third World Fascism* (Boston: South End, 1979).

61. See the more ample discussion in Gregor, *Marxism, China and Development*, chap. 8.

62. Karl Marx and Friedrich Engels, *The Communist Manifesto*, in *Collected Works* (New York: International, 1976), vol. 8, pp. 486–488.

63. Karl Marx, "The Future Results of British Rule in India," in Shlomo Avineri (ed.), *Karl Marx on Colonialism and Modernization* (New York: Doubleday, 1968), p. 131.

64. See Chomsky and Herman, *Washington Connection*, pp. x, xiii, 1, 10, 11, 15, *passim*.

65. See the collection in King C. Chen (ed.), *China and the Three Worlds: A Foreign Policy Reader* (White Plains, N.Y.: M. E. Sharpe, 1979).

66. See Lin Piao, *Long Live the Victory of People's War* (Beijing: Foreign Languages, 1968).

Chapter 4: Fascism and Marxism–Leninism in Power

1. See the account provided by Michael T. Florinsky, *Fascism and National Socialism* (New York: Macmillan, 1936), chap. 3. Some academics, after the Second World War, accepted essentially the same list of properties as characterizing fascism. Lloyd Eastman, e.g., employed the list to identify the Kuomintang as fascist. See Lloyd Eastman, *The Abortive Revolution: China under Nationalist Rule 1927–1937* (Cambridge, Mass.: Harvard University Press, 1974), pp. 80–81, and *idem*, "Fascism in Kuomintang China: The Blue Shirts," *China Quarterly*, no. 49 (Jan.–Mar. 1972): 28.

2. There were problems, of course. It was not clear whether Franco's Spain or Salazar's Portugal qualified as "fascism." See, e.g., Antonio Costa Pinto, *The Salazar "New State" and European Fascism* (Florence: European University Institute, 1991). Nor was it clear whether the wartime regimes in Hungary or Romania qualified as "fascist." See the discussion in Mariano Ambri, *I falsi fascismi: Ungheria, Jugoslavia, Romania 1919–1945* (Rome: Jouvence, 1980).

3. See, e.g., Dieter Dux (ed.), *Ideology in Conflict: Communist Political Theory* (Princeton: Van Nostrand, 1963); *A Mirror for Revisionists* (Beijing: Foreign Languages, 1963); *On Khrushchov's Phoney Communism and Its Historical Lessons for the World: Comment on the Open Letter of the Central Committee of the CPSU (IX)* (Beijing: Foreign Languages, 14 July 1964).

4. Harrison E. Salisbury, *War between Russia and China* (New York: Norton, 1969).

5. Both sides in the ensuing dispute produced an abundance of justificatory argument. Eventually, their respective allies joined in the enterprise, and much of the argument was generated in Albania, as an ally of China, and East Germany, as an ally of the Soviet Union. See, e.g., *Marxist–Leninist Ideology Will Certainly Overcome Revisionism*, 2 vols. (Tirana: Naim Frasheri, 1964), *China and Albania—Friends in a Common Struggle* (Beijing: Foreign Languages, 1964); Ernst Henry, *What Are They After in Peking?* (Moscow: Progress, 1979).

6. Soviet thinkers associated Maoism with "a petty-bourgeois nationalistic trend" that found "support, first and foremost, in the nationalistically-minded non-proletarian, petty-bourgeois . . . strata of Chinese society" (P. Fedoseyev, "Maoism: Its Ideological and Political Essence," in *A Destructive Policy* [Moscow: Novosti, 1972], p. 101).

7. See V. A. Krivtsov and V. Y. Sidikhmenov, *A Critique of Mao Tse-tung's Theoretical Conceptions* (Moscow: Progress, 1972), p. 167.

8. Ibid., pp. 193–195, 202–203; see Klaus Maehnel, "Economic Policy of the Mao Group," in V. I. Krivtsov (ed.), *Maoism through the Eyes of Communists* (Moscow: Progress, 1970), pp. 278–280.

9. Ibid., pp. 8, 9, 11.

10. See A. James Gregor, *Interpretations of Fascism* (New Brunswick, N.J.: Transaction, 1997).

11. Krivtsov and Sidikhmenov, *A Critique*, pp. 64, 66.

12. See Fedor Burlatsky, *Mao Tse-tung: An Ideological and Psychological Portrait* (Moscow: Progress, 1980), pt. 1.

13. Krivtsov and Sidikhmenov, *A Critique*, p. 199.

14. Krivtsov and Sidikhmenov, *A Critique*, pp. 144–145.

15. Burlatsky, *Mao Tse-tung*, p. 257.

16. Maoism, Soviet theoreticians decided, was "an ideological trend hostile to Marxism–Leninism" (A. Kruchinin and V. Olgin, *Territorial Claims of Mao Tse-tung: History and Modern Times* [Moscow: Novosti, n.d.], p. 6).

17. See Wlodzimierz Wowczuk, "Hieroglyphs of the Chinese Economy," in Krivtsov (ed.), *Maoism through the Eyes of Communists*, pp. 299–300.

18. Kruchinin and Olgin, *Territorial Claims*, pp. 8–10.

19. Ibid., p. 33.

20. See O. E. Vladimirov (ed.), *Maoism As It Really Is* (Moscow: Progress, 1981), pp. 220–256; and A. Malukhin, *Militarism—Backbone of Maoism* (Moscow: Novosti, 1970), p. 33.

21. "'Thought of Mao Tse-tung' versus Marxism," *Einheit*, nos. 4/5 (1968), repr. in Krivtsov (ed.), *Maoism through the Eyes of Communists*, pp. 33–48.

22. See the discussion in A. Zelochovtsev, *La Rivoluzione Culturale vista da un sovietico* (Milan: Rusconi, 1971).

23. See Boris Leibson, *Petty-Bourgeois Revolutionism (Anarchism, Trotskyism and Maoism)* (Moscow: Progress, 1970); and Malukhin, *Militarism*.

24. Vladimirov (ed.), *Maoism As It Really Is*, pp. 7, 9–11, 24, 28, 30–31, 34, 38.

25. "Tear Aside the Bourgeois Mask of 'Liberty, Equality and Fraternity,'" *People's Daily*, 4 June 1966, repr. in *The Great Socialist Cultural Revolution in China* (Beijing: Foreign Languages, 1966), vol. 4, p. 32.

26. Burlatsky, *Mao Tse-tung*, pt. 1.

27. Krivtsov and Sidikhmenov, *A Critique*, pp. 195–201.

28. Ibid., pp. 57f., 216f.

29. *A Destructive Policy*, p. 30; G. Apalin and U. Mityayev, *Militarism in Peking's Policies* (Moscow: Progress, 1980), p. 6; see the discussion in ibid., chap. 3.

30. Leonid Gudoshnikov and Rostislav Neronov, *China after Mao* (Moscow: Novosti, 1979), p. 9.

31. M. Sladkovsky (ed.), *Developments in China* (Moscow: Progress, 1968), p. 16; O. Leonidov, *Peking Divisionists* (Moscow: Novosti, 1971), pp. 104–110.

32. Pauly Parakal, *Peking's Betrayal of Asia* (New Delhi: Sterling, 1976), p. 113.

33. *China's Alliance with U.S. Imperialism* (New York: Spartacus Youth, Jan. 1976).

34. See the discussion in A. James Gregor, *The Fascist Persuasion in Radical Politics* (Princeton: Princeton University Press, 1974), chap. 6.

35. Chang Chien, "Imperialism on the Eve of the Social Revolution of the Proletariat: Notes on Studying Lenin's *Imperialism, the Highest Stage of Capitalism*," *Beijing Review*, no. 39

(1973), repr. in *Social Imperialism: Reprints from Peking Review* (Berkeley: Yenan Books, 1974), p. 2.

36. All this was already intimated in discussions conducted by Maoist theorists as early as 1960. See the essay prepared by the Editorial Department of *Hongqi: Long Live Leninism!* (Beijing: Foreign Languages, 1964), pp. 10–11 and *passim*.

37. Ming Sung, "Dire Consequences of Soviet Revisionsts' All-Round Capitalist Restoration," *Beijing Review*, no. 42 (18 Oct. 1974), repr. in *Social Imperialism*, pp. 5–7; "Carry the Great Proletarian Cultural Revolution through to the End," *People's Daily*, 1 Jan. 1967, repr. in *The Great Proletarian Cultural Revolution in China* (with the publication of the eighth pamphlet, Beijing changed the name of the series from *The Great Socialist Cultural Revolution* to *The Great Proletarian Cultural Revolution*), vol. 8, p. 1.

38. Zhang Chunqiao, *On Exercising All-Round Dictatorship over the Bourgeoisie* (Beijing: Foreign Languages, 1975), p. 3.

39. "Long Live the Great Proletarian Cultural Revolution," *Red Flag*, no. 8 (1966), repr. in *Great Socialist Cultural Revolution in China*, vol. 4, p. 8.

40. See Martin Nicolaus, *Restoration of Capitalism in the USSR* (Chicago: Liberator, 1975).

41. Ibid., pp. 12–14, 19.

42. "Soviet Revisionists' Fascist Dictatorship," *Beijing Review*, no. 4 (1974), repr. in *Social Imperialism*, pp. 16–18.

43. Chang Chien, "Imperialism," p. 2.

44. Ibid., p. 4.

45. See "Aid or Control and Plunder?," *Beijing Review*, no. 45 (1973), repr. in *Social Imperialism*, pp. 13–15.

46. Hsin Feng, "Mighty Ideological Weapon in the Struggle against Revisionism: A Study of Lenin's *Imperialism, the Highest Stage of Capitalism*," *Beijing Review*, no. 20 (17 May 1974), repr. in *Social Imperialism*, p. 9.

47. See Wang Chongjie, "The Acute Contradictions in the Economy of the Soviet Union," *Xinhua*, 26 Dec. 1980, trans. in *FBIS*, PRC International Affairs, Soviet Union, 2 Jan. 1981, pp. C2–C4.

48. "Soviet Revisionists once again Intrude into China's Territory Chenbao Island Area," *Xinhua*, 15 Mar. 1969, repr. in *Down with the New Tsars!* (Beijing: Foreign Languages, 1969), p. 18.

49. Chang Chien, "Imperialism," p. 2.

50. *On Khruschchov's Phoney Communism*, pp. 33–43.

51. *Leninism and Modern Revisionism* (Beijing: Foreign Languages, 1963). See Mao Zedong, "Talk with the American Correspondent Anna Louise Strong," in *Selected Works* (Beijing: Foreign Languages, 1967), vol. 4, pp. 97–101; *idem*, "Greet the New High Tide of the Chinese Revolution," in ibid., p. 120; *idem*, "The Present Situation and Our Tasks," in ibid., pp. 158–159.

52. See, e.g., *Long Live Leninism!*, pp. 15–16.

53. "Carry the Great Proletarian Cultural Revolution through to the End," *People's Daily*, 1 Jan. 1967, repr. in *Great Proletarian Cultural Revolution in China*, vol. 9, p. 2.

54. See the discussion in "A Great Revolution that Touches Peoples to Their Very Souls," *People's Daily*, 2 June 1966, repr. in *Great Socialist Cultural Revolution in China*, vol. 3, p. 8.

55. See the discussion in Yao Wenyuan, *On the Social Basis of the Lin Piao Anti-Party Clique* (Beijing: Foreign Languages, 1975), pp. 3, 8, 11–13.

56. Zhang, *On Exercising All-Round Dictatorship*, p. 10.

57. Ibid., p. 19.

58. Karl Marx, *Critique of the Gotha Program* (Beijing: Foreign Languages, 1972), p. 15.

59. See Chi Yen, "Ideological Weapon for Restricting the Bourgeois Right—Notes on Studying the 'Report to the Second Plenary Session of the Seventh Central Committee of the Communist Party of China,' " *Beijing Review*, no. 22 (1975): 8.

60. "Great Revolution that Touches Peoples to Their Very Souls," p. 9; "Mao Tse-tung's Thought is the Telescope and Microscope of Our Revolutionary Cause," *Liberation Army Daily*, 7 June 1966, repr. in *Great Socialist Cultural Revolution*, vol. 3, p. 13.

61. Zhang, *On Exercising All-Round Dictatorship*, p. 10.

62. "We must follow the instructions of the Central Committee of the Communist Party of China and never forget the class struggle, never forget the dictatorship of the proletariat, never forget to give prominence to politics. . . . We must firmly give prominence to politics" ("Mao Tse-tung's Thought is the Telescope," pp. 16–17).

63. Yao, *On the Social Basis*, pp. 7–8.

64. Kao Chu, "Open Fire at the Black Anti-Party and Anti-Socialist Line," in *Great Socialist Revolution in China*, vol. 2, p. 2.

65. "Mao Tse-tung's Thought is the Telescope," pp. 14–15.

66. Zhou Enlai, "Report to the Tenth National Congress of the Communist Party of China," in *The Tenth National Congress of the Communist Party of China (Documents)* (Beijing: Foreign Languages, 1973), as repr. in Raymond Lotta (ed.), *And Mao Makes 5: Mao Tsetung's Last Great Battle* (Chicago: Banner, 1978), p. 83.

67. "Carry the Great Proletarian Cultural Revolution," pp. 3, 12, 16, 19–20; "Take Firm Hold of the Revolution, Promote Production and Utterly Smash the New Counter-Attack Launched by the Bourgeois Reactionary Line," *Shanghai Wenhui Bao*, 5 Jan. 1967, repr. in *Great Proletarian Cultural Revolution*, vol. 10, pp. 7, 9; "Urgent Notice," *Shanghai Wenhui Bao*, 7 Jan. 1967, in ibid., p. 15, "Oppose Economism and Smash the Latest Counter-Attack by the Bourgeois Reactionary Line," *People's Daily*, 12 Jan. 1967, in ibid., p. 25.

68. "Hold Fast to the Main Orientation in the Struggle," *Red Flag*, no. 12 (1966), repr. in *Great Socialist Cultural Revolution*, vol. 7, pp. 24–25; "Raise High the Great Red Banner of Mao Tse-tung's Thought and Carry the Great Proletarian Cultural Revolution through to the End," in ibid., vol. 5, p. 25.

69. Ibid., p. 26.

70. "Oppose Economism," pp. 25–29.

71. "Revolutionary Youth Should Learn from the People's Liberation Army," *People's Daily*, 28 Aug. 1966, repr. in ibid., vol. 7, p. 19.

72. "Long Live the Great Proletarian Cultural Revolution," p. 17.

73. *People's Daily*, 16 June 1967, as cited in Krivtsov and Sidikhmenov, *A Critique*, p. 149.

74. Mao Zedong, *Chairman Mao Talks to the People: Talks and Letters, 1956–1971* (New York: Pantheon, 1974), pp. 118–120, 203–205, 211.

75. Ibid., p. 207.

76. Hung Yu, "History Develops in Spirals," *Beijing Review*, no. 43 (25 Oct. 1974), repr. in *And Mao Makes 5*, p. 159; see "Reversing Correct Verdicts Goes Against the Will of the People," *Beijing Review*, no. 11 (12 Mar. 1976), repr. in ibid., p. 261; Cheng Yueh, "A General Program for Capitalist Restoration—An Analysis of 'On the General Program for All Work of the Whole Party and the Whole Nation'," *Red Flag*, no. 4 (1976), repr. in ibid., pp. 274, 279.

77. Mao Zedong, *A Critique of Soviet Economics* (New York: Monthly Review, 1977), p. 34; see *Maoism As It Really Is*, p. 243.

78. Mao, *Critique of Soviet Economics*, pp. 41, 49–50; and *Maoism As It Really Is*, p. 243.

79. Mao, *Critique of Soviet Economics*, pp. 49–50.

80. Wang Li, *The Dictatorship of the Proletariat and the Great Proletarian Cultural Revolution* (Beijing: Foreign Languages, 1967), p. 16.

81. For an insightful biographical account of Chen Erjin, see Robin Munro, "Introduction: Chen Erjin and the Chinese Democracy Movement," in Chen Erjin, *China Crossroads Socialism* (London: Verso, 1984), pp. 1–68.

82. Ibid., pp. 72f.

83. Ibid., pp. 91–93. Wang Xizhe speaks specifically of "totalitarian" controls. See Wang Xizhe, "Mao Zedong and the Cultural Revolution," in Anita Chan, Stanley Rosen, and Jonathan Unger (eds.), *On Socialist Democracy and the Chinese Legal System* (Armonk, N.Y.: M. E. Sharpe, 1985), p. 185.

84. Ibid., pp. 98–109.

85. Ibid., p. 106. "Proletarian dictatorship? Nothing of the sort! On the contrary, this is out-and-out social-fascist dictatorship, out-and-out dictatorship by the bureaucrat class, out-and-out dictatorship *over* the proletariat" (ibid., p. 199).

86. Ibid., p. 180.

87. Ibid.

88. "As Marx and Engels said—'. . . the theory of the Communists may be summed up in the single sentence: Abolition of private property' " (Chen Erjin, *China Crossroads Socialism*, p. 191).

89. Wang Xizhe, "Mao Zedong and the Cultural Revolution," p. 206.

90. Ibid., pp. 140–141, 152–153. See the discussion of the "historic necessity" of dictatorship at the commencement of socialist rule in Chen Erjin, *Chinese Crossroads Socialism*, pp. 96–97.

91. See Ross Terril, *Madame Mao: The White-Boned Demon* (New York: Simon & Schuster, 1992), pp. 359, 389.

Chapter 5: Fascism and the Devolution of Marxism in the Soviet Union

1. See the relevant discussion in Adam B. Ulam, *The Communists: The Story of Power and Lost Illusions* (New York: Scribners, 1992), chaps. 2, 3, and 4.

2. While Khrushchev and his entourage were clearly prepared to accept the "self-evident truths" of Marxism–Leninism, it was equally evident that they immediately sought to clear away the "excrescences of Stalinism." See ibid., pp. 112, 114f. With *glasnost*, Soviet theoreticians made it very clear that, in their judgment, Stalin was an incompetent Marxist. See the essays, particularly those of Anatoly Butenko, "To Avoid Mistakes in the Future," and Boris Bolotin, "Dogma and Life," in the collection *The Stalin Phenomenon* (Moscow: Novosti, 1987), pp. 8, 10, 25, 27, 28.

3. See the discussion in Ulam, *Communists*, chap. 4.

4. See the discussion in John Gooding, *Rulers and Subjects: Government and People in Russia 1801–1991* (London: Arnold, 1996), chap. 8.

5. See the discussion in Martin Nicolaus, *Restoration of Capitalism in the USSR* (Chicago: Liberator, 1975), chap. 1.

6. Dmitry Volkogonov, "The Stalin Phenomenon," in *Stalin Phenomenon*, pp. 43, 49.

7. Palmiro Togliatti, the durable leader of Italy's Communists, recognized that Marxism–Leninism in the Soviet Union had "degenerated": quoted in *The Anti-Stalin Campaign and International Communism: A Selection of Documents* (New York: Russian Institute, Columbia University, 1956), p. 135.

8. As quoted in Kenneth Murphy, *Retreat from the Finland Station: Moral Odysseys in the Breakdown of Communism* (New York: Free Press, 1992), p. 195.

9. See David Floyd, *Mao against Khrushchev: A Short History of the Sino–Soviet Conflict* (New York: Praeger, 1963), chaps. 3 and 4.

10. From 1959 through 1964, Khrushchev embarked on a program of religious persecu-

tion and suppression. See Michael Bourdeaux, *Risen Indeed: Lessons in Faith from the USSR* (London: Darton, Longman, and Todd, 1983).

11. See John B. Dunlop, *The New Russian Revolutionaries* (Belmont, Mass.: Nordland, 1976), chap. 1.

12. *The People's Revolutionary Charter* of the Social-Christian Union for the Liberation of the People, appendix II, in Dunlop, *New Russian Revolutionaries*, pp. 247, 262.

13. Western specialists suggest that "Soviet patriotism" served as the functional equivalent of "Russian patriotism" for some considerable time in the USSR—and as a plausible surrogate for Russian nationalism. See the discussion in Walter Laqueur, *Black Hundred: The Rise of the Extreme Right in Russia* (New York: Harper, 1993), pp. 63–64.

14. See Alexander Yanov, *The Russian New Right: Right-Wing Ideologies in the Contemporary USSR* (Berkeley: Institute of International Studies, 1978), pp. 13–14.

15. *People's Revolutionary Charter*, pp. 278f. and points 13, 14, and 41 on pp. 282f. and 288. While the clear intent of the charter is politically liberal, it does speak of state intervention "when the initiative of citizens is insufficient to create enterprises vital to the populace." The state is also accorded the power "to set a ceiling on the price of basic commodities and to maintain control over foreign trade." See points 18 and 23 on pp. 283 and 284.

16. See ibid., points 29, 34, 43, and sec. 15 on pp. 286, 287, 289, and 290–292. See the discussion in Yanov, *Russian New Right*, pp. 28–30. The All-Russian Union included in its selected list of books Curzio Malaparte's *Coup d'Etat*. Malaparte was a prominent Fascist ideologue throughout the greater part of the Fascist regime.

17. See the discussion in Alexander Yanov, *The Russian Challenge and the Year 2000* (Oxford: Basil Blackwell, 1987), chap. 9.

18. See Laqueur, *Black Hundred*, p. 65.

19. Ibid., p. 91.

20. Viktor Chalmaev, "Inevitabity," *Molodaia gvardia*, no. 9 (1968). See the accounts provided by Yanov in *Russian New Right*, pp. 44–47, and *Russian Challenge*, pp. 109–113.

21. See the discussion in Dmitry V. Shlapentokh, "Bolshevism, Nationalism, and Statism: Soviet Ideology in Formation," in Vladimir N. Brovkin (ed.), *The Bolsheviks in Russian Society* (New Haven: Yale University Press, 1991), pp. 271–297.

22. It is clear that Gorbachev considered himself a committed Marxist–Leninist at that time. See, e.g., John B. Dunlop and Henry S. Rowen, "Gorbachev versus Ligachev, the Kremlin Divided," *National Interest*, Spring 1988, pp. 18–29.

23. See Robert C. Tucker, *Political Culture and Leadership in Soviet Russia: From Lenin to Gorbachev* (New York: Norton, 1987), and Moshe Lewin, *The Gorbachev Phenomenon* (Berkeley: University of California Press, 1989).

24. See the discussion in Philip Hanson, *From Stagnation to Catastroika: Commentaries on the Soviet Economy, 1983–1991* (New York: Praeger, 1992), chap. 7. See too, e.g., Abel Aganbegyan, *Inside Perestroika: The Future of the Soviet Economy* (New York: Harper and Row, 1989). Aganbegyan was the chief economic adviser to Gorbachev.

25. See the discussion in Andranik Migranian, "Dolgaia Doroga k Evropeiskomu Domu," *Novyi Mir*, no. 7 (July 1989), and *idem*, "Avtoritarizm—Mechta Dlia SSSR," *Latinskaia America*, 1, no. 3 (Mar. 1990), *passim*.

26. See the discussions of Kurginian in John Dunlop, *Rise of Russia and the Fall of the Soviet Empire* (Princeton: Princeton University Press, 1993), pp. 165–169; Laqueur, *Black Hundred*, pp. 134–136; Jeremy Lester, *Modern Tsars and Princes: The Struggle for Hegemony in Russia* (London: Verso, 1995), pp. 140–143, 148, 167–168; and Victor Yasmann, "Elite Think Tank Prepares 'Post-*Perestroika*' Strategy," *Report on the USSR*, 3, no. 21 (24 May 1991), pp. 1–6.

27. Kurginian joined the Communist Party only in 1987, apparently because he was convinced that the "Motherland" could be saved only by a rededicated party. Kurginian's program of 1990 is contained in Sergei Kurginian et al., *Post-Perestroika: Kontseptualnaia Model Razvitia Nashego Obshchestva, Politicheskikh Partii I Obshchestvennykh Organizatsii* (Moscow: Politzdat, 1990). *Post-Perestroika* was a group effort, involving Kurginian's colleagues at his Experimental Creative Center, Inc., an endowed "think-tank" in Moscow; but it is clear that the central ideas are those of Kurginian.

28. Ibid., p. 69.

29. It is very difficult to plausibly and easily distinguish "neo-Stalinists" from "National Bolsheviks" and both from "neo-Marxists" and "conservatives" using the current distinctions. See the suggestions of Yanov, *Russian Challenge*, pp. 52–53, and Dunlop, *Rise of Russia*, pp. 128–132. As will be argued, Kurginian continued to respect Stalin and Stalinism—with qualifications—although it would be hard to characterize him as a "neo-Stalinist." There are significant Marxist residues in Kurginian's thought; yet it would be difficult to identify him as a "neo-Marxist." That he sought to salvage the Soviet Union might qualify him as a "neo-conservative," but only with very significant qualifications.

30. Kurginian is a prolific, if unsystematic, author. His original articles appeared in *Literaturnaia Rossiia*, nos. 26, 27, 28, 35 (1989). Subsequent essays appeared in *Moskovskaia pravda*, 8 (June 1991); *Moskva*, no. 9 (1991); *Postfactum*, 1, no. 1 (1991); and other journals; see Laqueur, *Black Hundred*, p. 135, n. 24.

31. This is how he is generally characterized in Western commentaries. See Dunlop, *Rise of Russia*, chap. 4.

32. Kurginian nevertheless signaled his reservations about Stalinism. He argued that by the end of the 1940s, the Stalinist system required fundamental overhaul. See Kurginian, "O mekhanizme soskalzyvaniia: statia vtoraia," in *Sedmoi Stsenarii* (Moscow: ECC, 1992), vol. 1, pp. 16–17. But it is very clear that Kurginian saw the merits of Stalinism, whatever his reservations. See A. Podkopalov's interview with Kurginian entitled "Communism Begins Its Worldwide Triumph," *Komsomolskaia Pravda*, 13 Aug. 1991, in ibid., pp. 327–333.

33. See, e.g., the discussion in Ewa Berard-Zarzicka, "The Authoritarian Perestroika Debate," *Telos*, no. 89 (1990): 115–124.

34. See the discussion in Murphy, *Retreat from the Finland Station*, chaps. 24 and 25.

35. By the beginning of the 1990s, Kurginian seemed prepared to reject Marxism–Leninism in its entirety. As we shall see, he saw the future of the Soviet Union not in terms of "international class warfare" or "international proletarian revolution," but in terms of a "clash of culture vs. material civilization" in much the same fashion as conceived by Oswald Spengler. He saw the future of the Soviet Union in terms of a moral "communitarianism" versus the crass materialism of capitalism. See the exchanges in Podkopalov, "Communism Begins its Worldwide Triumph."

36. See Kurginian, *Post-Perestroika*, chaps. 7 and 9.

37. Ibid., pp. 11–17.

38. These concepts stem from Lenin's notions about imperialism, the final phase of capitalist development. They are reminiscent of New Left "dependency theory," which was very popular during Kurginian's youth. It is also very reminiscent of the Fascist distinction between "plutocratic" and "proletarian" nations. Kurginian's formulation differs insofar as he provides an elaborate taxonomy of dominant, semi-dependent, and dependent states, including (1) those that are "leaders," (2) those that are "insiders," (3) those that are "outsiders," and finally (4) those states that simply serve as "playgrounds" for the others. There is little point in pursuing the distinctions here.

39. See the discussion in *Post-Perestroika*, p. 40.

40. See the discussion in Kurginian, "O mekhanizme soskalzyvaniia: statia vtoraia," *Literaturnaia Rossiia*, no. 27 (1989).

41. See the discussion in Kurginian, *Post-Perestroika*, p. 56.

42. See ibid., pp. 17–34. Kurginian expounds, in considerable detail, on the development of the Soviet Union's "criminal bourgeoisie" who constitute the backbone for the subversion of the state and society. His notions share similarities with those of the Chinese critics of the "feudal fascism" of the People's Republic of China under the ministrations of the "Gang of Four." There is always a search for "bourgeois" culprits. In that sense, Kurginian's account is parasitic on his Marxist training in "class analysis."

43. Ibid., pp. 76–83.

44. Yasmann speaks of the productive system proposed by Kurginian as "a mixed market economy" ("Elite Think Tank," p. 1).

45. By that time it was fairly common to all "reformers" that "national salvation" was a matter of priority. The survival of Marxism–Leninism was no longer an issue of primary concern. See the discussion in Migranian, "Dolgaia Doroga k Evropeiskomu Domu," and *idem*, "Avtoritarizm." As will be argued, by the end of the 1980s, it was clear that there were those who were attempting to salvage the state system of the Soviet Union by separating it from its Marxist–Leninist rationale.

46. As quoted in Yasmann, "Elite Think Tank," p. 4.

47. See, e.g., Sergei Kurginian and Vladimir Ovchinsky, "Indulgentsia na Besporiadok, Ili Chto Takoe Kriminalnaia Burzhuazia?," *Literaturnaia Rossiia*, no. 51 (22 Dec. 1989), *passim*.

48. For many, Kurginian's "approach to the economy, and in particular its stress on a set of well-developed corporate principles [suggest] Mussolini's Italy as [a] . . . role model; an analogy that possesses a lot of substance" (Lester, *Modern Tsars and Princes*, p. 43). See the discussion in Vincenzo Nardi, *Il corporativismo fascista* (Rome: I.A.T., 1974).

49. See, e.g., the discussion in Guido Pighetti, "Notizie preliminari," in *Sindacalismo fascista* (Milan: Imperia, 1924), pp. 11–32, esp. p. 27.

50. See the detailed discussion in Giulio Scagnetti, *Gli enti di privilegio nell'economia corporativa italiana* (Padua: CEDAM, 1942).

51. In this context, see the discussion in Sergio Panunzio, *L'economia mista* (Milan: Hoepli, 1936), esp. pp. 8–9 and 17, where Panunzio speaks of "the approximation of Bolshevism . . . to Fascism . . . in terms of the realities of production" in a corporativist mixed economy under the juridical and political dominance of the state. Mussolini characterized the Fascist system in the following fashion: "The economic man does not exist. Man is complete: he is political, he is economic, he is religious, he is a saint, he is a warrior." He went on to indicate that the corporative economy implied a "regulated economy and therefore also [a] controlled economy," all of which, for its proper revolutionary function, required "an atmosphere of strong ideal tension" (Benito Mussolini, *The Corporate State* [Florence: Vallechi, 1938], pp. 31, 33, 35).

52. See, once again, Kurginian's interview with Podkopalov, "Communism Begins its Worldwide Triumph."

53. Kurginian speaks of a nation, in times of crisis, uniting in a sense of "a common destiny and mission, a community of blood shed and a brotherhood based upon them" (*Nezavisimaia gazeta*, 19 Feb. 1991).

54. Kurginian entertains a quaint notion of "fascism," which need not detain us. "Fascists," for Kurginian, are "criminals" who profit from having created a "society of civilized animals." This is a thoughtless inheritance from Soviet polemics. It does indicate, however, that Kurginian has studied little, if any, Fascist literature. His political, social, and economic thought is not derivative. See *Post-Perestroika*, pp. 43–47.

55. As quoted in Yasmann, "Elite Think Tank," p. 5.

56. Kurginian's Experimental Creative Center (ECC) was provided preferential funding from the central budget of the Marxist–Leninist state before its collapse. The ECC was afforded priority access to hard currency, and its personnel were provided with the opportunity for foreign travel. In effect, the leaders of the Marxist–Leninist state underwrote the making of fascism in the Soviet Union. See ibid., p. 1.

57. This is not to say that Western social and political scientists were any better at anticipating events. But they rarely claimed to be in possession of the "only true social science." In this regard, see John Lewis Gaddis, "International Relations Theory and the End of the Cold War," *International Security*, 17, no. 3 (Winter 1992–93): 5–58.

Chapter 6: Fascism and Post-Soviet Russia

1. The notable exception is Alexander Yanov, *The Russian New Right: Right-Wing Ideologies in the Contemporary USSR* (Berkeley: Institute of International Studies, 1978).

2. "The . . . unique feature of the Soviet transformation is that not a single Westerner predicted its occurrence" (Steven Kull, *Burying Lenin: The Revolution in Soviet Ideology and Foreign Policy* [Boulder, Colo.: Westview, 1992], p. 3). Jeremy Lester simply comments on the fact that, "given the track record of predictions by Sovietologists and Kremlinologists," Russia's past and present must have been "unfathomable" to them (*Modern Tsars and Princes: The Struggle for Hegemony in Russia* [London: Verso, 1995], p. 251).

3. See Mikhail Gorbachev's illuminating revelations in *The Ideology of Renewal for Revolutionary Restructuring* (Moscow: Novosti, 1988), pp. 35–36, as well as the discussion in Boris Kagarlitsky, *The Disintegration of the Monolith* (London: Verso, 1992).

4. *The Programme of the Communist Party of the Soviet Union* (Moscow: Novosti, 1986), pp. 7 and 23–24.

5. Gorbachev, as quoted in A. Mikhalyov, "USSR–Poland: Toward New Frontiers," in *FBIS: Soviet Union*, 30 Nov. 1988, p. 23.

6. See, e.g., Gorbachev, *Ideology of Renewal*, pp. 56, 61.

7. See Gorbachev, "Press Conference in Geneva, 21 November 1985," in Gorbachev, *The Coming Century of Peace* (New York: Richardson and Steinman, 1986), pp. 33–58.

8. Mikhail Gorbachev, *Political Report of the CPSU Central Committee to the 27th Congress of the Communist Party of the Soviet Union* (Moscow: Novosti, 1986), p. 81.

9. Mikhail Gorbachev, *Perestroika: New Thinking for Our Country and the World* (New York: Harper & Row, 1987), pp. 147–148.

10. See Steven Kull's report of an interview with a "prominent" leader in the entourage of Mikhail Gorbachev who insisted that Soviet foreign policy was hostage to the economy (Kull, *Burying Lenin*, p. 117).

11. Mikhail Gorbachev, "The Key Issue of the Party's Economic Policy," in *Coming Century of Peace*, p. 206.

12. See the discussion in Hanson, *From Stagnation to Catastroika, passim*.

13. Gorbachev, *Perestroika*, p. 12; see also "Presentation of Indira Gandhi Prize: Speech by Mikhail Gorbachev," cited in *FBIS: Soviet Union*, 21 Nov. 1988, p. 20.

14. See the report cited in *FBIS: Soviet Union*, 18 May 1989, p. 17.

15. "Text of the Spanish–Soviet Joint Political Declaration," *Pravda*, 28 Oct. 1990, p. 1, as cited in *FBIS: Soviet Union*, 29 Oct. 1990, p. 24. See the comment, "many of the values specified by new thinkers [in the Soviet Union of Mikhail Gorbachev were] basically the same as Western liberal values" (Kull, *Burying Lenin*, p. 35).

16. "Conversation between F. M. Burlatsky, Chairman of the Public Commission for

Humanitarian Cooperation, and Deputy Foreign Minister A. A. Adamishin," quoted in *FBIS: Soviet Union*, 27 Jan. 1989, p. 11.

17. See the discussion in Philip Hanson, *From Stagnation to Catastroika: Commentaries on the Soviet Economy, 1983–1991*.

18. As cited in ibid., p. 70.

19. See N. T. Glushkov, "Planovoe tsenoobrazovanie," *Voprosy ekonomiki*, no. 1 (1984): 3–15, as quoted in ibid., p. 80.

20. See the explicit account and implications of a collective work, *Problemy sobstvennosti v stranakh real'nogo sotsializma* (Moscow: IEMSS, 1987).

21. Gorbachev, *Ideology of Renewal*, p. 56.

22. Ibid., p. 54.

23. Gorbachev, as quoted in David Remnick, "I Cannot Go Against My Father," *Washington Post*, National Weekly Edition, 17–23 Dec. 1990, p. 25.

24. Ibid., p. 24.

25. See Kull, *Burying Lenin*, p. 156.

26. General V. Lobov, "Deputy's Opinion," *Sovetskaya Rossiya*, quoted in *FBIS: Soviet Union*, 19 Oct. 1989, pp. 101–102.

27. As early as the late 1970s, Alexander Yanov suggested that the emerging "new right" in the Soviet Union enjoyed some kind of Communist Party support. See Yanov, *Russian New Right*.

28. See the account in Paul Bellis and Jeff Gleisner, "After Perestroika: A Neo-Conservative Manifesto," *Russia and the World*, no. 19 (1991): 1–2.

29. *Proto-fascism* is used here to signify a collection of ideas, sharing similarities with those of paradigmatic Fascism, that have the potenial of maturing into full fascist expression under some set of circumstances.

30. For an excellent introduction to "Eurasianism," see Nicholas V. Riasanovsky, "Asia through Russian Eyes," in Wayne S. Vucinich (ed.), *Russia and Asia: Essays on the Influence of Russia on the Asian Peoples* (Stanford, Calif.: Stanford University Press, 1972), pp. 3–29, and *idem*, "The Emergence of Eurasianism," in Nicholas V. Riasanovsky and Gleb Struve (eds.), *California Slavic Studies* (Berkeley: University of California Press, 1967), vol. 4, pp. 39–72.

31. See Walter Laqueur, *Black Hundred: The Rise of the Extreme Right in Russia* (New York: Harper, 1993).

32. See the account in Stephen Carter, "*Pamyat* and Conservative Communism," *Russia and the World*, no. 19 (1991): 30–31.

33. The paramilitary branch of the Russian National Union was suppressed by legislation after it participated in the events of September–October 1993 which saw the burning of the Russian parliament building in Moscow. See Alexander Peresvet, "Fuehrer from St. Petersburg," *Moskovskie Novosti*, no. 14 (1994): 6. Lionel Dadiani, "Don't Ask Whether Fascism is Possible in Russia. It is Already There," *New Times*, Sept. 1994, p. 28. Barkashov has contested his identification with Hitler's National Socialism, but everything about his organization and its rationale suggests that such a characterization is appropriate.

34. The program of the Russian National Union advocates protection for the "genetic fund of the Russian nation," a proscription against "mixed marriages" between members of the Russian and non-Russian gene pools. See the account in Dadiani, "Don't Ask Whether Fascism is Possible in Russia," p. 27.

35. The "social patriotic" and "statist" forces included, during this period and at various times, such incompatibles as Dmitri Vasiliev's Pamiat, the Russian People's Front of Valeri Skurlatov, the Peoples' Constitutional Party of Sergei Vokov, the People's Information Party of Ivan Yuzvishin, the Sakharov Union of Democratic Forces of Vladimir Voronin, the

Liberal Democratic Party of the notorious Vladimir Zhirinovsky, the Russian All-Peoples' Union of Sergei Baburin, and the Russian Christian Democratic Union of Viktor Aksyuchits.

36. Nikolai Pavlov recognized the incongruity of the company when he applauded the fact that a "Russophile movement" could find among its leadership both a former Central Committee Secretary of the Communist Party of the Soviet Union, Gennadi Ziuganov, as well as a former General of the KGB, Alexander Sterligov. See Lester, *Modern Tsars and Princes*, p. 297, n. 95.

37. Kevin Fedarko, "Rising Czar?," *Time*, 11 July 1994, pp. 39–44; Vladimir Solovyov and Elena Klepikova, *Zhirinovsky: Russian Fascism and the Making of a Dictator* (New York: Addison Wesley, 1995).

38. See J. L. Black, introduction to chap. 3 of J. L. Black (ed.), *Russia and Eurasia Documents Annual 1994: The Russian Federation* (New York: Academic International Press, 1995), pp. 94–95.

39. See Solovyov and Klepikova, *Zhirinovsky*, pp. 16, 49, 52, 113, 114, 153, 160, 164, 178.

40. Ibid., pp. 156–157. See Ariel Cohen's excerpted translation of Zhirinovsky's *The Final Thrust South*, in *Zhirinovsky in His Own Words: Excerpts from* The Final Thrust South (Washington, D.C.: Heritage Foundation, 4 Feb. 1994), pp. 2–11; and Vladimir Zhirinovsky, *Poslednii Brosok na Iug* (Moscow: Pisatel, 1993), pp. 63, 66, 71, 73, 74, 76, 130. Zhirinovsky's *Final Thrust South* has been translated and published as *My Struggle* (New York: Barricade, 1996) in an apparent commentary on how Zhirinovsky's political views are considered in the West.

41. See Alexander Yanov, "The Zhirinovsky Phenomenon," *New Times International*, no. 2 (Oct. 1992): 10–13.

42. See the outline of Zhirinovsky's convictions in Fedarko, "Rising Czar?," pp. 38–44.

43. "Slovo k narodu," *Sovetskaia Rossii*, 23 July 1991, p. 1.

44. See the references in Joan Barth Urban and Valerii D. Solovei, *Russia's Communists at the Crossroads* (Boulder, Colo.: Westview, 1997), pp. 44–45, and James Carney, "A Communist to His Roots," *Time*, 27 May 1996, p. 61.

45. See Michael Specter, "Controversial Russian behind Communism's Revival," *San Francisco Chronicle*, 3 May 1996, p. A14.

46. See the discussion in Lester, *Modern Tsars and Princes*, p. 136, where the "Word to the People" is identified as anti-Gorbachev, anti-Western, and unqualifiedly nationalistic.

47. A. Prokhanov, "Sufficient Defense," *Nash sovremennik*, trans. in part in Mark Galeotti, "Life after the Party: Alexander Prokhanov's 'Sufficient Defense,'" *Russia and the World*, no. 18 (1990): 7.

48. Ibid., p. 8.

49. See the discussion in Lester, *Modern Tsars and Princes*, pp. 136–137.

50. See the discussion of Prokhanov's views in *Current Digest of the Post-Soviet Press*, 23 June 1993.

51. Alexander Yanov, "Political Portrait: The Empire's Last Soldier—Alexander Prokhanov, the Newspaper *Den* and the War Party," *Novoye vremya*, no. 19 (May 1993): 20–24.

52. Ibid.

53. This is the judgment of Yanov in his interview with Prokhanov. See ibid.

54. Sergei Kurginian, "Counteraction," *Nash sovremennik*, no. 17 (July 1992): 3–15. An excerpted English-language version is available in *Current Digest of the Post-Soviet Press*, 44, no. 40 (4 Nov. 1992): 13.

55. In his interview with Prokhanov, Alexander Yanov specifically emphasized the "corporativism" of Prokhanov's proposals. See his "Political Portrait."

56. See the discussion in Peter Reddaway, "On the Eve: Perceptions and Misperceptions from the Right," *Russia and the World*, no. 20 (1991): 4–10.

57. Sergei Kurginian, "Forum: If We Want to Win," *Den*, 1–9 Jan. 1993, p. 2, available in part in "Two Patriots Debate Threat of Fascism," *Current Digest of the Post-Soviet Press*, 45, no. 4 (24 Feb. 1993): 18.

58. Prokhanov, in Yanov, "Political Portrait," p. 20.

59. In his discussion with Prokhanov, Alexander Barkashov spoke of the millions of Russians who had died in the Stalin purges of the 1930s. Prokhanov did not object. See the discussion in "Under the Sign of a New Swastika," *Kommersant-Daily*, 25 Aug. 1995, p. 4. An English version is available in the *Official Kremlin International News Broadcast*, 25 Aug. 1995.

60. Prokhanov argued that existing Russian law proscribed efforts at "fascist political activity" or the dissemination of "fascist propaganda"; yet no Russian political group was charged with either infraction—which indicated either that there were no "fascists" in Russia or that the authorities really did not know how to identify fascism.

61. See John J. Stephan, *The Russian Fascists: Tragedy and Farce in Exile 1925–1945* (New York: Harper & Row, 1978), and Alexander Prokhanov and Alexander Barkashov, "Glory to Russia: A Dialogue," *Zavtra*, no. 12 (Mar. 1994): 1–2; available in English as, "Is a Mystical, Patriotic Russia in the Offing?," *Current Digest of the Post-Soviet Press*, 41, no. 17 (25 May 1994): 10.

62. Stephan, *Russian Fascists*, pp. 29, 338.

63. See Specter, "Controversial Russian behind Communism's Revival," p. A14.

64. "The Essential Zyuganov," *Newsweek*, 17 June 1996, p. 17; Carney, "Communist to His Roots."

65. See Matt Bivens, "Communist Party Platform is Odd Mix of 'Isms,' " *San Francisco Chronicle*, 11 June 1996, p. A6.

66. Sergei Skvortsov, "The Communist Party Still Has Not Fallen to Pieces," *Moscow News*, no. 8 (25 Feb. 1994): 13. The Russian version appears as "The Last Romantic," *Moskovskie novosti*, no. 8 (25 Feb. 1994): B6.

67. Gennadi Ziuganov, "Essay in Russian Geopolitics: The Merits of Rus," *Sovetskaia Rossiia*, 26 Feb. 1994, pp. 35–46. An English-language translation is available in Black (ed.), *Russia and Eurasia*, pp. 112, 114.

68. Ibid., p. 112.

69. Adrian Karatnycky, "The Real Zyuganov," *New York Times*, 5 Mar. 1996, p. A17.

70. Ziuganov insists that the gathering of peoples into a restored Union of Soviet Socialist Republics would be "voluntary."

71. Ziuganov, "Essay in Russian Geopolitics," pp. 112, 114. The theme of Russian humiliation recurs frequently in Ziuganov's writings and speeches; see, e.g., "Essential Zyuganov," p. 17.

72. Gennadi Ziuganov, "Geopolitical Fragments," *Izvestia*, 24 Sept. 1994. This appears in English translation in Black (ed.), *Russia and Eurasia*, pp. 124–127.

73. Ibid., pp. 126, 127.

74. Ibid., p. 127.

75. Riasanovsky, "Emergence of Eurasianism," p. 48.

76. Ibid., pp. 53–56.

77. Dmitry V. Shlapentokh, "Eurasianism: Past and Present," *Communist and Post-Communist Studies*, 30, no. 2 (1997): 144–145.

78. Leo Gumilev, *Ethnogenesis and the Biosphere* (Moscow: Progress, 1990).

79. Vadim Medish (ed.), *My Russia: The Political Autobiography of Gennady Zyuganov* (Armonk, N.Y.: M. E. Sharpe, 1997), pp. 47, 71–72.

80. Ibid., pp. 71, 75, 76.

81. See the comments in Shlapentokh, "Eurasianism," pp. 130–131.

82. Nikolai Trubetzkoi, "On the Idea Governing the Ideocratic State," in N. S. Trubetzkoi, *The Legacy of Genghis Khan* (Ann Arbor: University of Michigan Press, 1991), pp. 269, 270.

83. See, e.g., Medish (ed.), *My Russia*, pp. 93, 138.

84. Ivan A. Ilin, *Nashi Zadachi: statii 1948–1954 godov* (Paris: Izdanie Russkogo Oschche-Voinskogo Soiuza, 1956), vol. 1, p. 70.

85. Ibid., p. 71.

86. See A. James Gregor, "Fascism and the New Russian Nationalism," *Communist and Post-Communist Studies*, 31, no. 1 (1998): 1–15.

87. See discussion in Gennadi Ziuganov, "Gennadi Ziuganov Does Not Want to Stand in Line for the Presidency," *Argumenty i fakty*, no. 29 (June 1994): 3. An English-language version is available in *FBIS:USSR*, no. 071 (5 July 1994): 18–20. The program of the Communist Party of the Russian Federation refers to such a government upon the accession of the "President-Communist" to office.

88. See the discussion in *Zavtra*, 22 June 1994, as quoted in Veljko Vujacic, "Gennadiy Zyuganov and the 'Third Road,'" *Post-Soviet Affairs*, 12, no. 2 (1994): 143–144.

89. Ziuganov, "Essay in Russian Geopolitics," pp. 113–114.

90. Ibid., p. 114.

91. See the discussion in "Russia's Communist: A Dreadful Prospect," *Economist*, 16 Mar. 1996, pp. 53, 56; the suggestive comments by Franz Schurmann, "Why the Soviet Union Might Return to Neo-Communism," *San Francisco Chronicle*, 9 Jan. 1991, p. 2, and by Henry Kissinger, "Beware: A Threat Abroad," *Newsweek*, 17 June 1996, pp. 22–23.

92. Ziuganov consistently speaks of Russia's humiliation, and it is clear that this sense of humiliation motivates him. See, e.g., Medish (ed.), *My Russia*, pp. 13, 17, 20, 39, 80.

Chapter 7: Fascism and Bolshevism

1. See the discussion in Zeev Sternhell, *Neither Right nor Left: Fascist Ideology in France* (Berkeley: University of California Press, 1986), chaps. 4 and 5.

2. See, e.g., M. Rokeach, *The Open and Closed Mind* (New York: Free Press, 1960), and I. A. Taylor, "Similarities in the Structure of Extreme Social Attitudes," *Psychological Monographs*, 64, no. 2 (Feb. 1960): 1–36.

3. From a speech delivered 20 Jan. 1927, as quoted in "Cassius," in *Un Inglese defende Mussolini* (Rome: Riunite, 1946), p. 38.

4. Milford W. Howard, *Fascism: A Challenge to Democracy* (New York: Fleming H. Revell, 1928), pp. 46–47.

5. See, e.g., William Bolitho, *Italy under Mussolini* (New York: Macmillan, 1926).

6. See the discussions in Domenico Settembrini, *Fascismo controrivoluzione imperfetta* (Florence: Sansoni, 1978); Zeev Sternhell, *The Birth of Fascist Ideology* (Princeton: Princeton University Press, 1994).

7. The fullest account is that of Renzo De Felice, *Mussolini il rivoluzionario* (Turin: Einaudi, 1965). See A. James Gregor, *Young Mussolini and the Intellectual Origins of Fascism* (Berkeley: University of California Press, 1979).

8. See the discussion in A. James Gregor, *The Ideology of Fascism: The Rationale of Totalitarianism* (New York: Free Press, 1969), chaps. 2 and 3.

9. The most comprehensive history of Fascism, of course, is to be found in the monumental studies of Renzo De Felice.

10. See the discussion in A. James Gregor, *Italian Fascism and Developmental Dictatorship* (Princeton: Princeton University Press, 1979), chaps. 2 and 3.

11. See Gregor, *Ideology of Fascism*, pp. 72–85; and A. James Gregor, *Phoenix: Fascism in Our Time* (New Brunswick, N.J.: Transaction, 1999), chap. 2.

12. Gregor, *Phoenix*, pp. 100–104; Gregor, *Young Mussolini*, chap. 3.

13. Michels is rarely acknowledged as a scholar of traditional Marxism, but his work, while he was an acknowledged syndicalist, remains of substantial interest. See, e.g., Roberto Michels, *La teoria di C. Marx sulla miseria crescente e le sue origini* (Turin: Bocca, 1922).

14. See De Felice, *Mussolini il rivoluzionario*, chaps. 5–8.

15. A. O. Olivetti, "Presentazione," *Pagine libere*, 15 Dec. 1906. For reasons that need not concern us here, Olivetti's complete works were never published in Italy. His daughter, Livia Olivetti, made a two-volume, mimeographed collection of his writings available to me, entitled *Battaglie sindacaliste: dal sindacalismo al fascismo*, from which citations will be drawn. The above article is to be found in vol. 1, pp. 18–20.

16. See Olivetti, *Cinque anni di sindacalismo e di lotta proletaria in Italia* (Naples: Partenopea, 1914), p. 3.

17. Benito Mussolini, "Divagazione," in *Opera omnia* (Florence: La Fenice, 1953–64), vol. 11, p. 341.

18. Filippo Corridoni, *Sindacalismo e repubblica* (Rome: SAREP, 1945; originally pub. 1915), pp. 19, 23, 25–26.

19. Engels wrote that socialist revolution could only "be a revolution taking place simultaneously in all civilized countries, that is, at least in England, America, France and Germany. In each of these countries it will develop more quickly or more slowly according to whether the country has a more developed industry . . . and a more considerble mass of productive forces" ("Principles of Communism," in K. Marx and F. Engels, *Collected Works* [New York: International, 1976], vol. 6, p. 352).

20. See the discussion in A. James Gregor, *Marxism, China and Development* (New Brunswick, N.J.: Transaction, 1995), chap. 2.

21. See the discussion in A. James Gregor, *A Survey of Marxism* (New York: Random House, 1965), chap. 5. All this is explicit in *Communist Manifesto*.

22. Engels explicitly dismissed such revolutions as "untimely" and refused to consider them "socialist" in any serious Marxist sense. In this context, see Engels's letter to J. Weydemeyer, 12 Apr. 1853, in K. Marx and F. Engels, *Selected Correspondence* (Moscow: Foreign Languages, n.d.), p. 94.

23. See the discussion in A. O. Olivetti, "L'altra campana," *Pagine libere*, 5, no. 22 (15 Nov. 1911), and Paolo Orano, *Lode al mio tempo 1895–1925* (Bologna: Apollo, 1926).

24. See the discussion in Roberto Michels, *L'imperialismo Italiano* (Rome: Libraria, 1914), p. viii. Michels, himself an early syndicalist, regularly referred to Italy's political, miliary, and economic subordination to the more advanced industrial powers. He spoke eloquently of the industrial retardation of the Italian peninsula and affirmed that "it is industry that allows people to live and prosper in the modern world." Without a mature industrial base, a people finds itself the object of international disdain. See ibid., pp. xii, 3, 56f., 83–89.

25. Corridoni, *Sindacalismo e repubblica*, pp. 55–57.

26. See the discussion in Ivon de Begnac, *L'Arcangelo sindacalista (Filippo Corridoni)* (Verona: Mondadori, 1943), chap. 22; Tullio Masotti, *Corridoni* (Milan: Carnaro, 1932); and Vito Rastelli, *Filippo Corridoni: la figura storica e la dottrina politica* (Rome: "Conquiste d'impero," 1940).

27. See A. O. Olivetti, *Bolscevismo, communismo e sindacalismo* (published in Milan in 1919, but almost unobtainable; Olivetti's daughter was kind enough to supply a typescript copy of the manuscript, and references are to that copy), pp. 7–11.

28. Ibid., pp. 9, 11, 31.

29. Ibid., pp. 25, 31.

30. See the discussion in Edmondo Rossoni, *Le idee della ricostruzione: Discorsi sul Sindacalismo Fascista* (Florence: Bemporad, 1923), pp. 5, 30f., 57.

31. Ibid., pp. 74f.

32. There was a merger between the Italian Nationalists and the Fascists by the mid-1920s. See Romolo Ronzio, *La fusione del Nazionalismo con il Fascismo* (Rome: Italiane, 1943), and Sergio Panunzio, *Lo stato fascista* (Bologna: Cappelli, 1925), pp. 42f.

33. Corradini, as quoted in G. Petracchi, *La Russia revoluzionaria nella politica italiana 1917–1925* (Bari: Laterza, 1982), pp. 226f.

34. Friedrich Engels, *The Peasant War in Germany*, in Marx and Engels, *Collected Works*, vol. 10, p. 470.

35. See the discussion in Rossoni, *Le idee della ricostruzione*, pp. 82–83, and Sergio Panunzio, *Che cos'è il fascismo* (Milan: Alpes, 1924), pp. 24–25.

36. See the discussion in Vincenzo Zangara, *Rivoluzione sindacale: lo stato corporativo* (Rome: Littorio, 1927), pp. 113f.

37. Ibid., chap. 3. Mussolini argued that what Bolshevik Russia required was increasing conformity to "objective economic realities." He held that economic production and development necessitated "order, discipline and work," those "verities" familiar to anyone who has had to deal with productive realities (Mussolini, "Ritorno all'antico," in *Opera omnia*, vol. 17, pp. 199–200).

38. See the discussion in Panunzio, *Che cos'è il fascismo*, pp. 88f., 102.

39. Thus Mussolini argued that once Lenin recognized that development of the productive forces and the expansion of the economy were, in fact, the tasks of Bolshevism, he had to concede that order, discipline, and hierarchy were necessary. See the discussion in Mussolini, "Fascismo e sindacalismo" and "Timori infondati," in *Opera omnia*, vol. 18, pp. 225f., 371f.

40. Lenin, in his *State and Revolution*, had argued that the political state would begin to "wither away" immediately after the socialist revolution. Compare those notions with Mussolini's discussion in "Mentre il PUS siede: Lenin, Vanderlip e c." and "Il primo discorso alla Camera dei Deputati," in *Opera omnia*, vol. 16, pp. 118–121, 442; "Dove impera Lenin" and "Fame e Russia," in ibid., vol. 17, pp. 76–78, 98f.; and "La Russia all'asta," in ibid., vol. 18, pp. 404–406.

41. See the discussion in Sergio Panunzio, "Contro il regionalismo," in *Stato nazionale e sindacati* (Milan: Imperia, 1924), pp. 72–91, and pp. 117–118 and 122 dealing with National Syndicalism.

42. "Fascist syndicalism is national and productivistic.... A syndicalism has arisen in Italy that does not ignore the nation ... [it] educates men to labor ... in a national society in which labor becomes a joy, an object of pride and a title to nobility" (Mussolini, "Commento," in *Opera omnia*, vol. 18, pp. 228–229).

43. See the discussion in ibid.

44. See the discussion in Mussolini, "Fascismo e sindacalismo," p. 226; and Ezio Maria Olivetti, *Sindacalismo nazionale* (Milan: Monanni, 1927), pp. 41–45.

45. See the instructive discussions in Panunzio, *Stato nazionale e sindacati*, and A. O. Olivetti, *Il sindacalismo come filosofia e come politica: lineamenti di sintesi universale* (Milan: Alpes, 1924).

46. Panunzio, *Che cos'è il fascismo*, pp. 29, 40, 52–53, 62–63.

47. See the discussion in Panunzio, *Stato nazionale e sindacati*, pp. 102–105, 115–123; Guido Pighetti, *Sindacalismo fascista* (Milan: Imperia, 1924), pp. 69–90. The accounts in Panunzio and Pighetti are a reflection of the more emphatic version found in the works of the Nationalist Enrico Corradini, written as early as 1913. See Corradini, "Le nuove dottrine

nazionali e il rinnovamento spirituale," in *Discorsi politici (1902–1923)* (Florence: Vallecchi, n.d.), pp. 203–209.

48. See the discussion in Ardengo Soffici, *Battaglia fra due vittorie* (Florence: "La Voce," 1923), pp. 126–137.

49. Nikolai Bukharin, *Economia del periodo di trasformazione* (Milan: Jaca, 1971).

50. The Fascists emphasized the incredible privation that had settled on "socialist" Russia. See, e.g., Mussolini, "Nel paradiso Bolscevico: Il ritorno dell'antropofagia in Russia," in *Opera omnia*, vol. 18, pp. 397–398.

51. Bukharin, *Economia*, pp. 9f.

52. Marx and Engels both anticipated that the transition from capitalist to socialist society would be largely peaceful, with the transitional society inheriting the mature economic system produced by modern capitalism. See Gregor, *Survey of Marxism*, chap. 5. Karl Kautsky described the postrevolutionary economic restructuring of socialist society in his *Die soziale Revolution: Am Tage nach der sozialen Revolution* (Berlin: Vorvaerts, 1904). For classical Marxists, capitalist society had developed into a monopoly economy that had instituted extensive planning. The socialist revolution needed only to abolish private property and the market in order to sketch the principal outlines of the future society. There was no suggestion that the period of transition would be burdened by a devastating economic collapse.

53. See Bukharin, *Economia*, chaps. 2 and 3.

54. Ibid., p. 42.

55. Ibid., p. 105. Thus, Bukharin sought to charge the economic devastation of the post-Bolshevik revolution in Russia to the account of the "inevitable collapse" of the world capitalist system. It was not the episodic, contingent result of civil war or the intervention of foreign capitalists. It was the result of the "final crisis" of capitalism.

56. See the variation of Bukharin's account provided by Leon Trotsky, *The Revolution Betrayed: What is the Soviet Union and Where is it Going?* (Garden City, N.Y.: Doubleday, 1937), pp. 22–23.

57. Bukharin, *Economia*, p. 171; see the discussion in chap. 11.

58. Thus Mussolini insisted that the effort to "sovietize" Western Europe had failed, and that there was every indication that "Marxist" revolution would fail everywhere else. See Mussolini, "Italia e Russia," in *Opera omnia*, vol. 17, pp. 204f., and the discussion in "L'azione e la dottrina fascista dinnanzi alle necessità storiche della nazione" and "Discorso di Cremona," in ibid., vol. 18, pp. 411–424.

59. See, e.g., Enrico Corradini, "Le opinioni degli uomini e i fatti dell'uomo," "La vita nazionale," and "La morale della guerra," in *Discorsi politici (1902–1923)* (Florence: Vallecchi, 1923), pp. 24–31, 36–50, 142f.

60. The entire discussion concerning the empirical origins of nationalism goes back to the beginning of the twentieth century among Fascist and proto-fascist thinkers. See, e.g., Enrico Corradini's discussion in "Le opinioni degli uomini e i fatti dell'uomo" and "La vita nazionale," esp. pp. 24–25 and 36–50. These themes remained central to the interpretation of nationalism and recur throughout the Fascist period. See, e.g., Corrado Gini, *Nascita, evoluzione e morte delle nazione* (Rome: Littorio, 1930), esp. pp. 86, 100; M. Canella, *Lineamenti di antropobiologia* (Florence: Sansoni, 1943), esp. p. 8.

61. "Fascism does not believe in the vitality and the principles that inspire the so-called League of Nations. In that League the nations do not stand as equals. The League is a kind of Holy Alliance of plutocratic nations . . . [assembled] to guarantee the exploitation of the larger part of the world" (Mussolini, "Il fascismo e i problemi della politica estera Italiana," in *Opera omnia*, vol. 16, p. 158). See Corradini's discussion, "Nazionalismo e socialismo," in *Discorsi politici*, pp. 213–229, esp. pp. 226–229.

62. Mussolini argued that because of its exploitative practices, it would be necessary for "proletarian" Italy to disengage itself from the "Western plutocratic nations" if it intended to "develop its own internal productive forces." As for "proletarian internationalism," Mussolini dismissed it as totally unrealistic, the product of "artificial and formalistic constructions" ("Il fascismo e i problemi della politica estera Italiana," pp. 158, 159).

63. Mussolini, "Il 'PUS' al Congresso," in *Opera omnia*, vol. 16, pp. 116–117.

64. Soffici, *Battaglia*, p. 137.

65. See the discussion in Celestino Arena, *L'espansione economica in regime corporativo* (Rome: Diritto del Lavoro, 1929), chaps. 1 and 2, and Mussolini's comments on "late developers" in "La politica estera al Senato," in *Opera omnia*, vol. 22, p. 151.

66. Frederick C. Barghoorn, *Soviet Russian Nationalism* (New York: Oxford University Press, 1956), p. 29.

67. There were Marxists who refused to countenance such a possibility. Trotsky argued that "the contradictions in the position of the Workers' Government in a backward country . . . can find a solution only on an international scale. . . . [The] Russian Revolution [must] become the prologue to world revolution. . . . Of this there cannot be any doubt for a single moment" (quoted in Nikolai Bukharin, *Building Up Socialism* [London: CPGB, 1926], pp. 34f.; see Trotsky, *The Permanent Revolution and Results and Prospects* [New York: Pathfinder, 1970], p. 31).

68. V. I. Lenin, *State and Revolution*, in *Collected Works* (Moscow: Foreign Languages, 1966), vol. 25, pp. 420–421.

69. It is clear that Lenin understood that socialism could not be imposed on a primitive economic base. He expected that the Russian "proletariat" might begin the "work which the British, French, or German proletariat will consolidate" (Lenin, "Address to the Second All-Russia Congress of Communist Organizations of the Peoples of the East," in *Collected Works*, vol. 30, p. 162).

70. As quoted in Louis Fischer, *The Life of Lenin* (New York: Harper and Row, 1964), p. 258.

71. Lenin, "Better Fewer, But Better," in *Collected Works*, vol. 33, pp. 498–499, 501; see *idem*, "Tenth All-Russia Conference of the R.C.P. (B)," in ibid., vol. 32, p. 408.

72. Lenin, "The New Economic Policy and the Tasks of the Political Education Departments," in ibid., vol. 33, pp. 63, 66.

73. Nikolai Bukharin, "Critica della piattaforma economica dell'opposizione," in Nikolai Bukharin and Evgeni Preobrazenski, *L'accumulazione socialista* (Rome: Riuniti, 1972), p. 113. Bukharin took his cues on class collaboration from Lenin; see Lenin, "How We Should Reorganize the Workers' and Peasants' Inspection," in *Collected Works*, vol. 33, pp. 485–487.

74. Both Leon Trotsky and Evgeni Preobrazhenski recognized that peasants and proletarians alike would have to submit to state authority as part of the program of "primitive socialist accumulation." The state would extract "surpluses" from both peasants and workers in order to fuel capital expansion and industrialization. See Evgeni Preobrazhenski, *The New Economics* (London: Clarendon Press, 1965), and the discussion of Trotsky's position in Curtis Stokes, *The Evolution of Trotsky's Theory of Revolution* (Washington, D.C.: University Press of America, 1982), p. 98.

75. As cited in Ian Grey, *Stalin: Man of History* (London: Lawrence, 1979), pp. 199f.

76. See the discussion in Kenneth Murphy, *Retreat from the Finland Station: Moral Odysseys in the Breakdown of Communism* (New York: Free Press, 1992), pp. 73–76.

77. Drieu La Rochelle, *Socialismo fascista* (Rome: E.G.E., 1973), p. 215; see La Rochelle's discussion in "Contro Marx" and "La prossima guerra," in ibid., pp. 78–86 and 161–168.

78. Trotsky, *Revolution Betrayed*, p. 278.

79. M. Ardemagni, "Deviazioni Russe verso il fascismo," *Gerarchia*, 15 (July 1934): 571.

80. In his Sixteenth Report to the leadership of the Communist Party in June 1930, Stalin affirmed: "We stand for the withering away of the state. At the same time we stand for the strengthening of the dictatorship of the proletariat, which is the mightiest and strongest state power that has ever existed. The highest development of state power with the object of preparing the conditions for the withering away of state power—such is the Marxist formula. Is this 'contradictory'? Yes, it is 'contradictory.' But this contradiction is bound up with life, and it fully reflects Marx's dialectics" (J. Stalin, "Political Report of the Central Committee to the Sixteenth Congress," in *Works* [Moscow: Foreign Languages, 1952–55], vol. 12, p. 381).

81. A. Nasti, "L'Italia, il bolscevismo, la Russia," *Critica fascista*, 15, no. 10 (15 Mar. 1937): 162.

82. Sergio Panunzio argued that "statocrazia" represented the Fascist conception of the "dictatorship of the state," as distinct from the Marxist notion of the "dictatorship of a class." He argued that Fascism had committed itself to the "political and juridical dominion of the state over all classes," rather than one class over another (*Il sentimento dello stato* [Rome: Littorio, 1929], p. 215). By the mid-1930s, it was clear that the Soviet, like the Fascist, state exercised "political and juridical dominion" over all classes, strata, and organized interests.

83. B. Ricci, "Il 'fascismo' di Stalin," *Critica fascista*, 15, no. 18 (15 July 1937): 317–319.

84. T. Napolitano, "Il 'fascismo' di Stalin ovvero l'U.R.S.S. e noi," *Critica fascista*, 15, no. 23 (1 Oct. 1937): 397. Classical Marxism anticipated the "withering away of the state." Fascist theoreticians pointed to the fact that Stalinism had created a "political army" to support the state, eloquent evidence that the "Marxists" of the Soviet Union were not prepared to supervise the disappearance of the state. See Panunzio, *Il sentimento dello stato*, p. 47, n. 18.

85. See, e.g., the discussion in Renzo Bertoni, *Russia: trionfo del fascismo* (Milan: "La prora," 1937), pp. 150–153, 214, 220, 231–232.

86. Fascist intellectuals argued that the invocation of a collective sense of mission represented a tacit admission that a "sentiment of nationalism" inspired organized communities. Such a sentiment was the overt manifestation of "the moral unity of a people." Those were the sentiments to which Fascism appealed. Similarly, the appeal to those sentiments among the Marxists of Stalin's Soviet Union signaled their recognition of some of Fascism's critical beliefs. See Panunzio, *Il sentimento dello stato*, pp. 65–66, and *idem*, *Popolo, nazione, stato (esame giuridico)* (Florence: "La nuova Italia," 1933), pp. 15–16. The argument was that the concept of a "citizen-soldier," united to that of a "citizen-producer," distinguished Fascism from any of its alternatives, because it captured both the nationalism and the productivism that had come to characterize the regime. See Panunzio, *Teoria generale dello stato fascista* (Padua: CEDAM, 1939), pp. 61–62.

87. Bertoni, *Russia*, p. 173. For Panunzio, all this signified the "exhaustion" of Marxist and "Bolshevik" ideology and the clear vitality of Fascism. See Panunzio, *Teoria generale dello stato fascista*, pp. xiv, 8f., 10, 22 n. 1.

88. Sergio Panunzio, *L'economia mista: dal sindacalismo giuridico al sindacalismo economico* (Milan: Hoepli, 1936), pp. 8–9. See Panunzio's discussion of the single-party state and its clear manifestation in the Soviet Union (*Teoria generale dello stato fascista*, pp. 459–463).

89. See the discussion in Felice Guarneri, *Battaglie economiche tra le due grandi guerre* (Milan: Garzanti, 1953), vol. 1, pp. 61–70; Gianni Toniolo, *L'economia dell'Italia fascista* (Rome: Laterza, 1980), chap. 2; and the comments by Ugo Spirito, *Capitalismo e corporativismo* (Florence: Sansoni, 1933), p. 56. Mussolini's principal writings of the period on the Fascist corporative state are available in English in *The Corporate State* (Florence: Vallecchi, 1938), p. 8.

90. Arena, *L'espansione*, p. 18.

91. Panunzio, *L'economia mista*, p. 64.

92. Spirito, *Capitalismo e corporativismo*, pp. 14–15. See his later comments in *La filosofia del comunismo* (Florence: Sansoni, 1948), pp. 56–57.

93. Mussolini, "Atto quinto finora," in *Opera omnia*, vol. 29, p. 63.

94. Mussolini, *Corporate State*, pp. 40, 48. In this regard see Franco Angelini (ed.), *La concezione fascista della proprieta privata* (Rome: Confederazione fascista dei lavoratori dell'agricoltura, 1939).

95. Mussolini, *Corporate State*, pp. 96–97.

96. See, e.g., Mussolini's comments on the "elephantiasis and paralysis" that afflicted the "Bolshevik State" because of its bureaucratization of the national economy (Mussolini, "To the National Assembly of the Corporations," 5 May 1937, in *Corporate State*, pp. 96–97). As early as 1934, Mussolini insisted that nationalization and its attendant bureaucratization would impair, rather than sustain, economic and industrial development, none of which would preclude direct state intervention in critical industries and critical sectors of the economy. See his comments in Mussolini, "Before the Assembly of the Councils of Corporations," 23 Mar. 1936, in ibid., esp. p. 77. See in this context the professional exposition in Arrigo Serpieri, *Principi di economia politica corporativa* (Florence: Barbera, 1944).

97. Mussolini, "Il piano regolatore della nuova economia Italiana," in *Opera omnia*, vol. 27, pp. 241–248.

98. See Mussolini, "Alla terza assemblea generale delle corporazioni," in ibid., vol. 28, pp. 175–181.

99. Fascist propaganda literature justifying Italy's entry into the Second World War is abundant. See, e.g., Vito Beltani, *Il problema delle materie prime* (Rome: Tupini, 1940); Guido Puccio, *Lotta fra due mondi* (Rome: Edizioni italiane, 1942); Domenico Soprano, *Spazio vitale* (Milan: Corbaccio, 1942).

Chapter 8: Fascism, Marxism and Race

1. Lev Gumilev, *Ethnogenesis and the Biosphere* (Moscow: Progress, 1990), pp. 9, 29, 37, 44, 57–58, 76–77, 79 n. 20, 146 n. 3, 147 n. 23, 164–165, 170 n. 12, 204–207.

2. See the account in Alexander Yanov, *Weimar Russia and What We Can Do About It* (New York: Slovo-World, 1995), chap. 9.

3. Gumilev, *Ethnogenesis*, pp. 31, 66, 112, 132, 136.

4. Ibid., pp. 31, 50, 131. See the discussion at p. 205.

5. Ibid., pp. 206–240.

6. Ibid., pp. 80, 90, 172, 177. See ibid., pp. 98, 105, 109.

7. Ibid., pp. 74, 143, 146.

8. See the discussion in A. James Gregor, *Ideology of Fascism: The Rationale of Totalitarianism* (New York: Free Press, 1969), chap. 6 and appendix A.

9. Benito Mussolini, "L'Italia e le grandi potenze," in *Opera omnia* (Florence: La Fenice, 1953–64), vol. 19, p. 3. This was affirmed only a few days after the march on Rome, on 3 Nov. 1922.

10. See Dino Grandi, *Giovani* (Bologna: Zanichelli, 1941), pp. 39–42.

11. See the discussion in Edmondo Rossoni, *Le idee della ricostruzione: discorsi sul sindacalismo fascista* (Florence: Bemporad, 1923), pp. 5, 9, 17–18, 30–31, 41–42, 63, 91; Sergio Panunzio, *Che cos'è il fascismo* (Milan: Alpes, 1924), pp. 28–29, 31.

12. Sergio Panunzio, *Il fondamento giuridico del fascismo* (Rome: Bonacci, 1987), pp. 180–186.

13. It would be useful to provide a definition of "totalitarianism" as Fascists understood it, but this would require more space than I have here. The treatment by Giovanni Gentile is instructive; see Gentile, *Genesi e struttura della società* (Florence: Sansoni, 1946).

14. "Myth" was understood to be the necessary elemental motivator of popular mobilization. Individual and collective action, informed by reason and interest, was inspired by sentiment and moral incentive. See the discussion in Sergio Panunzio, *Il sentimento dello stato* (Rome: Littorio, 1929). Like religious faith, political action was a union of sentiment and reason. For that reason, Fascists often spoke of the state as an *ecclesia*. See the discussion in Sergio Panunzio, *La teoria generale dello stato fascista* (Podua: CEDAM, 1939), pt. 1; and Carlo Costamagna, *Dottrina del fascismo* (Tutin: UTET, 1940), chap. 4.

Mysticism, for Fascists, referred to the sentiment that inspired self-sacrifice on the part of individuals in the service of the larger community. It referred to the selfless dedication of "humane and heroic figures" in the service of others. "Fascist mysticism" meant "the readiness to expose oneself to risk . . . , to the total sacrifice of one's very being, to the most absolute dedication to the Cause of the Regime" (G. S. Spinetti, *Mistica fascista nel pensiero di Arnaldo Mussolini* [Milan: Hoepli, 1936], p. ix).

This kind of mysticism and its implied discipline and self-sacrifice were functional in circumstances that demanded arduous and continuous labor in a program of extensive economic growth and intensive technological development. Sacrificial devotion recommended itself where a less developed community conceives itself forever threatened by the armed might of more powerful "imperialist" neighbors.

15. Even before the seizure of power with the march on Rome, Mussolini spoke of the nation as "our myth . . . a faith, a passion. . . . Our myth is the nation; our myth is the greatness of the nation" (Benito Mussolini, "Il discorso di Napoli," in *Opera omnia* [Florence: La Fenice, 1963], vol. 18, p. 457). The Fascist use of the term *myth* is a Sorellian derivative and refers to a kind of conceptual language that includes facts and invokes sentiment calculated to generate the energy and commitment necessary for revolution. See Giovanni Gentile, *Che cosa è il fascismo* (Bologna: Vallecchi, 1924), p. 96; cf. Gregor, *Ideology of Fascism*, pp. 64–68. "Fascist politics turns entirely on the concept of the national state" (Giovanni Gentile, *Origini e dottrina del fascismo* [Rome: Littorio, 1929], p. 43). See Sergio Panunzio, *Popolo, Nazione, Stato* [Florence: "La nuova Italia," 1933], p. 7.

16. See F. T. Marinetti, "Definizione dello squadrista," in Asvero Gravelli (ed.), *Squadrismo* (Rome: "AntiEuropa," 1939), p. 107; and Gentile, *Che cosa è il fascismo*, p. 33, when he speaks of the state.

17. This material varies in quality and focus. There are excellent historical treatments of the concepts in books like that of Renato Soriga, *L'idea nazionale italiana dal secolo XVIII all'unificazione* (Modena: Soliani, 1941), together with discursive and analytic assessments to be found among the Italian nationalists at the turn of the century until the First World War. This is particularly true of the work of Enrico Corradini, some of whose more insightful writings and speeches are collected in *Discorsi politici* (1902–23) (Florence: Vallecchi, 1923) and *La rinascita nazionale* (Florence: Le Monnier, 1929). See the ample account of the development of the ideology of the Italian Nationalist Association in Paola Maria Arcari, *Le elaborazioni della dottrina political nazionale fra l'unità e l'intervento (1870–1914)* (Florence: Marzocco, 1934–39). The Nationalists merged with the Fascists in February 1923.

Fascists never denied that they could provide rational support for nationalist policies; what they denied was that the masses could be mobilized and sustained in their efforts by such arguments.

18. By the end of the 1920s, Michels was recognized as a "comrade" in the ranks of the

Partito Nazionale Fascista and one of Fascism's most able intellectuals. See Paolo Orano, "Roberto Michels: l'amico, il maestro, il camerata," in *Studi in memoria di Roberto Michels* (Padua: CEDAM, 1937), pp. 9–14. In the preface to his *L'imperialismo italiano* (Rome: Libraria, 1914), p. v, Michels reported that he had long been intellectually occupied with problems related to "the fatherland, the nation, and nationality." Thus, long before his conversion to Fascism, Michels occupied himself with the historical, political, psychological, and moral problems of nationality and nationalism. See his *Patriotismus und Ethik* (Leipzig: Felix Dietrich, 1906); *idem*, "Le Patriotisme des Socialistes Allemands et le Congres d'Essen," *Le Movement Socialiste*, 3rd ser., 10, no. 2 (1908): 5–13; *idem*, "Zur historischen Analyse des Patriotismus," *Archiv fuer Sozialwissenschaft und Sozialpolitik*, 36, nos. 1 and 2 (1913): 14–43.

19. See A. James Gregor, *Phoenix: Fascism in Our Time* (New Brunswick, N.J.: Transaction, 1999), chaps. 3 and 4.

20. See Michels, "Neue Polemiken und Studien zum Vaterlandsproblem," *Archiv fuer Sozialwissenschaft und Sozialpolitik*, 66, no. 1 (1931): 98. All this had been part of the revolutionary syndicalist tradition that provided much of the doctrinal substance of Fascism. See the discussion in Sergio Panunzio, *La persistenza del diritto* (Pescara: Abruzzese, 1910), chaps. 2 and 3.

21. One of the central convictions of Fascist theory was that human beings were not "isolated atoms," but were, in essence, "social beings." Fascism was, in principle, collectivistic, rejecting the "bourgeois" notion that individuals were self-contained "monads," entering into social relations only through calculated contract. In this context see the philosophical arguments of the neo-idealism of Giovanni Gentile which Mussolini allowed to appear as part 1 of the official *Doctrine of Fascism*. See the general arguments in Gentile, *Che cosa è il fascismo*.

Michels early rejected the notion that "class" might be the collectivity with which individuals might identify. While human beings are understood to be essentially social animals, disposed to live in association, it was the nation, not an economic class, that provided the outlet. See Michels's essay "Patriotism," in *First Lectures in Political Sociology* (New York: Harper, 1949), pp. 156–166. See also the discussion in Alfredo Rocco, "La dottrina politica del fascismo," in Rocco, *Scritti e discorsi politici* (Milan: Giuffre, 1938), vol. 3, pp. 1100–1101.

22. See the discussions in Michels, *First Lectures*, chaps. 2, 3, 6, and 8.

23. See Panunzio's reference to the study of groups in *Appunti di dottrina generale dello stato: Realità e idea dello stato* (Rome: Castellani, 1933), pp. 83–84. Panunzio's account reflects that of Enrico Corradini, "La vita nazionale," in *Discorsi politici*, pp. 35–50.

24. See the discussion in Roberto Michels, *Der Patriotismus: Prolegomena zu seiner soziologishcen Analyse* (Munich: Duncker & Humblot, 1929), pp. 1, 10–12, and the early formulations of Enrico Corradini, *L'ombra della vita* (Naples: Ricciardi, 1908), pp. 285–287. These notions were repeated regularly in standard Fascist literature; see, e.g., Gentile, *Che cosa è il fascismo*, pp. 18–21, 27; Dino Grandi, *Le origini e la missione del fascismo* (Bologna: Cappelli, 1922), pp. 52–53.

25. See, e.g., Panunzio's discussion of the First World War having "incited" the "national idea" (*Lo stato fascista* [Bologna: Cappelli, 1925], p. 70).

The humiliations suffered by the nation were a constant theme in Fascist literature. See, e.g., Panunzio, *Che cos'è il fascismo*, pp. 14–15; Gentile, *Che cosa è il fascismo*, pp. 18, 19, 21, 26–27; see the discussion in Paolo Orano, *Lode al mio tempo 1895–1925* (Bologna: Apollo, 1926), esp. pp. 74–86; Grandi, *Le origini e la missione del fascismo*, pp. 52–54; Rossoni, *Le idee della ricostruzione*, pp. 32, 56.

Panunzio put the entire discussion in the context of contacts and conflicts between groups organized as nations. The "sentiment of nationality" as nationalism arises in the modern world in "antithesis to other nations" (Panunzio, *Popolo nazione stato*, p. 43, n. 10).

26. Corradini advanced very much the same argument early in the century. See the entire

discussion in Enrico Corradini, "Le nazioni proletarie e il nazionalismo," in *Discorsi politici*, pp. 105–118.

27. Michels, "Neue Polemiken," pp. 130–131.

28. See Panunzio, *Teoria generale*, p. 54, and the early characterizations by Corradini, *L'ombra della vita*, pp. 285–287.

29. See in this context Michels, "La guerra Europea al lume del materialismo storico," *La Riforma Sociale*, 3rd ser., 25 (1914): 945–957.

30. Thus, Sergio Panunzio speaks of a "national sentiment" that is a function of time and circumstances. See Panunzio, *Il sentimento dello stato*, pp. 65–66. See also his remarks on the necessities of survival in a world of competition in *Che cos'è il fascismo*, p. 62.

31. All this echoes the rationale for nationalism and a strong state embodied in the Nationalist thought of the turn of the century. See Corradini, "La vita nazionale." Michels, like most Fascist theoreticians, was familiar with an entire body of literature dealing with "mass" or "crowd" psychology and the disposition of humans to organize themselves in aggregates of "similars." Treatments of group psychology were common among pre-Fascist Italian Syndicalists and Nationalists. See, e.g., Paolo Orano, *La psicologia sociale* (Bari: Laterza, 1902), and Corradini, "Nazionalismo e imperialismo," in *La rinascita nazionale*, pp. 143–172; see Gregor, *Ideology of Fascism*, pp. 72–85.

32. See Benito Mussolini, *Dottrina del fascismo* (Milan: Hoepli, 1935), chap. 1, para. 2; and Gentile, *Genesi e struttura della società*, p. 41. Gentile was the author of pt. 1 of the *Dottrina del fascismo*.

33. This, of course, was a constant theme of Fascist theoreticians. See, e.g., Gioacchino Volpe, *History of the Fascist Movement* (Rome: Novissima, 1936), pp. 17, 26, 28. For the more abstract, metaethical version of elitism, see Gentile, *Origini e dottrina del fascismo*, p. 59.

34. This idea appears in the official *Dottrina del fascismo*, chap. 1, para. 2, authored by Gentile. It is an idea that is intrinsic to the traditional German Idealism of Hegel and was adopted and adapted by Gentile. In this context, see H. S. Harris, *The Social Philosophy of Giovanni Gentile* (Urbana: University of Illinois, 1960).

35. The basic rationale for Fascist totalitarianism was the same for all its apologists. The differences between them turned on ontological, epistemological, and methodological orientations. While critics have made much of the differences between ontological idealists like Gentile, sociological positivists like Michels, and legal philosophers like Panunzio, it is hard to argue that Fascist ideology was "inconsistent" or "incoherent" as a consequence. Fascist ideology was as coherent as any revolutionary ideology in the twentieth century (one need only consider the ideological curiosities of the "Marxism" of Fidel Castro or Mao Zedong to recognize the truth of this claim). In this context, see Nino Tripodi's discussion of the distinctions between Gentile's "immanent idealism" and Mussolini's "positive realism" (*Il fascismo secondo Mussolini* [Rome: Borghese, 1971]). One comes away with a sense that for all political purposes the differences are no differences.

Michels's rejection of the Marxist treatment of both concepts marked his final alienation from traditional socialism and his increasing approximation to what would ultimately become Fascism. Consider Michels's discussion in "La guerra Europea al lume del materialismo storico."

36. Perhaps the most important of Gentile's works in defense of Fascism is his posthumously published *Genesi e struttura della società*; perhaps the most important of Panunzio's works is his *Teoria generale*; see Costamagna, *Dottrina del fascismo*.

37. On the influence of elites, see, e.g., Camillo Pellizzi, *Fascismo—Aristocrazia* (Milan: Alpes, 1925); Michels, *Der Patriotismus*, chap. 1, esp., pp. 50–53; and Gentile, *Origini e dottrina del fascismo*, pp. 9–11.

38. Mussolini, "La Carta del Lavoro," in *Dottrina del fascismo*, p. 278.

39. This argument can be traced back to the first revolutionary syndicalist discussions of law and society. See Panunzio, "Prefazione," in *Persistenza del diritto*.

40. See Panunzio, *Teoria generale*, p. 27, and *idem*, *Lo stato fascista*, p. 49. "Without the state, there is no nation" (Costagmagna, *Dottrina del fascismo*, p. 183).

41. Panunzio, *Teoria generale*, p. 40; see, e.g., Rossoni, *Le idee della Ricostruzione*, esp. pp. 17, 32, and 20. See, e.g., Costamagna, *Dottrina del fascismo*, pp. 105–111. Panunzio, in this context, refers to the pedagogical obligations of the modern state. See *Teoria generale*, p. 59; Gentile speaks of "Fascist education" as "national education" intended to generate a "common fundamental national conscience" (Giovanni Gentile, *Fascismo e cultura* [Milan: Treves, 1928], pp. 70–71).

42. Mussolini, "Direttive," in *Opera omnia*, vol. 9, p. 259. See A. James Gregor, *Young Mussolini and the Intellectual Origins of Fascism* (Berkeley: University of California Press, 1979), pp. 215–220.

43. See Michels, *L'imperialismo italiano*, pp. 56–57.

44. See Virginio Gayda, *L'economia di domani* (Rome: Giornale d'Italia, 1941), esp. pp. 13f., 23, 24, 28, 40, 82, 83. This was a constant theme in Fascist literature and became a major argument in the rationale for Italy's participation in the Second World War. For the earlier period, see Celestino Arena, *L'espansione economica in regime corporativo* (Rome: "Diritto del lavoro," 1929), pt. 1.

45. See Arthur Livingston's "Introduction" to Gaetano Mosca, *The Ruling Class* (New York: McGraw-Hill, 1939). Mosca regularly alludes to the fact that individuals are "guided" by both their "passions and [their] needs" (p. 287), a conviction central to Fascist strategies for governance. Fascist theoreticians always argued that the appeal to "passions" was critical to the rule of populations. This is not, in and of itself, "irrational."

Pareto regularly alluded to the "nonlogical" sources of individual and collective political action. See, e.g., Dino Fiorot, *Politica e scienza in Vilfredo Pareto* (Milan: Communità, 1975), pt. 2, chap. 1, and Luigi Montini, *Vilfredo Pareto e il fascismo* (Rome: Volpe, 1974).

Gustav Le Bon, *Psychology of the Crowd* (London: Benn, 1952) repeats the same views. All Italian syndicalists were influenced by such views, and some of them, like Paolo Orano, passed directly into the Fascist ranks after the conclusion of the First World War. In this context, see Orano, *La psicologia sociale*.

46. See the discussion in Guido Bortolotto, *Massen und Fuehrer in der faschistischen Lehre* (Berlin: Hanseatische Verlaganstalt, 1934).

47. There is a variety of Fascist accounts of charismatic leadership, but Bortolotto's *Massen und Fuehrer in der faschistischen Lehre* is among the better ones. Michels's comments are instructive and provide insights into the Fascist notions of elite and charismatic leadership. See Michels, *First Lectures*, chap. 6.

48. Panunzio, *Il sentimento dello stato*, pp. 65–66, 73 n. 29, and *Teoria generale*, p. 34.

49. Benito Mussolini, "Discorso di Bologna," in *Opera omnia*, vol. 16, pp. 240, 243.

50. Mussolini, "La politica interna al Senato," in ibid., vol. 21, p. 201; *idem*, "Il venticinquennio del Regno di Vittorio Emanuele III," in ibid., p. 343; *idem*, "Discorso a Genoa," in ibid., vol. 22, p. 138.

51. See Roberto Michels, *Lavoro e razza* (Milan: Vallardi, 1924), p. lx; cf. p. 1, n. 1.

52. See the discussion in Gregor, *Ideology of Fascism*, chap. 6.

53. See Corrado Gini, *Nascita evoluzione e morte delle nazioni* (Rome: Littorio, 1930), esp. p. 100, n. 31; G. Acerbo, *I fondamenti della dottrina fascista della razza* (Rome: Unione Editoriale d'Italia, 1940), p. 25; and N. Timofeeff-Ressowsky, "Genetica ed evoluzione" and

"Sulla questione dell'isolamento territoriale entro popolazione specifiche," *Scientia genetica*, 1 (1939).

54. See the discussion in the "Introduction" to Mario F. Canella, *Razze umane estinte e viventi* (Florence: Sansoni, 1942); *idem, Lineamenti di antropobiologia* (Florence: Sansoni, 1943), chap. 1; and *idem, Princip di psicologia razziale* (Florence: Sansoni, 1941), chap. 1.

55. Aldo Capasso, *Idee chiare sul razzismo* (Rome: Augustea, 1942), p. 21; see Guido Landra, "La razza Italiana nella teoria dell'ologenesi," *Difesa della razza*, 2 (5 Apr. 1939): 10.

56. The authors of the official "Manifesto of Fascist Racism" referred, therefore, to an "Italian race." While there was a clear insistence that the "race" not be "contaminated" by "miscegenation" with "alien" types, these authors refused to attribute "superiority" to any given race or races. They urged the "Italian race" to entertain an "Aryan–Nordic" ideal, so as to provide a "normative model" that would circumvent any extra-European attachments. See "The Manifesto of Fascist Racism," trans. in Gregor, *Ideology of Fascism*, paras. 5–10, pp. 384–386.

57. Antonio Banzi insisted that Fascist racism specifically rejected the "theories of De Gobineau, [Houston S.] Chambelain, [Madison] Grant, [Ludwig] Woltmann and [Alfred] Rosenberg" (*Razzismo fascista* [Palermo: Agate, 1939], p. 13). Banzi was reaffirming a judgment made by Mussolini early in his career. See Mussolini's discussion of "Pan-German racial theories" in "Il trentino veduto da un socialista," in *Opera omnia*, vol. 33, pp. 153–161. See the treatment in Leone Franzi, *Fase attuale del razzismo tedesco* (Rome: Istituto nazionale di cultura, 1939).

Costamagna's comments were specific and unqualified. There was a simple rejection of biological racism and its determinism (*Dottrina del fascismo*, pp. 84–85, 189–210, 235). See the comments by Capasso, *Idee chiare*, p. 21.

There were, of course, some minor theoreticians who accepted the National Socialist interpretation of race; see, e.g., Enzo Leoni, *Mistica del razzismo fascista* (Padua: CEDAM, 1941).

58. This is one of the major thrusts of the curious volume by Julius Evola, *Sintesi di dottrina della razza* (Milan: Hoepli, 1941), and probably explains Mussolini's recommendation.

59. See Banzi, *Razzismo fascista*, p. 66, and Costamagna, *Dottrina del fascismo*, pp. 203–208.

60. Panunzio's theoretical contribution to the development of Fascist racism was compatible with the general account that received official sanction. Paolo Orano, on the other hand, became notable for his anti-Semitic posturing. See his "Introduction" to *Inchiesta sulla razza* (Rome: Pinciana, 1939) and his *Gli ebrei in Italia* (Rome: Pinciana, 1938).

61. See "Introduction" by Auguste Cornu and Wolfgang Moenke (eds.) in Moses Hess, *Philosophische und sozialistische Schriften 1837–1850* (Berlin: Akademie Verlag, 1961), p. lxvii.

62. In the mid-1840s Hess collaborated with Marx and Engels on the preparation of *The German Ideology*, and in 1847 he joined the League of Communists. See Shlomo Avineri, *Moses Hess: Prophet of Communism and Zionism* (New York: New York University Press, 1985), pp. 15–16.

See the discussion in Hess, "Die Folgen einer Revolution des Proletariats," in *Philosophische und sozialistische Shriften*, pp. 427–433; *idem*, "Dritter Artikel," in ibid., pp. 438–441; *idem*, "Schluss von Nr. 89," in ibid., pp. 441–444; and *idem*, "Rother Kathechismus fuer das deutsche Volk," in ibid., pp. 447–457.

63. The primary source is Moses Hess, "Rom und Jerusalem," in Horst Lademacher (ed.), *Ausgewaehlte Schriften* (Cologne: Akademische Verlag, 1962), which I have used as a guide to retranslate Moses Hess, *Rome and Jerusalem* (New York: Philosophical Library, 1958). Page references will be given to the English edition. See Hess, *Rome and Jerusalem*, p. 31; cf. "Rome and Jerusalem," in Arthur Herzberg (ed.), *The Zionist Idea* (New York: Atheneum, 1979), p. 119.

64. Ibid., p. 123.

65. Hess, *Rome and Jerusalem*, p. 71.

66. The principal theme of Hess's 1837 volume *Die heilige Geschichte der Menschheit* was written to convince his European readers that Spinoza was the "herald of the New Age." See Avineri, *Moses Hess*, chap. 2 and p. 125. Cf. Hess, *Rome and Jerusalem*, p. 61.

67. Hess, *Die heilige Geschichte der Menschheit*, in *Philosophische und sozialistische Schriften*, p. 73.

68. Hess, *Rome and Jerusalem*, pp. 80–81, and *idem*, "Rome and Jerusalem," pp. 136–137.

69. Hess, "Rome and Jerusalem," pp. 124, 126–127, 130, and *idem*, *Rome and Jerusalem*, p. 80.

70. Hess, *Rome and Jerusalem*, pp. 28, 44, 51–52, 56, 79.

71. Ibid., p. 85.

72. Ibid., p. 59.

73. Ibid., pp. 85–88.

74. Ibid., p. 26; see p. 63 for references to "original races."

75. Ibid., pp. 10, 44.

76. See ibid., pp. 10, 24, 41, 44, 62, 68–69.

77. Balbino Giuliano, *Elementi di cultura fascista* (Bologna: Zanichelli, 1929), pp. 120, 122.

78. Mussolini himself spoke of an ultimate world at peace, enjoying the "real and radical abolition of armies . . . , with national boundaries of exclusively historic character, without tariff restrictions, with a free flow of trade between them" (Benito Mussolini, *Testamento politico di Mussolini* [Rome: Pedanesi, 1948], p. 35).

79. Lenin recommended Woltmann's *Der historische Materialismus* (Duesseldorf: Michels, 1899) in the bibliography appended to his expository article on Karl Marx (V. I. Lenin, "Karl Marx," in *Collected Works* [Moscow: Foreign Languages, 1960], vol. 21, p. 87).

80. See Ludwig Woltmann, *Die Germanen in Frankreich* (Leipzig: Doerner, 1936), and *Die Germanen und die Renaissance in Italien* (Leipzig: Doerner, 1936), originally published in 1907 and 1905 respectively.

81. Ludwig Woltmann, *Politische Anthropologie* (Leipzig: Doerner, 1936), chap. 2, esp. p. 83.

82. "The biological history of human races is the real and fundamental history of states" (Ludwig Woltmann, "Die sozialistischen Parteien," in ibid., p. 35; see the discussion concerning Marxism in ibid., pp. 381–393).

83. Marx's reference to race as a condition of development can be found in Karl Marx, *Capital* (Moscow: Foreign Languages, 1954), vol. 1, p. 512. See Woltmann's comment in *Der historische Materialismus*, pp. 326–327. See the discussion in Ludwig Woltmann, *Die Darwinische Theorie und der Sozialismus* (Duesseldorf: Michels, 1899).

84. See Otto Reche's biographical introduction to Woltmann, *Politische Anthropologie*, pp. 7–23, and the discussion in A. James Gregor, *Contemporary Radical Ideologies: Totalitarian Thought in the Twentieth Century* (New York: Random House, 1968), pp. 181–189.

85. See the discussion in Bogdan Denitch, *Ethnic Nationalism: The Tragic Death of Yugoslavia* (Minneapolis: University of Minnesota Press, 1994).

86. See Patricia Golden Steinhoff, "Tenko: Ideology and Social Integration in Prewar Japan" (Ph.D. diss., Harvard University, 1969).

87. *Minzoku* translates as people, nation, or race, much as the Italian term *stirpe* can be translated as either people or race. The discussion that follows is based largely on Germaine A. Hoston, "Tenko: Marxism and the National Question in Prewar Japan" (unpublished paper).

88. See the discussion in Crowley, "A New Deal for Japan and Asia: One Road to Pearl Harbor," in James B. Crowley (ed.), *Modern East Asia: Essays in Interpretation* (New York:

Harcourt, Brace & World, 1970), pp. 235–264, and *idem, Japan's Quest for Autonomy* (Princeton: Princeton University Press, 1966).

89. See the discussion in Miles Fletcher, *The Search for a New Order: Intellectuals and Fascism in Prewar Japan* (Chapel Hill: University of North Carolina Press, 1982).

90. See the Fascist discussion in Carlo Avarna di Gualtieri, *La politica giaponese del "Nuovo Ordine"* (Milan: Principato, 1940).

91. See the discussion in Charles Tilly, "Reflections on the History of European State-Making," in Tilly (ed.), *The Formation of National States in Western Europe* (Princeton: Princeton University Press, 1975), pp. 3–83, in which both Japan and Germany are seen as having embarked on nation building as a consequence of external threat. See as well John Dower, *War without Mercy: Race and Power in the Pacific War* (New York: Pantheon, 1986), p. 329, and Cullen Hayashida, "Identity, Race and the Blood Ideology of Japan" (Ph.D. diss., University of Washington, 1976).

92. See the discussion in Mikhail Agursky, *Contemporary Russian Nationalism: History Revised* (Jerusalem: Hebrew University Press, Jan. 1982).

93. See the account in François Ponchaud, *Cambodia: Year Zero* (New York: Holt, Rinehart and Winston, 1977); David Hawk, "The Killing of Cambodia," *New Republic*, 15 Nov. 1982, pp. 17–21.

94. See the commentary by Alexander Yanov, *Weimar Russia and What We Can Do About It* (New York: Slovo-World, 1995).

95. "I was not bluffing when I affirmed that the Fascist idea will be the idea of the twentieth century" (Mussolini, *Testamento politico*, pp. 27–28).

Chapter 9: "Fascisms"

1. Sergio Panunzio, A. O. Olivetti, and Paolo Orano were among them. Later they were joined by Roberto Michels, a former Marxist theoretician and one of the major political thinkers of the early twentieth century. See A. James Gregor, "Giovanni Gentile and the Philosophy of the Young Karl Marx," *Journal of the History of Ideas*, 24, no. 2 (1963): 213–230; see V. I. Lenin, "Karl Marx," in *Collective Works* (Moscow: Foreign Languages, 1964), vol. 21, p. 88. In this context, see Ugo Spirito, *La filosofia del comunismo* (Florence: Sansoni, 1948).

2. See the discussion in Giovanni Gentile, "La filosofia di Marx: studi critici," in *I fondamenti della filosofia del diritto* (Florence: Sansoni, 1955), pp. 163–164, esp. pp. 226–229, n. 2.

3. In the official *Dottrina del fascismo* the thesis was expressed as: "The human being [in the conception of] Fascism is nation and Fatherland, a moral law that unites individuals and generations in a tradition and in a mission" (Benito Mussolini, *Dottrina del fascismo* [Milan: Hoepli, 1935], pt. 1, para. 2). See the discussion in A. James Gregor, *Contemporary Radical Ideologies: Totalitarian Thought in the Twentieth Century* (New York: Random House, 1968), chap. 2.

4. See the insightful discussion in Curzio Malaparte, "Improprietà naturale e storica del socialismo nostrano," in *L'Europa vivente e altri saggi politici (1921–1931)* (Florence: Vallecchi, 1961), pp. 381–395; see esp. pp. 384 and 394–395.

5. It was not forgotten by many in Fascist Italy. There was a constant complaint that Fascism was moving closer and closer to Marxism and Bolshevism. See, e.g., Guido Cavallucci, *Il fascismo e sulla via di Mosca?* (Rome: Cremonese, 1933). In this context see the discussion of Ugo Spirito, *Capitalismo e corporativismo* (Florence: Sansoni, 1933).

6. Ernst Nolte, *Three Faces of Fascism: Action Française, Italian Fascism, National Socialism* (New York: Holt, Rinehart and Winston, 1966), pp. 20–21.

7. See the interesting discussion in Domenico Settembrini, *Fascismo controrivoluzione imperfetta* (Florence: Sansoni, 1978), chap. 1. Recently Richard Pipes has commented, "No prominent European socialist before World War I resembled Lenin more closely than Benito Mussolini" (*Russia under the Bolshevik Regime* [New York: Vintage, 1995], p. 245).

8. See the account in Fabio Gabrielli, *"La Verità" e la sua avventura* (Milan: n.p., 1984).

9. A. James Gregor, *An Introduction to Metapolitics: A Brief Inquiry into the Conceptual Language of Political Science* (New York: Free Press, 1971), pp. 368–369.

10. See Gilbert Allardyce, "What Fascism is Not: Thoughts on the Deflation of a Concept," *American Historical Review*, 84, no. 2 (Apr. 1979): 367–388.

11. Jaroslav Krejci, "Introduction: Concepts of Right and Left," in Luciano Cheles, Ronnie Ferguson, and Michalina Vaughan (eds.), *Neo-fascism in Europe* (New York: Longman, 1991), p. 3.

12. A publication blurb on the book jacket of Roger Griffin's *The Nature of Fascism* (New York: Routledge, 1993).

13. Benito Mussolini, "On the Corporate State (14 November 1933)," in *The Corporate State* (Florence: Vallecchi, 1938), p. 35.

14. See the discussion in Griffin, *Nature of Fascism*, pp. 36f.

15. As early as 1914, Enrico Corradini identified nationalism as a reactive response to collective threat and humiliation. See "Nazionalismo e socialismo," in *Discorsi politici (1902–1923)* (Florence: Vallecchi, 1923), pp. 216–217. Corradini's ideas passed directly into Fascism.

16. In 1917, Sergio Panunzio referred to the "absurd and iniquitous system . . . in which the minority of powerful states exploit all the others . . . who suffer as little more than servants" (*Diritto, forza e violenza: lineamenti di una teoria della violenza* [Bologna: Cappelli, 1921], p. xxiv).

17. See R. J. Rummel, *Death by Government: Genocide and Mass Murder since 1900* (New Brunswick, N.J.: Transaction, 1994), and the comments in Irving Louis Horowitz, *Taking Lives: Genocide and State Power* (New Brunswick, N.J.: Transaction, 1997), pp. 28–29, 227.

18. Over half a century ago, Sir Arthur Keith argued thus in *A New Theory of Human Evolution* (New York: Philosophical Library, 1949).

19. See the entire discussion concerning "self-transcendence," nationalism, and fascism in Griffin, *Nature of Fascism*, chap. 7.

20. The literature on collective life goes back well into the nineteenth century. Ludwig Gumplowicz, e.g., spoke eloquently of the role of "social elements" in the articulation of personality and their impact on political behavior. See Gumplowicz, *Der Rassenkampf* (Innsbruck: Universitaet, 1883), and *idem*, *Outlines of Sociology* (Philadelphia: American Academy of Social and Political Science, 1899). All the major social thinkers of the late nineteenth and early twentieth centuries allude to the identification of individuals with selected groups of "similars" as critical to the evolution of personality. See the discussion in A. James Gregor, *The Ideology of Fascism: The Rationale of Totalitarianism* (New York: Free Press, 1969), chap. 2.

21. This is not the place to rehearse social-scientific thought concerning ethnocentricity and its relationship to nationalism. One of the foremost theoreticians concerned with just this issue was the late Sir Arthur Keith, whose books on the relationship between human beings as group animals and nationalism are many and illuminating. See Keith, *New Theory*, which contains an extensive bibliography. For an extensive and reasonably detailed discussion of the relationship between group consciousness and nationalism, see Eugen Lemberg, *Nationalismus* (Hamburg: Rowohlt, 1964), vol. 1.

22. See the discussion in Griffin, *Nature of Fascism*, chap. 7.

23. See the discussion in Francis Fukuyama, *The End of History and the Last Man* (New York: Free Press, 1992), "Introduction" and chap. 31.

24. Griffin, *Nature of Fascism*, p. 195.

25. Fukuyama, *End of History*, p. 270.

26. Griffin, *Nature of Fascism*, p. 195.

27. Long before his adherence to Fascism (in 1914) and early in the Fascist period (1920), Dino Grandi, one of the architects of the movement, conceived of the world as divided between "the rich and the poor nations"—a division which necessarily produced conflict. For Grandi, the entire twentieth century would be beset by wars between "proletarian" and "plutocratic" nations. See his discussion in "La guerra non risolvera nulla" and "Lettera a un socialista," in *Giovani* (Bologna: Zanichelli, 1941), pp. 39, 225. In articulating the position of the first Fascism, Mussolini outlined his conception of the world as a place dominated by national "egoisms," in which nations were obliged to struggle for a place in the sun. See Mussolini, "La nuova politica estera," in *Opera omnia* (Florence: La Fenice, 1953–64), vol. 19, p. 130; see *idem*, "Prime basi dello stato corporativo," in ibid., vol. 20, p. 133. At the end of the Fascist period, the struggle between poor and rich nations served as a rationale for the Second World War. See the discussion in Guido Puccio, *Lotta fra due mondi* (Rome: Edizioni Italiane, 1942), chap. 2.

28. Domenico Soprano, *Spazio vitale* (Milan: Corbaccio, 1942), p. 23. As early as Panunzio's *Diritto, forza e violenza* in 1921, one finds the same theme.

29. This thesis goes back at least to 1916 in Corradini's "diritti e doveri nazionali dei produttori" (*Discorsi politici*, pp. 341f., and *idem*, *La marcia dei produttori* [Rome: "L'Italia," 1916], p. 60). This is not to suggest that only proto-fascists recognized the connection. It is clearly addressed in the writings of Sun Yat-sen about the same time and in those of the intellectuals around him. Traces of these elements are found in the writings of Chinese "proto-communists" as well.

30. This has been understood by Marxist–Leninists and Fascists alike. In addressing the First Conference of Russian Industrial Managers in 1931, Josef Stalin pointed out that "the history of old Russia is the history of defeats due to backwardness." See the same sentiments in the Fascist account of L. Fontana Russo, *Preparazione e condotta economica della guerra* (Rome: Cremonese, 1942), esp. p. 21.

31. See the discussion in Italo Lunelli, *Pagine della nostra fede* (Milan: Varese, 1942), chaps. 9 and 11. At its very commencement, Mussolini identified the League of Nations as a "sort of holy alliance of plutocratic nations designed to guarantee—their episodic conflicts of interest notwithstanding—exploitation of the major part of the world" ("Le linee programmatiche del partito fascista," in *Opera omnia*, vol. 17, pp. 177–178).

32. See, e.g., the summary description of the policies of Vargas and Peron in the context of the peculiar economic and political conditions of Latin America in the first half of the twentieth century by Gullermo A. O'Donnell, *Modernization and Bureaucratic-Authoritarianism: Studies in South American Politics* (Berkeley: Institute of International Studies, 1973), pp. 55–60.

33. One of the more insightful discussions of some of these issues is to be found in Ludovico Garruccio, *L'industrializzazione tra nazionalismo e rivoluzione: le ideologie politiche dei paesi in via di svilupppo* (Bologna: Il mulino, 1969).

34. See Peter F. Sugar, *Native Fascism in the Successor States, 1918–1945* (Santa Barbara, Calif.: Clio, 1971); Nicholas M. Nagy-Talavera, *The Green Shirts and the Others: A History of Fascism in Hungary and Rumania* (Stanford, Calif.: Hoover Institution Press, 1970); and Mihai Fătu and Ion Spălătelu, *Garda de fier: Organizaţie terorista de tip fascist* (Bucharest: Editura politica, 1971).

35. Andrew C. Janos, *The Politics of Backwardness in Hungary 1825–1945* (Princeton: Princeton University Press, 1982), p. 259.

36. See the discussion in Ion I. Motza, one of the principal ideologues of the Romanian

"Legion of the Archangel Michael" (*L'uomo nuovo* [Padua: Edizioni di Ar, 1978]; the original Romanian edition was entitled *Cranii de Lemn*).

37. Corneliu Zelea Codreanu, *Guardia di ferro* (Padua: Edizioni di Ar, 1972), a translation of *Pentru Legonari*.

38. As quoted in Eugen Weber, "Romania," in Hans Rogger and Eugen Weber (eds.), *The European Right: A Historical Profile* (Berkeley: University of California Press, 1966), p. 504.

39. In this context see Mariano Ambri, *I falsi fascismi: Ungheria, Jugoslavia, Romania 1919–1945* (Roma: Jouvence, 1980), pp. 222–223.

40. Motza, *L'uomo nuovo*, p. 247.

41. Weber, "Romania," p. 524.

42. Corneliu Zelea Codreanu, *Il capo di cuib* (Padua: Edizioni di Ar, 1974), pp. 65–66.

43. Codreanu maintained that Fascism was predicated on the "principle of the state," and National Socialism rested, in the last analysis, on the notion of biological racism, whereas the legion found its impulse in religious mysticism. See Julius Evola, *Il fascismo: saggio di una analisi critica dal punto di vista della destra* (Rome: Volpe, 1964), p. 32, n. 1.

44. Codreanu, *Il capo di cuib*, p. 21. See in this context the writings of one of the more important ideologues of the legion, Motza, *L'uomo nuovo*.

45. See Julius Evola, "Nazionalismo e ascesi: La Guardia di Ferro," *Corriere Padano*, 14 Apr. 1938, pp. 1–2, repr. in Carlo Sburlati (ed.), *Codreanu e la Guardia di Ferro* (Rome: Volpe, 1977), pp. 71–75.

46. See Carlo Sburlati, *Codreanu il capitano* (Rome: Volpe, 1970), p. 165.

47. See, e.g., Motza, "Il senso del nostro nazionalismo," in *L'uomo nuovo*, pp. 229–233; and Codreanu, *Guardia di ferro*, pp. 130–132.

48. See the discussion in Motza, "La fase precorporativa," in *L'uomo nuovo*, pp. 207–209.

49. For a history of "fascism" in Hungary and Romania, see Nagy-Talavera, *Green Shirts*.

50. Horia Sima assumed leadership of the legion upon the death of Codreanu. For Sima's views, see Maurizio Cabona (ed.), *Horia Sima: Intervista sulla Guardia di Ferro* (Palermo: Edizioni Thule, 1977).

51. Mihail Manoilescu, *Le siècle du corporatisme: doctrine du corporatisme integral et pur* (Paris: Felix Alcan, 1938), esp. pt. 1, chaps. 1 and 2; see also *idem*, *Die einzige Partei* (Berlin: Otto Stollberg, 1941).

52. That Manoilescu did not address the Jewish question directly rendered his ideas fatally flawed in the judgment of the leaders of the legion. See the comments of Motza, "Sotto il peso delle rimanenze," in *L'uomo nuovo*, pp. 210–220.

53. Members of the legion would donate their time and efforts to assist peasants in the construction of roads and bridges in rural areas. They would work to beautify the rural villages. Codreanu admonished all legionaries to serve the needs of the peasants, because they represented the "True Romania." See Ernst Nolte, *Die faschistischen Bewegungen: Die Krise des liberalen Systems und die Entwicklung der Faschismus* (Munich: DTV, 1966), pp. 219–220.

54. Stalin's anti-Semitism, unlike Mussolini's, was not formalized in legislation in the Soviet Union. Nonetheless, Jews were discriminated against almost everywhere. See Gennadi Kostyrchenko, *Out of the Red Shadows: Anti-Semitism in Stalin's Russia* (Amherst, N.Y.: Prometheus, 1995), and Arkady Vaksberg, *Stalin against the Jews* (New York: Knopf, 1994). See the comments of Renzo De Felice, *Interpretations of Fascism* (Cambridge, Mass.: Harvard University Press, 1977), pp. 10–11.

55. The issue of Fascism's Lateran Accords with the Roman Catholic Church is far too complicated to review here, but some of the principal Fascist ideologues objected to the

implications of the relationship. See, e.g., the discussion in Spirito, *La fine del comunismo* (Rome: Volpe, 1978), pt. 2, esp. pp. 111–115.

56. Stalin insisted that "in ten years at most we must make good the distance that separates us from the advanced capitalist countries" ("The Tasks of Business Executives," in *Works* [Moscow: Foreign Languages, 1954], vol. 13, p. 43).

57. J. V. Stalin, "Industrialisation of the Country and the Right Deviation in the C.P.S.U. (B.)," in ibid., vol. 11, p. 256.

58. Stalin, *Works*, vol. 11, pp. 296–297, as quoted in Mikhail Agursky, *The Third Rome* (Boulder, Colo.: Westview, 1987), p. 205.

59. Grandi, *Giovani*, p. 225.

60. Stalin, "Letter to Chugunov," in *Works*, vol. 9, p. 206.

61. "It would be most difficult to support the clear distinction . . . between nationalism and Communism. Does the evidence of the new states suggest that whoever gains power in these countries—be they nationalist or Communist—are required by the overwhelming difficulties of maintaining their own power while creating a new and viable nation to adopt those policies which best facilitate that task: nationalist economic and political policies?" (Robert F. Dernberger, "The Role of Nationalism in the Rise and Development of Communist China," in Harry G. Johnson (ed.), *Economic Nationalism in Old and New States* [London: George Allen and Unwin, 1968], p. 70).

62. See A. James Gregor, *Marxism, China and Development* (New Brunswick, N.J.: Transaction, 1965), chaps. 4 and 5.

63. See the discussion in Chen Xi, "The Nationalism of Chinese Intellectuals," *Beijing zhichun (Beijing Spring*, published in New York), no. 39 (Aug. 1996): 38–43; "China Prints Book to Educate Farmers," *San Francisco Chronicle*, 28 Nov. 1995, p. A11.

64. See Wang Shan, *Disanzhi yanjing kan zhongguo* (Taipei: Zhouzhi wenhua, 1994). This book, *Looking at China through the Third Eye*, originally published in the People's Republic as though it were a translation of a work by a German author, was recommended by the leadership in Beijing. In the last chapter the author speaks of international competition in terms of a Darwinian struggle for existence; see pp. 267–295, esp. pp. 274–280.

65. George Wehfritz, "China: Springtime Perennial," *Newsweek*, 10 June 1996, p. 17; Marcus W. Brauchli and Kathy Chen, "Nationalist Fervor," *Wall Street Journal*, 23 June 1995, pp. A1 and A5.

66. Among intellectuals in the People's Republic of China there has been an increasing emphasis on the glories of Chinese culture. Where the Maoists tended to distinguish the "reactionary" past from the "progressive" revolutionary, Marxist–Leninist present, the disposition among the increasingly nationalistic Chinese is to celebrate Chinese culture in its historic entirety.

67. See, e.g., G. B. Marziali, *Fascismo educatore* (Palermo: Palumbo, 1939); Augusto Turati, *Ragioni ideali di vita fascista* (Rome: Berlutti, n.d.); G. A. Fanelli, *Idee e polemiche per la scuola fascista* (Rome: Cremonese, 1941).

68. Recently, the Chinese Communist Party published "instructional pamphlets" for the citizens of the People's Republic that enjoin them to "love their country" and never forget the humiliations heaped upon China by the imperialists. See "China Prints Book to Educate Farmers," p. A11.

69. In this context see Felice Guarneri, *Battaglie economiche tra el due grandi guerre* (Milan: Garzanti, 1953), vol. 1, chaps. 9–11; Gianni Toniolo, *L'economia dell'Italia fascista* (Rome: Laterza, 1980), chaps. 4–6.

70. Thus Otto-Ernst Schueddekopf affirms that "if we take the concept of 'fascism' in its

strictest sense, it can only be applied to Italy" (*Revolutions of Our Time: Fascism* [New York: Praeger, 1973], p. 17).

71. One of De Felice's clearest statements of this position is found in "Il fenomeno fascista," which serves as an introduction to Ambri, *I falsi fascismi*.

72. See Walter Laqueur's critique of Sovietology in *The Dream that Failed: Reflections on the Soviet Union* (New York: Oxford University Press, 1994), chaps. 5 and 6.

73. Pipes, *Russia under the Bolshevik Regime*, p. 253. "Between us and the Communists there are no political affinities but there are intellectual ones. Like you, we consider necessary a centralized and unitary state which imposes iron discipline on all persons, with this difference, that you reach this conclusion by way of the concept of class, and we by way of the concept of nation" (Mussolini, "Per la vera pacificazione," in *Opera omnia*, vol. 17, p. 295). Mussolini argued that "in fact, both [the Russian and the Fascist] revolutions supercede all the ideologies and, in a certain sense, the liberal and democratic institutions that found their origin in the French revolution" ("La riforma elettorale," in *Opera omnia*, vol. 19, p. 310).

74. The postrevolutionary United States displayed many of the properties of reactive, developmental nationalism. It was also democratic in intent. The question arises of whether Sun Yat-sen's Kuomintang was a member of the subspecies "fascism" or not, since Sun Yat-sen's ultimate intention was democratic. There is no simple answer to such questions. The classification of political ideologies, political movements, and political regimes is reasoned, but not "objective." For the period after Sun's death in 1925 until the introduction of democratic modalities under Chiang Ching-kuo, the rule of the Kuomintang on Taiwan could be classified either as "fascism" or, should that irritate the sensibilities of democratic Chinese, as a "developmental authoritarianism."

75. G. Lowell Field, *Comparative Political Development* (London: Routledge & Kegan Paul, 1967), p. 15.

76. David E. Apter, "A Comparative Method for the Study of Politics," in H. Ekstein and D. E. Apter (eds.), *Comparative Politics* (New York: Free Press, 1963), p. 82.

Index